BR
THE SPELL

Contemporary Realism under Discussion

Edited by Sarah De Sanctis and Anna Longo

MIMESIS
INTERNATIONAL

© 2015 – MIMESIS INTERNATIONAL
www.mimesisinternational.com
e-mail: info@mimesisinternational.com

Book series: *Philosophy*, n. 10
Isbn: 9788857526591

© MIM Edizioni Srl
P.I. C.F. 02419370305

MIMESIS INTERNATIONAL

PHILOSOPHY

n. 10

TABLE OF CONTENTS

ACKNOWLEDGEMENTS

This book is the result of long discussions on the philosophical positions that go under the name of 'Speculative Realism' in the U.K., France and U.S.A., and 'New Realism' in Italy and Germany. This work does not claim to offer any solution or unifying perspective, but is meant as a platform collecting reflections, critiques and propositions regarding the most problematic and unresolved issues; it is an invitation to try to answer compelling questions about our philosophical present. I thank first of all my co-editor Sarah De Sanctis, who improved the original project and provided the enriching interviews that you will find at the end of this volume. Secondly, I thank the director of Mimesis International, Luca Taddio, who offered us the possibility of producing this book and played an active role in promoting the debate on realism. Finally, I want to express my gratitude to all the authors who contributed to this collection, providing the general debate with new sharp observations and promising propositions.

Anna Longo

INTRODUCTION

Why Contemporary Realism Is Not Just Another "Ism"

SARAH DE SANCTIS

Part I: After Anthropocentrism, or, the Meaninglessness of Life

> I think human consciousness is a tragic misstep in evolution. We became too self-aware. Nature created an aspect of nature separate from itself. We are creatures that should not exist by natural law. We are things that labor under the illusion of having a self, this accretion of sensory experience and feelings, programmed with total assurance that we are each somebody, when in fact everybody's nobody. I think the honorable thing for our species to do is to deny our programming. Stop reproducing. Walk hand in hand into extinction. One last midnight, brothers and sisters opting out of a raw deal.

These are not the words of a contemporary philosopher, although they sound very much like that. The quote, in fact, comes from the first episode of the popular TV series *True Detective*, and this fairly depressing passage belongs to Detective Rust Cohle. Now, there are a few interesting things about this. Firstly, a deeply pessimistic, philosophical show has managed to gain unprecedented popularity, and as good as Matthew McConaughey and Woody Harrelson may be, I doubt it's just because of them. It probably means that there is something about this series (about the views it expresses) that struck a nerve in the audience.

Secondly, the show was written by Nic Pizzolatto, a former Professor of Fiction and Literature who became a writer and was strongly influenced by Thomas Ligotti and Ray Brassier (see the essay by Anna Longo in this volume). In fact, in August 2014, an article alleged that Pizzolatto actually plagiarized Thomas Ligotti's book *The Conspiracy Against the Human Race: A Contrivance of Horror*, even mentioning eleven examples that apparently included word-for-word quotations. HBO and Pizzolatto stated that they regard those allegations groundless, arguing that philosophical ideas can never be plagiarized. According to Wikipedia, the issue remains unresolved. This is important because Brassier is one of the main targets of the present book, and he wrote the introduction to Ligotti's book that much inspired the creation of *True Detective*.[1]

---

1   For an in-depth analysis of *True Detective* and philosophy, see E. CONNOLE, P. J.

Thirdly, Detective Rust Cohle describes himself as being a realist; although, philosophically speaking, he'd probably see himself as a pessimist. Now, there seems to be a bond, lately, between realism and pessimism. How did we get to this?

Ever since Quentin Meillassoux's influential *After Finitude,*[2] much discussion has been devoted to the so-called 'end of correlationism'. This means that, unlike what Kant's legacy has led us to believe, it is not true that we can only know the *relation* between reality and our thought of it. Reality is out there, and doesn't really care what we think. A chair does not disappear if I stop looking at it or thinking about it. It is not our conceptual schemes and perceptual apparatuses that shape reality: reality is brutally there. Fair enough, you'll say. But what this truly means is that, to put it in Maurizio Ferraris' words, reality is unamendable: it cannot be corrected, it's just what it is.[3]

Here's another way to look at the issue: both Ferraris and Meillassoux have resorted to very ancient ('ancestral', Meillassoux would say) times to remind us of the utter contingency of our lives. As a matter of fact, the Earth existed perfectly well without us for billions of years: think of the dinosaurs or the famous arche-fossil. Brassier, on the contrary, has referred to the future, when the Sun will stop shining and life on Earth will cease to exist.[4] This is the same scenario depicted by Rust Cohle in *True Detective*. So, whether in the past or in the future, *at some point in time* human life did not, or will not, exist. This makes our life contingent – and therefore, pointless. This is how, from the refutation of correlationism, we get to pessimism – or rather, nihilism.

Now, how does this all connect with realism? I think here it might be worth looking at what contemporary realists are largely opposing, operating a negative definition *à la* Parmenides, so that realism will be defined by what antirealism is not. In fact, the landscape of new realisms is very broad and vague, and I believe it is held together by a common enemy, rather than by a specific shared view on what reality is. The common enemy of contemporary realism, in my opinion, is postmodern antirealism.

ENNIS, N. MASCIANDARO (eds.), *True Detection* (London: Schism Press, 2014).

2   Q. MEILLASSOUX, *After Finitude* (London: Continuum, 2008). French original *Après la finitude*, (Paris: Seuil, 2006).

3   M. FERRARIS, *Manifesto of New Realism* (New York: SUNY Press, 2014).

4   R. BRASSIER, *Nihil Unbound* (New York: Palgrave Macmillan, 2007).

Part II: After Postmodernism

As I said, the 'declared enemy' of new realisms is 'correlationalism,' namely, 'any current of thought which maintains the unsurpassable character of [correlation]', where 'by correlation we mean the idea according to which we only ever have access to the correlation between thinking and being.'[5] This stance is clear enough, as it has been reinstated in several books, conferences and articles on the topic. There is something broader, though, that new realists set themselves against, something that is often merely (and vaguely) referred to as 'postmodern philosophy' or 'antirealism'. For example, object-oriented ontologist Graham Harman speaks of 'the "postmodernist"' view 'that everything is a poetic fiction inside the mind'.[6] The polemical target is often left rather indefinite, and the reader might feel the need to understand who exactly it is that these realists are talking about, when they use such broad terms.[7]

Now, what I would like to do is try to understand better what the true object of dispute is within the broad horizon of postmodernism. I shall start with a useful quote from Meillassoux's influential *After Finitude*. Once he has defined correlationism, the French theorist goes on to state the following:

> [...] intersubjectivity, the consensus of a community, supplants the adequation between the representations of a solitary subject and the thing itself as the veritable criterion of objectivity, and of scientific objectivity more particularly. Scientific truth is no longer what conforms to an in-itself supposedly indifferent to the way in which it is given to the subject, but rather what is susceptible of being given as shared by a scientific community.[8]

---

5   Q. MEILLASSOUX, *After Finitude*, p. 5.
6   Interview with Graham Harman in ASK/TELL (http://eeevee2.blogspot.co.uk/2011/10/interview-with-graham-harman.html), Sunday, October 23, 2011.
7   One might also refer to the so-called "straw man fallacy" here. In fact, much criticism of new realist positions has claimed that their declared enemy was but a straw man and didn't really exist in the terms in which it is portrayed by those thinkers. The new realist attack on postmodernism might seem to be based on single, clamorous quotes, such as the unfortunate remark by Bruno Latour that Ramses II could not have died of tuberculosis, since the disease was only discovered in 1882 (Bruno Latour, 'Ramses II est-il mort de la tuberculose?', in *La Recherche*, 307, March 1998). Yet, such far-fetched claims do not seem to provide sufficient grounding for accusing postmodernism in general of endorsing a somehow Berkleyan antirealism. This is why, as I will try to argue, I believe what new realism opposes is really the general atmosphere of 'culturalism' (the focus on language, hermeneutics, cultural practices and biases) that was the Zeitgeist of those years.
8   Q. MEILLASSOUX, *After Finitude*, pp. 4-5.

He then specifies that 'during the twentieth century, the two principal "media" of the correlation were consciousness and language.'[9]

I want to focus on this point. As unspecific as they might be, the references to postmodernism made by new realist thinkers share the belief that postmodernists denied objectivity *per se*, and regarded truth as rather dependent on intersubjective consensus or linguistic coherence. I believe that we can therefore specify postmodern philosophy, as it is understood by new realists, as:

1)   social dependence of truth;
2)   linguistic construction of truth.

Famously, what postmodernity and deconstruction taught us is that (1) many things that were considered to be natural and objective (e.g. that women are inferior to men) are actually far from being so. Part of this view consists in the commonsensical consideration that even scientific research, supposedly the objective knowledge *par excellence*, is not exempt from biases: why research something rather than something else? Money is obviously involved, as well as a number of other interests. This is clearly acknowledged by new realists (see Paul Boghossian[10] and Ferraris himself, who refers to this as the 'fallacy of knowledge-power'[11]). Except that Ferraris then goes on to say that 'in postmodernism the Nietzschean view prevailed according to which knowledge is an instrument of domination and a manifestation of the will to power', which has led to the Foucauldian perspective according to which 'the only critical knowledge is a form of counterpower that is committed to systematically doubting knowledge, exercising a deconstruction without reconstruction,'[12] which he considers to be futile and counter-productive.

---

9   *Ibid.*, p.6.
10   'The idea at the core of these new "postmodern" conceptions of knowledge [... is that] knowledge necessarily depends at least in part on the contingent social and material setting in which that belief is produced (or maintained).' P. Boghossian, *Fear of Knowledge* (New York: Oxford University Press, 2007), p. 6.
11   Ferraris defines the weak version of this fallacy as 'that which, by radicalizing the connection between knowledge and interest, simply aims at calling into question the idea that there are disinterested reasons at the basis of knowledge.' M. Ferraris, *Manifesto of New Realism*.
12   *Ibid.*

I believe this is not the real issue at stake. Rather than an equivalence between knowledge and power, the real problem arises when this 'weak' form of social dependence of knowledge turns into the claim that (2), in the words of Boghossian, we 'emphasize the dependence of any fact on our contingent social needs and interests'[13] and we reach the extreme conclusion that truth depends on language and cannot escape it. So on the one hand we have Rorty positing that 'nothing counts as justification unless by reference to what we already accept, and [...] *there is no way to get outside our beliefs and our language* so as to find some test other than coherence.'[14] On the other hand, we have Gianni Vattimo proclaiming his Weak Thought, weak because it entails the impossibility to believe in one prevailing way of seeing the world:

> At the root of this weakness of thought with regard to that which exists – and according to which to think means only an enjoyable taking in of the spiritual forms that were handed down – there would seem to be an *obfuscation of the very idea of truth*. In fact the link between weak thought and hermeneutics makes such a suspicion credible, for if Being is not but is instead handed down [si tramanda], to think being would be only to rethink what has been said and thought thus far.[15]

Not only is the very concept of truth questioned, whoever claims to have reached it is actually ridiculed: for Rorty, the philosopher who asserts to have reached the Truth is an arrogant 'ascetic priest' in search of power.

> My description of the ascetic priest is deliberately pejorative and gendered. I am sketching a portrait of a phallocentric obsessive [...] he is inclined both to keep women in their traditional subordinate place, out of sight and out of mind, and to favour a caste system [...] what is important in not the fleshly phallus but the immaterial one [possessed by the ascetic priest] – the one which penetrates through the veil of appearances and makes contact with true reality...[16]

---

13   P. Boghossian, *Fear of Knowledge*, p. 39.
14   R. Rorty, *Philosophy and the Mirror of Nature* (Princeton, NJ: Princeton University Press, 1979), p. 178. My emphasis.
15   G. Vattimo, 'Dialectics, Difference, Weak Thought', in *Weak Thought*, (New York: SUNY Press, 2012), p. 48. My emphasis.
16   R. Rorty, 'Heidegger, Kundera and Dickens' in *Essays on Heidegger and Others*, vol.2, (Cambridge: Cambridge University Press, 2006), p. 72.

Part III: Not Only Philosophy

At the beginning of this essay, I stressed the fact that the very much 'contemporary realism-oriented' TV series *True Detective* was probably so popular also because it struck a nerve in the audience. This is because, I believe, what contemporary realism opposes is not just a philosophical squabble as per whether the truth exists or not. Postmodern antirealism as I described it above has had some significant 'existential' consequences, so to speak. Today's thought is connoted by nihilism and pessimism just like its predecessor was characterized by irony and playfulness. And this was not just in philosophy, but in culture as a whole. Ever since the end of the seventies (when the most influential 'postmodern' books were written, e.g. Richard Rorty's *Philosophy and the Mirror of Nature* and François Lyotard's *La condition postmoderne*) popular culture was suddenly filled with scepticism, cynicism and a kind of snobbish, savvy attitude.

To have an opinion suddenly meant being a fascist (remember Rorty's view on truth?) or something of the sort, so the great age of political correctness arrived. To make an example, T.S. Eliot could write something like the following: 'No poet, no artist of any art, has his complete meaning alone. [...] You *cannot* value him alone; you *must* set him, for contrast and comparison, among the dead'[17] and be perfectly fine notwithstanding the long list of imperatives in his sentence. In postmodern years, on the contrary, academic papers were suddenly filled with phrases like 'I might risk the hypothesis that' or 'I would almost argue that'. Nothing was to be taken too seriously, as there was no ultimate truth. After all, it's all cultural, isn't it? God being gone, and having taken all metanarratives with him, there was no Upper Source of Knowledge to refer to, and, to put it again with Rorty, there was '*no way to get outside our beliefs and our language.*'[18]

---

17   T. S. ELIOT, *Tradition and the Individual Talent*, in Frank Kermode (ed.) *Selected Prose of T. S. Eliot* (New York: Farrar, Straus, and Giroux, 1975). The essay dates back to 1919.

18   Of course, this does not mean that postmodernists are liberal democrats while realists are nazis. Both assert their views and are certainly convinced of being right, so even when Rorty says there is no truth, he paradoxically thinks that there is truth to what he is saying. My point is rather that postmodernism was very much focused on the *human subject* (culture, language and so on) and posited there is no way for the subject to be outside of itself. This is why we will be forever biased and can't speak in terms of universal truths. Realism, on the contrary, focuses on the *human and non-human object*, and therefore to all that is *not* tied to cultural or linguistic practices. Cultural relativism gives way to the universal objectivity of the real – even if this objectivity lies in the pointlessness of all things.

This was obviously very liberating – no one can criticize me too much if I am merely 'risking hypotheses.' And to gain everyone's respect it was enough to just snort at all those who were still so naïve as to talk about things like ethics, or religion. *I mean, seriously?* To give you an idea of what I am talking about, I'll copy here a long quote by American writer David Foster Wallace, one of the most stern endorsers of the end of post-modernism (and whom I regard as a 'new realist' precisely for this reason):

> For me, the last few years of the postmodern era have seemed a bit like the way you feel when you're in high school and your parents go on a trip, and you throw a party. You get all your friends over and throw this wild disgusting fabulous party. For a while it's great, free and freeing, parental authority gone and overthrown, a cat's-away-let's-play Dionysian revel. But then time passes and the party gets louder and louder, and you run out of drugs, and nobody's got any money for more drugs, and things get broken and spilled, and there's a cigarette burn on the couch, and you're the host and it's your house too, and you gradually start wishing your parents would come back and restore some fucking order in your house. It's not a perfect analogy, but the sense I get of my generation of writers and intellectuals or whatever is that it's 3:00 A.M. and the couch has several burn-holes and somebody's thrown up in the umbrella stand and we're wishing the revel would end. The postmodern founders' patricidal work was great, but patricide produces orphans, and no amount of revelry can make up for the fact that writers my age have been literary orphans throughout our formative years. We're kind of wishing some parents would come back. And of course we're uneasy about the fact that we wish they'd come back--I mean, what's wrong with us? Are we total pussies? Is there something about authority and limits we actually need? And then the uneasiest feeling of all, as we start gradually to realize that parents in fact aren't ever coming back--which means we're going to have to be the parents.[19]

Part IV: A New Era?

So what about new realism? New Realism is not here to bring back the parents, but acts as a sort of wise (and very serious) stepfather who tells us that the party is over. He is also here to tell us that it's OK to talk about truth, but careful – it's not a truth we will like. The freedom of culture is thus replaced with the brute constraints of nature, and our thought is regarded no longer as the expression of our soul but as the

---

19 S. Burn, *Conversations with David Foster Wallace*, (Jackson: University Press of Mississipi, 2012) p. 52.

mere outcome of chemical reactions in our brain. To put it once again with Rust Cohle, human consciousness is a tragic misstep in evolution. This is why I believe New Realism (with which I broadly refer to contemporary forms of philosophical realisms) is not just another "ism". I think it's a movement (as vague as its predecessor) that truly captures the Zeitgeist. Many new realists focus on the concepts of object, which has been neglected in the history of philosophy (Harman speaks of "overmining" and "undermining")[20] in the light of an anthropocentric perspective. Jane Bennett argues for the need to think "human and nonhuman actants on a less vertical plane" and critiques "fantasies of a human uniqueness in the eyes of God, of escape from materiality";[21] Tristan Garcia analyses time, animals, humans, history, gender as different *kinds* of objects.[22] Markus Gabriel, similarly, posits the equivalence of all things, which exist in different fields of sense (the only thing that doesn't exist being the totality of all things, which he calls the World).[23] All these thinkers propose a "flat ontology" or a "democracy of objects".[24] Humans are regarded as an object like any other, and lose their ontological primacy.

It is interesting to note that correlationism – the view, opposed by all new realists, that we only ever have access to the relation between the human subject and reality – is made to begin with Kant's *Critique of Pure Reason* (1781), while the anthropocene – the geological era shaped by human interventions over nature – is taken to begin with the Industrial Revolution (1760s). There is a connection between anthropocentric views in philosophy and the human exploitation of the world. This underlies the connection between new realisms and ecological views (in particular in Timothy Morton). Precisely in the light of ecological catastrophes (which are far from unlikely), today the idea of our disappearance from the planet is not mere conjecture. If Cohle is right, nature would in fact be better off without us.

---

20   G. HARMAN, *The Quadruple Object* (London: Zero Books, 2011).
21   J. BENNETT, *Vibrant Matter: A Political Ecology of Things* (Durham and London: Duke University Press 2010), p. xi.
22   T. GARCIA, *Forme et objet*, (Paris: PUF, 2011).
23   M. GABRIEL, *Il senso dell'esistenza* (Roma: Carocci, 2012).
24   The latter is actually the title of a book by L. BRYANT, *The Democracy of Objects* (Ann Arbor: OPEN HUMANITIES PRESS, 2011). There has also been a sort of revival of Alexius Meinong, who could be regarded as the forefather of flat ontology itself.

Part V: The Present Book

As I have said before, contemporary realism – while generally setting itself against postmodern antirealism - is far from homogeneous. The texts included in the present work, coming from heterogeneous scholars, focus on many different aspects that have emerged in the past few years and constitute a critical commentary to the whole 'movement.' The meaninglessness of life – and the utter indifference of everything to the needs of the living – is, as I have outlined, the starting point from which the general pessimistic nihilism derives. This 'eliminative materialism', which reduces the human (and life as a whole) to the status of mere organic matter, is somewhat opposed to the vitalist approach that, on the contrary, attributes agency to inorganic matter as well. In any case, the least common denominator of both positions is that the human is pushed off the pedestal where Kantian and post-Kantian philosophy had placed it, rendering it nothing more than an object like any other.

The question that opposes a certain nihilistic approach to vitalism is addressed by Paul Ennis, who highlights its risks and potential. The prospect of a bleak reality completely indifferent to human needs is taken into account also by the co-editor of this book Anna Longo, who highlights the links with the horror stories of Ligotti (the inspiring source of True Detective). Longo stresses that realist speculation somewhat tends to fiction by imagining scenarios in which the human subject is not included, such as the worlds of Meillassoux, in which the laws of physics are such that we could never experience them. The question of vitalism is also addressed by Ben Woodard: while proposing a comparison with cognitive theories such as enaction, he argues for the philosophical views of Schelling and Hamilton Grant as they emphasize the need to think of the real as a process in which life and thought emerge.

The question of the conditions of knowledge is also addressed by Gabriel Catren, who offers a sophisticated meta-observation of the way in which the real determines its own modes of observation. Indeed, the question of the conditions of possibility of objective knowledge of reality is of crucial importance to contemporary realism. This issue was introduced by Kant who, while being responsible for the subjectivist revolution in Western thought through his very Ptolemaic Copernican revolution, has also the merit, as rightly stressed by Fabio Gironi, of having given us the tools for the realist turn of contemporary philosophy. Kant has often been taken as the polemical target of contemporary philosophy – he is considered to be the one who started correlationism. However, the fiercest critic of corrélationisme, Quentin Meillassoux, might actually be closer to Kant's positions that he is willing to admit. This is the object of Liam Sprod's essay, which shows us how Meillassoux's claim of the contingency of everything (including the laws of physics) comes from an attempt to answer the same questions as those tackled by Kantian criticism itself.

When establishing the conditions of knowing a subject-independent reality, realist philosophy has to come to terms with scientific knowledge, as well as the ethical and political consequences it implies. This issue is addressed by Sjoerd van Tuinen and Matthijs Kouw, who take into analysis the thought of Manuel de Landa and Isabelle Stengers, whose views are fundamental in this respect. Stengers is also critically analysed by Erik Bordeleau, who offers a comparison between Stengers' position (admittedly opposed to speculative realism) and that of Bruno Latour, whose location within the landscape of realism is rather problematic. Finally, Andrea Zhok and Luca Taddio tackle the question of philosophical realism through a phenomenological approach, the former with the aim of rejecting Meillassoux's charges of anti-realism to phenomenology, the latter arguing in favour of a naïve realism *à la* Paolo Bozzi, reiterating the direct and immediate relationship with the phenomenal reality underlying experimental phenomenology.

Since contemporary realism is a very dynamic 'movement', the purpose of the present book was that of offering a critical commentary by heterogeneous interpreters and scholars who are not immediately associated with a specific brand of realism. However, we have also included four interviews with some of the most important thinkers of the contemporary philosophical landscape: Lee Braver, Maurizio Ferraris, Tristan Garcia and Graham Harman. We hope we have provided the reader with a comprehensive and up-to-date tool to tackle the issue of contemporary realism, giving space not only to the 'usual suspects' of the movement but also to younger scholars from different schools and traditions. Speculative realism indeed needs to be discussed as, we feel, it will stay with us for long.

I

ANTI-VITALISM AS A PRECONDITION FOR NIHILISM

PAUL J. ENNIS

1. Everything's Already Dead

In this paper I examine the anti-vitalist arguments of Ray Brassier's *Nihil Unbound*.[1] This anti-vitalism is what Brassier explored in his early thought and it is expressed neatly in the Preface as follows: 'Thinking has interests that do not coincide with those of the living; indeed, they can and have been pitted against the latter.'[2] My ambition is to capture this sentiment through what appears to be the least philosophical moment in the text, namely the poetic evocation of the heat-death of the universe, and then reveal the rationalist arguments motivating the following flourish:

> sooner or later both life and mind will have to reckon with the disintegration of the ultimate horizon when, roughly one trillion, trillion, trillion (101728) years from now, the accelerating expansion of the universe will have disintegrated the fabric of matter itself, terminating the possibility of embodiment. Every star in the universe will have burnt out, plunging the cosmos into a state of absolute darkness and leaving behind nothing but spent husks of collapsed matter. All free matter, whether on planetary surfaces or in interstellar space, will have decayed, eradicating any remnants of life based in protons and chemistry, and erasing every vestige of sentience – irrespective of its physical basis. Finally, in a state cosmologists call 'asymptopia', the stellar corpses littering the empty universe will evaporate into a brief hailstorm of elementary gravitational particles. Atoms themselves will cease to exist. Only the implacable gravitational expansion will continue, driven by the currently inexplicable force called 'dark energy', which will keep pushing the extinguished universe deeper and deeper into an eternal and unfathomable blackness.[3]

---

1   R. BRASSIER, *Nihil Unbound: Enlightenment and Extinction* (London: Palgrave Macmillan, 2007).
2   *Ibid.*, p. xi.
3   Here I quote the flourish in full and ask the reader to keep it in mind throughout what follows. BRASSIER, *Nihil Unbound*, p. 228.

Heat-death is, I argue, Brassier's aesthetic coda that opens out into his philosophical nihilism proper. It is a moment that, as we will see, closes off all vitalist counters to a relentless pull of a thinking uncoupled from life. Now, those with an interest in continental realism will know that Brassier's work has tailed off in a new direction.[4] I will briefly address some of the connections between his early nihilism and his more recent and mature work, which is inspired principally by his engagement with Wilfrid Sellars.[5] However, I still believe there is much of value to be found in Brassier's *Nihil Unbound* and, in particular, that the road he first took tells us much about the path he is currently travelling on.

Let us begin with the most striking claim of *Nihil Unbound*: that everything is dead already. What precisely does that mean? To find out I will highlight some both implicit and explicit arguments that allow this statement to carry weight. It is only persuasive, I claim, when we contextualize the book through its acknowledged and unacknowledged influences. Now, just before beginning the remarkable section on solar catastrophe (7.3), where the claim to our being already dead occurs, Brassier asks two questions: (1) 'How does thought think a world without thought?' and (2) 'How does thought think the death of thinking?'[6] The former question is the anti-correlationist one he shares with the influential French philosopher Quentin Meillassoux.[7] What would it be like to think an absolutely

---

4   The term is my own and I use it as an alternative to speculative realism since the latter term is broadly disavowed by many of the thinkers associated with it. I use it to designate simply those thinkers working on realism, but with an emphasis on what we consider traditionally the thinkers of continental philosophy. See P. J. ENNIS, *Continental Realism* (Winchester: Zero Books, 2011). Brassier's 'turn' can be traced, roughly, back to 'Concepts and Objects', in *The Speculative Turn: Continental Materialism and Realism*, ed. By Levi Bryant, Graham Harman, and Nick Srnicek (Melbourne: re-press, 2010), pp. 47-65.

5   See R. BRASSIER, 'Nominalism, Naturalism, and Materialism: Sellars' Critical Ontology', in *Contemporary Philosophical Naturalism and its Implications*, ed. by Bana Bashour and Hans D. Muller (London and New York: Routledge, 2014).

6   BRASSIER, *Nihil Unbound*, 223, italics removed.

7   This is the 'the idea according to which we only ever have access to the correlation between thinking and being, and never to either term considered apart from the other.' Q. MEILLASSOUX, *After Finitude: An Essay on the Necessity of Contingency*, trans. by Ray Brassier (London: Continuum, 2008), p. 5. Brassier glosses the meaning of the correlationist circle as follows: 'Correlationism is subtle: it never denies that our thoughts or utterances *aim at* or *intend* mind-independent or language-independent realities; it merely stipulates that this apparently independent dimension remains internally related to thought and reality.' BRASSIER, *Nihil Unbound*, p. 51.

de-subjectivated world?[8] Brassier begins with how to think the death of thinking. The reason is that if we can think the elimination of thinking then we should be able to envision a de-subjectivated world. What is aimed at here is the disarticulation of correlationism through the elimination of its apparent indispensability. In other words, we must break the bond between thinking and being, mind and world, and the many other variations of correlationism. To think the world without thought you have think the death of thinking. One must learn to de-couple thinking from its association with life. This is why it is imperative that we eviscerate all forms of meaning subservient to our self-image from our considerations.

Brassier begins this thought-process by way of François Lyotard's remarkable essay 'Can Thought go on without a Body?'[9] He engages the 'He and She' dynamic, but it is the implications of the 'He' section that Brassier is truly concerned with. There Lyotard seems to challenge a certain terrestrial myopia that is operative in Continental philosophy.[10] It is here that the crucial line occurs: 'everything's dead already if this infinite reserve from which you now draw energy to defer answers, if in short thought as quest, dies out with the sun.'[11] Lyotard delivers a straightforward reminder of how Continental philosophy consistently disavows the question of matter considered at the most abstract cosmological scale.[12] His target is the

---

8   In the second part of the Berlin lecture, entitled 'Essay on the Derivation of Galileanism,' Meillassoux discusses his own desire for a vision of the de-subjectivated as follows, '…can we found the capacity of mathematics to grant us access to the Kingdom of death, and then to return so as to recount to the living the discoveries of our voyage? The principle of materialism is infernal: it supposes that the Hell of the inorganic world – those deep, subterranean realms where life and subjectivity are absent – can nevertheless become the object of human knowledge.' Q. MEILLASSOUX, 'Iteration, Reiteration, Repetition: A Speculative Analysis of the Meaningless Sign', *Spekulative Poetik* (Freie Universität, Berlin, 20 April 2012), p. 19.

9   Jean-François LYOTARD, *The Inhuman: Reflections on Time,* trans. by Geoffrey Bennington and Rachel Bowlby (Stanford: Stanford University Press, 1991), pp. 8-23.

10   Brassier, in fact, radicalises Lyotard's position here and pushes it far beyond the thought-experiment function it has in the original text.

11   LYOTARD, *The Inhuman*, p. 9.

12   That is, 'Matter taken as an arrangement of energy created, destroyed and recreated over and over again, endlessly. On the corpuscular and/or cosmic scale I mean. I am not talking about the familiar, reassuring terrestrial world or the reassuring transcendent immanence of thought to its objects… In 4.5 billion years there will arrive the demise of your phenomenology and your utopian politics, and there'll be no one there to toll the death knell or hear it.' Lyotard, *The Inhuman*, p. 9.

long-standing tradition within Continental philosophy of valorizing the
'familiar, reassuring terrestrial world.'[13] Brassier adds that here the Earth
acts as a quasi-transcendental horizon that has been built on the Nietzschean imperative to remain true to it.[14] This is a self-imposed limitation
with a quite specific function: it signals an allegiance to the local field,
the only vital one we are aware of, against all over-arching schematics,
whether in the form of rationalism, metaphysics, or cosmology, that are not
sufficiently anchored to immediate, terrestrial concerns.[15]

In this way Continental philosophy carves out a niche for itself as
the defender of the lifeworld against those who would reduce it or
abstract from it.[16] However, the matter is complicated by the emphasis
on death in that same tradition, as it was introduced by Martin Heidegger.[17] Despite this apparent morbidity, the motif of death in the
post-Heideggerian tradition tends to focus on how *personalized* death
is, as a topic, to be considered the core focus of the 'life of the mind':
'If, as a limit, death really is what escapes and is deferred and as a
result what thought has to deal with, right from the beginning — this
death is still only the life of our minds.'[18] It is that which gives human life meaning and significance, and it is thus the most pressing
of all problems. It is, then, death considered in the light of life or the
living. Against abstraction and reduction the motif of death brings us
back down to earth. In this manner a demarcation is generated between
earth and cosmos, particular and universal, chronological and temporal time, ontic passing and existential death and more besides. Even
Meillassoux, often considered the thinker most opposed to the current
configurations of Continental philosophy, eventually returns to this

13   *Ibid.*
14   Nietzsche is the subject of the preceding section, 7.1. Nietzsche's Fable, and is cri-
      tiqued for lapsing back into a quasi-vitalist affirmationism. See BRASSIER, *Nihil
      Unbound*, pp. 205-223.
15   Of course, this is another connection between Brassier and Meillassoux. The lat-
      ter explicitly chooses to focus on statements about events '...sometimes older than
      any form of *life* on earth' in order to challenge this terrestrial focus in his own way.
      MEILLASSOUX, *After Finitude*, p. 9, my italics.
16   The preeminent defence of the lifeworld and the critique of abstract/reduction
      remains that of E. HUSSERL, *The Crisis of European Sciences and Transcenden-
      tal Phenomenology*, trans. by David Carr (Evanston: Northwestern University
      Press, 1970).
17   Beginning properly with Martin Heidegger, *Being and Time*, trans. by John Mac-
      quarrie and Edward Robinson (Oxford: Basil Blackwell, 1962), §47.
18   LYOTARD, *The Inhuman*, p. 10.

theme when he considers unmourned deaths to be the most important philosophical dilemma.[19]

Lyotard's provocation is to re-focus not on personal annihilation, but the cessation of all human traces. This is in order to stave off any recourse to sublation or deferral: '...solar death implies an irreparably exclusive disjunction between death and thought: if there's death, then there's no thought.'[20] What Lyotard invites us to think is what happens to thought when we subsume the time of the terrestrial horizon under the logical relations of cosmological time. One obvious complication is that the Earth finds itself in a dependency relation to a sun that will, in the distant future, die; and this process of dying will render our own planet inhospitable, albeit 4.5 billion years from now. The death of the sun is a far-off catastrophe not just in this blunt sense, but also because, for the life of the mind, such knowledge disrupts the earthly temporality that Continental philosophers think in accordance with. What has not properly been countenanced is temporality thought from this inevitable solar catastrophe. From that particular perspective we can view terrestrial history as belonging, and not in any significant sense, to a process within which the history of life on Earth can be read as an 'elaborately circuitous detour from stellar death.'[21]

In the last instance, then, terrestrial history is rendered insignificant when situated within this wider relationship between the Earth and its Sun. Stellar catastrophe as inevitable end-point stretches our philosophical fascination for the terrestrial until we begin to gain a meta-perspective whereby thought begins to think relations wider than itself. At this point Brassier has already gone much further than Lyotard, for whom this widening of relations is ultimately a prompt to an entirely different discussion.[22] What Brassier isolates and considers relevant for his project is the possibility of flattening conceptions of death such that one cannot privilege existential death and its conception of futurity (a terrestrial perspective) over, as in this instance, the extinction of the sun. Inexistence at the scale of the Earth-

19   See Q. MEILLASSOUX, 'Spectral Dilemma', in *Collapse IV: Concept Horror*, ed. by
      Robin Mackay (Falmouth: Urbanomic, 2008), pp. 261-275. The echoes to Derri-
      da's work of mourning are difficult to overlook here and the spectral dilemma ar-
      guably re-situates Meillassoux back into the more recent concerns of postmodern
      theology. See, J. DERRIDA, *The Work of Mourning*, ed. by Pascale-Anne Brault and
      Michael Naas (Chicago: University of Chicago Press, 2001).
20   LYOTARD, *The Inhuman*, p. 11.
21   BRASSIER, *Nihil Unbound*, p. 223.
22   This is carried out in the second 'She' segment of the essay which focuses on em-
      bodiment and gender. LYOTARD, *The Inhuman*, pp. 16-23.

Sun relationship recognises no such privilege: 'the sun is *dying* precisely to the same extent as human existence is bounded by *extinction.*'[23] Extinction at this scale undermines the implicit placement of the human at the heart of its own terrestrial narrative, free from the trace of inevitable solar catastrophe. This is to say the exterior proper, what is truly inhuman, is pushed outside the remit of philosophy (*qua* correlationism) and thus we find ourselves transcending a false limit: that of terrestrial death as the 'motor of philosophical speculation.'[24]

The point is direct: 'the extinction of the sun is not *of* or *for* thought.'[25] It is not simply an image or concept or internality that we can incorporate into our experience. It is not a question of my death and how this might act as the most pressing question for a life of the mind. Lyotard drives the point home: '...the death of the sun is a death of mind, because it is the death of death as the life of the mind.'[26] One solution, as outlined by Lyotard's 'He' voice, would be to separate the mind from the body such that the loss of the planet would not spell extinction for us.[27] This would simply reflect the general pattern of evolutionary strategy operative since the beginning of terrestrial history. This 'vitalist eschatology' refuses to face up properly to the consequences of extinction, at least in Brassier's strong sense.[28] It defers the truth of extinction such that we can point to the endless adaptability of terrestrial life as a potential that will win out against any catastrophe it might face. Here vitalism becomes allied with the desire to live and, in a manner not dissimilar to Meillassoux's critique of vitalists, we find in this position a refusal to follow the 'will to know' to its less charming conclusions.[29] Hinted at here is the desire to link the will to know with the will to nothingness and, for Brassier, the latter is to be understood as the 'the compunction to become equal to the in-itself.'[30] The deferring tactics expressed by vitalism in the face of solar catastrophe are given a final condemnation by Brassier. Even if we were to survive the death of the sun there is no surviving the heat-death of the universe. Nothing escapes this final moment and no exit, no matter how far we go, can out-circle it.

Each new horizon can only be construed as temporary. In imagining

---

23   BRASSIER, *Nihil Unbound*, p. 224.
24   BRASSIER, *Nihil Unbound*, p. 224.
25   *Ibid.*, p. 224.
26   LYOTARD, *The Inhuman*, p. 10.
27   *Ibid.*, p. 225.
28   *Ibid.*, p. 227.
29   *Ibid.*
30   *Ibid.*

that adaptability will let us live in perpetuity we fail to accept 'the transcendental scope of extinction' which names an annihilation with no exceptions.[31] Transcendental extinction is a true exterior that cannot be encompassed within correlationist coordinates. Contra death as transcendable 'internalized exteriority', extinction externalises the apparent interiority of the mind such that it joins all other entities as an object ('as a perishable thing in the world like any other').[32] Here the correlation is undone. The externalising of thought into object is connected to the posterior nature of extinction which cannot be rendered 'for us' in the manner that Meillassoux's ancestrality, according to Brassier, can.[33] There can be no circling around extinction after the fact that would turn it into a correlated event. The object for thinking when it comes to extinction is the 'absence of correlation' *tout court*.[34] Whereas Meillassoux is famously concerned with how thought can index a reality prior to humans, no such posterior reality is indexed by extinction. This is, then, to think an in-itself, corresponding to unqualified annihilation, which indexes 'the thought of the absence of thought' and answers Brassier's query as to how to think a world without thought through the prism of the death of thought.[35]

2. Death Drive

Let us turn now to some of the motivations guiding Brassier's argument. His adherence to nihilism is based on two fundamental convictions: (1) disenchantment through the use of reason is a positive outcome of the Enlightenment[36] and (2) philosophy should not be beholden to human 'self-esteem.'[37] In essence, Brassier accepts the curious fact that our species has worked out its own insignificance. The bulk of his criticism in *Nihil Unbound* is directed at the attempts at vitalist re-enchantment of the world found in much Continental philosophy. For instance, we see it

---

31　*Ibid.* p. 229.
32　*Ibid.*
33　See BRASSIER, *Nihil Unbound*, pp. 49-94.
34　*Ibid.*, p. 229.
35　*Ibid.*
36　Brassier tells us that 'The disenchantment of the world deserves to be celebrated as an achievement of intellectual maturity, not bewailed as a debilitating impoverishment.' BRASSIER, *Nihil Unbound*, p. xi.
37　In an increasingly famous line he states, 'Philosophy should be more than a sop to the pathetic twinge of human self-esteem.' BRASSIER, *Nihil Unbound*, p. xi.

when Deleuze and Guattari defend vitalism in order to render life ceaseless becoming or production or creativity.[38] Even Nietzsche's active response to nihilism is seen by Brassier as ultimately a betrayal.[39] In this manner Brassier remains consistently virulent in his anti-vitalism. Inasmuch as a subject exists in his thinking it is one who 'carries out a 'voiding' of being' which he reads as a speculative or cosmological 're-inscription of Freud's account of the death drive.'[40] Simplified Brassier names here a subject allied to the will to know or one that is on the side of thinking *against* life. The will to know is, furthermore, allied to the will to nothingness helping us to explain the seemingly irrational impulse evident in our species to pursue the interests of thinking over our own.[41]

Here I do not wish to reiterate Brassier's conclusion to *Nihil Unbound*, but I would like to provide some context that can help explain his allegiance to thinking over life. We know from the 'Preface' that Brassier embraces the disenchanting tendencies of Enlightenment rationalism and that he refuses to accommodate attempts to rescue human self-esteem from the 'coruscating potency of reason.'[42] Counter-enlightenment tendencies can be, from this position, read as blockages attempting to disrupt the malignant insights that reason reveals. The subject that embraces the truth of extinction will be capable of merging with the will to know (the thinking 'form' of the will to nothingness) and will no longer present itself as a barrier to knowledge of the in-itself. This would allow for the intensification or acceleration of philosophy as 'the organon of extinction.'[43] The nihilist will act as a mere vector, an already dead subject, allied with a process pursuing its own interests.[44] Readers of *Nihil Unbound* will no doubt have experienced the feeling that Brassier has reached an impasse. The intensification of the processes of disenchantment leave us as vectors for an alien process (the will to know/will to nothingness) that actively undermines attempts to provide our species

---

38   As Brassier reminds us, Deleuze goes as far as to extricate organic death from the Freudian conception of the death-drive. BRASSIER, *Nihil Unbound*, p. 163.
39   BRASSIER, *Nihil Unbound*, section 7.2.
40   *Ibid.*, p. 204.
41   Developed in more detail in the conclusion to *Nihil Unbound* in sections 7.5-7.6.
42   BRASSIER, *Nihil Unbound*, p. xi.
43   *Ibid.*, p. 239.
44   The kernel of this idea comes, I would argue, from Nick Land; albeit not uncritically. Nick Land is an important figure in the prehistory of continental realism. However, it is only recently that his articles were properly edited and collected. See N. LAND, *Fanged Noumena: Collected Writings 1987-2007*, ed. by Ray Brassier and Robin Mackay (Falmouth: Urbanomic, 2011).

with a unique, special status within the cosmos. The more our knowledge grows, the less significant our deeply local story becomes.

The tension found in *Nihil Unbound* is, then, that between the desire to facilitate the emergence of truth no matter the implications for our self-esteem, and the awareness that the intensification of the process of disenchantment is nonetheless dependent upon rational agents with the capacity to articulate such truths.[45] Drawing on Wilfrid Sellars, Brassier accepts that the manifest image denotes the site of our self-understanding *as* rational agents. We are concept-users and affected – or gripped – by concepts: which is to say, we are 'concept-governed creatures engaged in giving and asking for reasons.'[46] Only within such a medium it is possible to make sense of scientific explanation and description. Without a conceptual net (normativity) within which to assess claims, the scientific image could not be sense *of*. This is why Brassier is content to accept that, neurobiologically speaking, although there is no 'self', it is nonetheless impossible that we can eliminate the 'category of agent' as the locus of sense-making.[47] In this manner, Brassier asserts the significance of the manifest image not in order to shore up defences against the scientific image, but precisely because he believes the corrosive influence of the latter is contingent upon the former, in terms of its gaining traction at all.[48]

A mature manifest image is, then, the greatest ally to the flowering of the scientific image. This is important because it is traditional in Continental philosophy for one to read the manifest image, broadly speaking, as akin to the 'human' field of experience that is at risk of a dehumanising elimination by, for instance, neuroscience.[49] Brassier takes a middle path:

---

45   On the latter point Brassier is allied with the 'normativity' Sellarsian position defended by Robert Brandom. See R. BRASSIER, 'The View from Nowhere', *Identities: Journal for Politics, Gender, and Culture* 8:2 (2011), 7-23. However, his commitment is strongly prefigured in his critique of the eliminative materialist strain of Sellarsian thinking in BRASSIER, *Nihil Unbound*, pp. 3-31.

46   R. BRASSIER, 'The View from Nowhere', *Identities: Journal for Politics, Gender, and Culture* 8:2 (2011), 6.

47   *Ibid.*, 22.

48   See R. BRASSIER, 'Concepts and Objects', in *The Speculative Turn: Continental Materialism and Realism*, ed. By Levi Bryant, Graham Harman, and Nick Srnicek (Melbourne: *re-press*, 2010), pp. 47-65.

49   Perhaps the strongest example of this tendency is the 'no self' argument of Thomas Metzinger. See T. METZINGER, *Being No One: The Self-Model Theory of Subjectivity* (Massachusetts: MIT Press 2003). Metzinger, along with Paul Churchland, are both rigorously examined in BRASSIER, *Nihil Unbound,* pp. 3-31. Churchland's most robust defence of eliminative materialism, albeit without his stressing that

the self is eliminable, but rational agency is not. The quandary of motivation remains in place: one might agree that, according to advancements
in neuroscience, we will come to see self-hood as an illusion and perhaps
even as a necessary one in our evolution. The surviving rational agent
persists, but why should it? One escape route is to consider that, drawing on the inevitability of the heat-death of the universe, one is already
dead.[50] In such circumstances the distinction between localised 'life' and
'death' collapse and opting to align oneself with the will to know or not
is a decision undertaken (perhaps unconsciously) by a depersonalised rational agent.[51] Towards the end of *Nihil Unbound* the speculative thesis
undergirding Brassier's vision becomes explicit. Borrowing from Freud's
own speculative thesis that present within us is a desire to return to an
inorganic state (death-drive), Brassier adds that the will to know can be
read as thinking's *expression* of that will to nothingness.[52]

Specifically, the will to know takes the form of a marriage between a
dispassionate merger of the scientific and manifest images that refuses
to place either on a higher perch. This standpoint refuses to buttress our
sense of significance or centrality *qua* human beings, without negating
the extraordinary fact that we *think*. We find ourselves returning here to
a historical lineage closer to the Enlightenment rationalism that has been
under attack by generations of Continental philosophy.[53] We can call this
the contextual form of the wider argument about our being already dead,
since it provides the historical framework: the Enlightenment set in motion an irreversible process of disenchantment that philosophy, even if it
undermines our specialness, must pursue if they truly do love wisdom.
Allied to the contextual argument is the speculative (death-drive) framework within which the claim can make libidinal sense. If there is an innate drive within us to return to the in-itself, then there is a reason why

---

term's importance is, P. M. CHURCHLAND, *Plato's Camera: How the Physical Brain
Captures a Landscape of Abstract Universals* (Massachusett: MIT Press, 2012).

50   To recap, at the cosmological scale, since extinction is inevitable there is a sense in
which it has already happened. This renders our existence less significant and places us on the same scale, absolutely, as all other matter. This ontic fact is a cure for
our anthropocentric near-sightedness and has the aim of disarticulating our correlationist myopia. But the most forceful part is the idea that, all things being equal,
we are retroactively dead inasmuch as this truth is an uncircumventable fact.

51   It is not Brassier's position but I would consider suicide in this context to be rendered contingent within the map of cosmological time since one is, from that me-
ta-position, already dead. One simply chooses, in this context, the localised timing.

52   BRASSIER, *Nihil Unbound*, section 7.5.

53   This context is clearest in the short Preface to BRASSIER, *Nihil Unbound*, pp. x-xiii.

some forms of knowledge are pursued even when they jar against the biological imperative. Both frames help to explain the self-subversion exhibited in the compulsion toward demonstrating our own insignificance. It is not that some aspect of ourselves is alien to us *per se*, but that we oftentimes refuse to accept that a constitutive element of our makeup is inherently self-destructive.

The royal road to the inhuman can be read, then, as one entered through the aperture of a self-less rational agent pursuing knowledge without concern for the revivification of our humanity, broadly construed. If philosophy is truly the pursuit of knowledge then it must operate at the widest possible scale. The scientific image, our Enlightenment heritage, forces the issue with a cosmological vision that forces us to expand the parameters of the localised, terrestrial field. The imagery of the heat-death of the universe will, surely, always be linked with the Brassier of speculative realism, but as we have seen it is no mere rhetorical or aesthetic device. To state explicitly that we are already dead is to argue implicitly that philosophy is no longer a discipline concerned with the good life. If thinking has interests of its own then we must accept when these depart from the vitalist line. There is no denying that recourse to heat-death has an eschatological teleology, but it is one with no room for redemption or hope. It is in the recognition that this is not all about us that ensures the pre-condition for nihilism is a vigilant anti-vitalism.

II

THE REALITY OF THE END OF THE WORLD: OUT-SCIENCE-FICTION AND HORROR STORIES

Anna Longo

Beyond the world that is given within our experience, speculative realism has revealed a rationally accessible real that is totally different from what we expected. Since it is the metaphysical condition of the empirically given reality we are in relation with, the real can be accessed only by thinking of the state that precedes or follows the circle of correlation: how can we know what there was before humans appeared? How can we know what will be there after the extinction of humanity? In other words, to rationally access the real, we have to imagine a situation where the correlation between us and objects is *not yet* or *no longer*, since we have to think of the metaphysical condition which allows for our relation to objects and our representation of the world – a condition that cannot be actually experienced but that could be rationally conceived. Once rationally accessed, the real is revealed to be different from the phenomenal appearance we were used to: things look weird like in fiction. And in fact there is proximity between speculative realism and fiction since the real, as it is accessed by speculation, does not look familiar at all, being rather the secret dimension that lays beyond our subjective relation to the objects. In the first part of this paper I am going to outline the relation between fiction and speculative realism by taking into account Quentin Meillassoux and Ray Brassier's speculations: while the former clearly indicates a proximity between his philosophy and a particular genre of science-fiction, the latter, by writing the foreword of Thomas Ligotti's last book, has declared his interest in horror stories. Then, in the second part, I am going to show that both the fictional scenarios can be considered as antinomic solutions to the same speculative problem concerning the real genesis of thought and objects and I will focus the dilemma that is challenging any speculative realist philosophical position.

1. Out-Science-Fictions And The God To Come

In May 2008, Quentin Meillassoux gave a conference at the École Normale Supérieure where he explained the reasons for his interest in fiction: "Métaphysique et fiction des mondes hors-science"[1] (Metaphysics and fictions of the out-science worlds). Beside the genre known as science-fiction, he claimed that we have to account for another, more philosophically relevant, genre: what he calls *out-science-fiction*. Science-fiction is usually about possible future evolutions of our world where, thanks to the discovery of natural phenomena that would have seemed impossible before, we obtain an improvement of scientific knowledge allowing for very advanced technology. Accordingly, science-fictional future worlds do not resemble the present world, even though the physical laws are unchanged: these worlds are different only regarding our knowledge of the natural phenomena that can be lawfully produced, facts that we could not have predicted before and which would have been considered impossible. This is why, referring to David Hume's famous example of the billiard balls, Meillassoux says that science-fiction corresponds to Karl Popper's epistemological solution to the problem of the induction of causality. In this example, Hume asks if we can establish any reason for excluding any unpredictable behavior of billiard balls being hit on a table, and his conclusion is that we cannot. According to Hume, we have to rely on habits: we have to state that they will *probably* keep behaving according to the laws of mechanics. Popper's solution to the problem is that an unpredictable behavior of the balls could actually be observed since our knowledge of the laws is not perfect but perfectible. This means that it can be possible that our knowledge is not developed *enough* to allow for the prediction of all possible events, thus the observation of an unusual behavior would imply that we have to find better theories to explain what seemed inexplicable. In other words, for Popper, any unusual behavior of the balls, i.e. any unpredictable fact, is not determined by a change of the laws, but is rather a demonstration of our imperfect knowledge of the laws: it is not unpredictable in itself, it is just that *we* are not able to predict it. Thus science-fictional worlds are not characterized by different physical laws, but by a better knowledge of them. This allows for things that would have been considered impossible before.

---

1   The record of the conference is available on the ENS website: www.diffusion.ens. fr/index.php?res=conf&idconf=1286. The text was transcribed and published together with Isaac Asimov's short story "The billiard ball" in Q. MEILLASSOUX, *Métaphisique et fiction des mondes hors science* (Paris: Aux forges du volcan, 2013).

Accordingly, Meillassoux states that science-fiction describes a Popperian future where facts that would be considered impossible according to present knowledge are part of the common representation of the world, allowing for an amazingly developed technology. However, from this point of view, the belief in the necessity of natural laws is not dismissed, even though unpredictable events can force us to disregard our theories. Nevertheless, Meillassoux claims there is another kind of fiction, which he calls *out-science-fiction*, that is adequate to the correct understanding of Hume's problem (which is actually an ontological question concerning the necessity of the laws rather than an epistemological question regarding our knowledge of them). Hume does not ask if our knowledge can be so perfect as to predict any possible event. Instead, he asks if we can prove that the laws are necessary, i.e. if there is reason to infer that, given the same cause, the same effect will always follow. So, Meillassoux explains, Kant was the one that actually understood Hume's problem as an ontological issue and provided an appropriate, even if not definitive, solution. In the *Transcendental deduction* Kant claims that if the laws were contingent, then representation would be impossible: not only the billiard balls in Hume's example would behave in a strange way, but the same would also go for all the elements that in Hume's example constitute the stable frame allowing us to imagine the scene. Accordingly, if representation is possible, then laws cannot change, i.e. they are necessary: we would not be able to represent a scene where all the elements change continuously. However, as Meillassoux notices, Kant's mistake consists in supposing that contingent laws (laws deprived of a reason to be as they are) must change continuously, although nothing prevents us from thinking *they* can be stable for a while: if there is no reason for them to be necessary and eternal, there is no reason for them to change frequently. In Kant's hypothesis laws cannot be contingent since, if they were, then representation would be impossible; but, according to Meillassoux, since contingent laws can be stable for a while, their lack of necessity does not prevent representation. Thus transcendental deduction is proof that the necessity of the laws can be refuted. And this is the answer to Hume: we cannot prove that laws are necessary, but rather that they behave as though they were necessary. We can actually claim that they are contingent since this does not prevent the order of the world: non-necessary laws can determine a stable situation that, without any reason, could persist (although it does not *have* to).

For Meillassoux, as it is not possible to prove the necessity of the laws, we have to accept their contingency and this implies that the unusual behavior of the billiard ball can be considered the unpredictable consequence of a possible change of the laws. A fiction narrating such an event, where at a certain point a strange event is determined by the change of contingent laws, would be what Meillassoux calls *out-science-fiction*. Contrary to science-fiction, where the events that happen in a fictional future are explained as the necessary consequences of physical laws that we do not know in our present, out-science-fiction narrates events which are determined by a change of the laws, so they are ontologically unpredictable rather than epistemologically unpredictable. In other words, rather than relying on the idea of possible evolutions of our knowledge of necessary laws, out-science-fiction is based on the idea of the contingency of the laws, and this is why this kind of fiction is adequate to Meillassoux's solution to the problem of the induction of causality. I am not going into the detail of Meillassoux's demonstration of the absolute contingency of everything, which actually derives from his solution to Hume's problem to support the claim that only contingency is absolutely necessary.[2] I will limit myself to showing how this rational achievement brings about the convergence of philosophy and out-science-fiction. Once established that natural laws are actually contingent, then we are allowed to think of other virtually possible worlds beside the one that our science is able to describe with the use of mathematics, worlds where the laws are different from the ones we know, even if they constitute rational and coherent wholes. For Meillassoux, in fact, philosophy, as realist speculation, must be concerned with the contingent worlds that could be actualized within a change of the present set of physical laws: it has to determine what scenarios are actually thinkable as absolutely contingent, since to be contingent does not mean to be whatever. As science is the discipline that describes our world according to its known laws, science-fiction is a narration concerning a future where our knowledge is improved. On the contrary, since realist speculation is about the conditions allowing for the actualization of virtually possible facts (not simply possible according to the laws of our world) that could be actualized within a change of the laws, out-science-fiction is the narration of events that are ontologically unpredictable.

But how can philosophy deal with the actualization of laws that must determine facts that are actually contingent? It is important to notice that, for Meillassoux, science provides us with a subject-independent description of the contingent fact that is our world, thanks to mathematical formalization. For Meillassoux all contingent facts, and only contingent

---

2   For the demonstration see Q. MEILLASSOUX, *After Finitude: An essay on the necessity of contingency* (London: Continuum, 2007).

facts, can be mathematically described since mathematics, in particular set theory, entails an ontology of contingent facts. Since we cannot think of any reason for preferring one set of functions describing possible laws and since any of them is susceptible of describing a contingent fact, we are can imagine all the virtually possible worlds. However, the set of all the virtually possible worlds is not totalizable: this means that we cannot consider it as a defined totality of possibilities, according to which we could apply the calculus of probabilities. For this reason, Meillassoux calls the virtual set of all the contingent facts 'Hyperchaos', and he claims that it is a crazy time that, without any reason, can destroy one contingent world to substitute it with another one. I would like the reader to notice that, since there is no principle of reason that would render one actualization necessary rather than another, we do not have to imagine that the same world can become what it was not, as this would entail that there is a superior law forcing everything to become. Such a world would be necessary, and necessary beings cannot exist since, according to the principle of factuality, only contingent facts can be actualized. Thus, one contingent world can be actualized only after the destruction of the previous, as it is not rational to think of the existence of something being already everything without being contradictory: this something would be necessary. In this way, since we know that the virtual Hyperchaos can actualize only contingent and non-contradictory facts that can be mathematically representable, we also know that the God of metaphysics cannot exist. In fact, he is the reason for the necessity of the laws and, being such reason, he is responsible for the totality of the possible events that can happen in the world that he decided to create. Thus the God of metaphysics cannot exist as he would be a necessary and contradictory being, and, according to the principle of factuality, only contingent facts can be actualized.

We now have all the elements to understand why it is possible to speculate imagining other virtually possible worlds, that could be actualized after the end of the world in which we live: we just have to imagine their contingent and non-contradictory laws. I would like the reader to notice that these virtually possible worlds are not mere fictions, but facts that could be actually produced and that can be considered as realities whose existence does not depend on the subject who thinks them: they can actually come to existence and they are not just a production of the human mind, moreover their mathematical description guarantees the objectivity of their representation. However, it is clear that there is a proximity between Meillassoux's realist speculation and out-science-fiction, the latter becoming a philosophically relevant genre. To understand this we just need to consider the article "Spectral Dilemma,"[3] where we are invited to think of a virtually possible world in which a contingent God would allow for the resurrection of the dead and the accomplishment of Justice. Since Meillassoux established that God cannot exist as the reason that makes this world necessary, he elaborates the notion of a contingent God that could be actualized within a world of perfect justice where the laws are such that the victims of terrible deaths can come back to life. In this way we are invited to produce a realist out-science-fiction, to imagine the virtually possible world that our hope for justice deserves. Thus, once liberated from the irrationality of the principle of reason (i.e. the belief in a cause rendering the order of the world necessary), philosophy is rationally allowed to create its own *out-science-non-fictions*, to think of virtually possible worlds the laws of which are not the same as those of the world we experience. However, what is at stake here is not the role of philosophy but the nature of thought. I will deal with this issue later, after having explained why Ray Brassier's realist speculation is very close to another fictional genre: that of horror stories.

2. The Horrific Meaninglessness Of The Real

In *Nihil Unbound*,[4] Brassier exposes a strategy to access the last instance of reality outside the circle of correlation by carrying on the Enlightenment rational process of disenchantment that, to him, culminates in Nihilism. For Brassier, Nihilism is not a mere form of skepticism towards values, but a rational achievement revealing truth about reality: its meaninglessness and indifference to human purposes. Thus, Nihilism does not express a skeptical impossibility to access the real but refuses to consider the real as the foundation of our purposes and meanings. The fact that things in themselves are independent from human narratives and interpretations is, according to Brassier, the most important achievement of reason and it constitutes the starting point to re-elaborate the image of man according to scientific knowledge: we are objects like any other rather than special or privileged beings. Therefore, thought should be considered as an object whose functioning can be explained starting from brain structures, as it happens in reductionist cognitive sciences. This knowledge of objects as independent from our

---

3   MEILLASSOUX, "Spectral Dilemma", in *Collapse IV* (London: Urbanomic, May 2008), pp. 261-75.

4   R. BRASSIER, *Nihil Unbound. Enlightenment and extinction* (New York: Palgrave Macmillan, 2007).

values and purposes compels us to dismiss our traditional view of thought, provided by folk psychology, according to which intelligent activity is determined by feelings, desires and beliefs rather than by the interaction of physical structures reacting in a determined and mechanical way.

It is only by understanding how thought, as an object, is determined by other objects – rather than by human purposes, beliefs and values – that it would be possible to pursue the Enlightenment project of disenchantment and to know the real as subject-independent. Then, as Brassier claims, 'philosophers would do well to desist from issuing any further injunctions about the need to re-establish the meaningfulness of existence, the purposefulness of life, or mend the shattered concord between man and nature. Philosophy should be more than a sop to the pathetic twinge of human self-esteem.'[5] To follow rationality means to dismiss the old representation of a meaningful world in order to recognize that the real 'despite the presumptions of human narcissism, is indifferent to our existence and oblivious to the 'values' and 'meanings' which we would drape over it in order to make it more hospitable.'[6] Brassier's realist position, then, addresses a world which is totally indifferent to us, a world that has not been made for supporting our life: in such world we struggle, suffer and die without any predetermined finality.

This description could fit the scenario of a horror story. In fact we find something very similar in Thomas Ligotti's latest non-fiction book, *The Conspiracy Against The Human Race*,[7] which is opened by Brassier's foreword. Ligotti is a very well known horror stories writer, a master of this genre, and it is significant that this last work of his should be theoretical rather than fictional. Following a pessimistic philosophy *à la* Schopenhauer, Ligotti shows that the truth about the real is far scarier than any fiction. Rational knowledge reveals the world to be a cold place that does not support any projection of meaning or purpose, a place that constitutes no reason for preferring life over death: nature has not been made for our wellbeing or pleasure. It is only because we usually prefer to believe that our existence has a value that we irrationally want to survive, while reason clearly indicates that reality does not provide any base for our hopes. If we want to be rational and to consider reality for what it actually is, Ligotti suggests that the best solution is to cause the extinction of humanity, to stop

---

5   BRASSIER, *Nihil Unbound*, p. X.
6   *Ibid.*, p. XI.
7   T. LIGOTTI, *The conspiracy against the human race*, (New York: Hippocampus Press, 2010).

reproducing and to commit suicide: this is the only way to avoid useless suffering and irrational illusions. This conclusion is very close to Brassier's claim that 'thinking has interests that do not coincide with those of living; indeed, they can and have been pitted against the latter,'[8] since for reason the real must be considered as totally independent from the subjective belief that the world is there for supporting our desires. Objective knowledge of objects in themselves leads us to dismiss our will to consider life as the purpose of nature, as it is nothing but a non-necessary and unessential effect whose essence is a dead and purposeless mechanism. This is quite frightening, mostly if not taken as fiction but as a rational truth about reality. In order to better understand what is at stake here, I will explain how Brassier arrives to this conclusion.

As I've said before, for Brassier Nihilism achieved the awareness that the real is different from our representations of it, in the sense that it cannot be considered as supporting our subjective will to find meaning and value in life. Thus, the occasion to think of the real as subject-independent is provided by the actual necessity of the extinction of humanity: in order to figure out what the real is, we have to imagine it as it would be when no subject is there to interpret it according to his or her needs. Moreover, we have to think of it as able to cause the destruction of humanity without being affected by it. Extinction, in this sense, is not merely fiction but a *fact* that will actually happen when the Sun stops shining – this truth can help us stop believing that objects depend on our relations with them and that they are what we need them to be. In other words, extinction has the power of revealing that thought itself is a contingent object that will disappear, so that it cannot be conceived of as the *condition* for knowing the real but as a (subject-independent) non-necessary *product* of the metaphysical real, which determines thought together with the other objects thought represents. After the extinction of humanity, the circle of correlation (the relation within which objects are determined according to our capacities and needs) will no longer be there and the thought of this absence reveals that the real is situated outside the circle and is the actual condition of the circle's very existence. The extinction of humanity reveals thought to be an object that can be scientifically known like any other, since it is not the condition for determining objects but is an object that is determined by the real, a real that is the condition of correlation rather than a correlate of the subject's representational set. In this way, we are allowed to take into account a reductionist description of cogni-

---

8   Brassier, *Nihil Unbound*, p. XI.

tion, according to which desires and beliefs can be reduced to states of the brain that can be studied as effects of specific stimulations rather than as a-priori structures determining our knowledge.

The extinction of humanity, which entails the end of the world as a correlate of our narrations or meaningful interpretations, represents the opportunity to realize that we can conceive thought as being determined by the real rather than as the condition of the determination of objects: in other words, the real is the condition of the *existence* of objects and of the *representation* of objects in thought. Since it is the condition of the nonnecessary being of correlation (the representation of objects in thought), the real must be conceived as what lays outside the circle of determination: the real is the non-determined allowing for every determination, the nonconceptualizable allowing for any conceptualization. Thus the real cannot be a correlate of thought and it cannot be known as an object. For this reason, it has to be conceived as *being-nothing*. *Being-nothing*, as the last instance of the real, is the *zero degree* of being that does not correspond to a negative non-being as dialectically opposed to the positivity of being.

Being-nothing is the immanent condition of being, the *zero degree* of being from which any being differentiates itself without the former differentiating from the latter in return. This non-dialectical process of differentiation is what François Laruelle, one of Brassier's most important references, calls non-dialectical unilateral determination. Accordingly, since thought cannot objectify the real, it cannot actually 'know' it but can recognize that objects differentiate themselves from the real, without the real differentiating from them in return. Thus, thought itself can be known as one of these objects differentiating themselves from the real without being actually different from being-nothing. In other words, thought can conceive the real as being-nothing, thus it can recognize being-nothing as its own immanent and non-representable condition. In this way, thought realizes that the process of differentiation of objects in thought follows the same non-dialectical process of unilateral determination: thought is the zero degree of the differentiation of objects in thought, thus thought is itself the being-nothing which is the non-representable condition of representation. In other words, thought can grasp the real only by thinking according to it, by recognizing itself to be essentially nothing. This entails that knowledge is a will to nothing, the will to be equal to the real as being-nothing, as the non-determinable condition of determination.

Beside thought, life can also be analyzed like an object determined by the real beyond all our narrations and beliefs – in particular beyond the vitalist idea that the will to life is the immanent cause of the productive

becoming which is the finality of being. According to Brassier's interpretation of Freud's death drive, in fact, life does not aim at producing
life, but at repeating the trauma of its differentiation from the inorganic, a
trauma which is its non-experienceable condition. So, life aims to experience the death which is its condition; in other words, it aims to be equal to
the inorganic from which it is differentiated. In this sense, death cannot be
merely considered as a previous or a future state with respect to life, but
as the inexperienceable condition of the experience of life itself. Thus, by
wanting itself, life actually wants death: not as its origin, nor as its end,
but as the zero degree from which it differentiates itself without being
different in nature. Once established the logic of unilateral determination,
according to which beings are mere contractions of the zero degree of
being which is being-nothing or death, Brassier can easily demonstrate
that the truth of everything is that everything is already nothing or already
dead: the fact that beings are different from being-nothing does not imply
that the reality of beings is different from being-nothing. This metaphysical assumption provides the base for Brassier's project of a transcendental
realism consisting in understanding how the representation of objects in
thought is determined by the real – in other words, how scientific knowledge is possible as a representation that is independent from the subjective
pursuit of meaning and value for life.

In fact, for Brassier, reductionist science knows objects, thought and
life as independent from human needs and purposes: as differentiations of
the metaphysical real which is being-nothing, the zero degree of being. It
is clear that Brassier's conclusion is very similar to Ligotti's non-fictional
horror story where, by giving an account of all the philosophically rational demonstrations of the meaninglessness and purposelessness of life, the
world is revealed to be totally indifferent to life's needs. The question is:
are we sure that the meaninglessness of reality is not just another metaphis-
ical narration? Before answering, I will go back to Meillassoux's speculation in order to better understand its relation to fiction and its consequences
for our engagement in the world.

3. Out-Science-Fiction And The Genesis Of Thought

If we accept Meillassoux's impressive demonstration of the absolute
contingency of everything, then, as seen above, philosophy becomes a sort
of out-science-fiction that consists in thinking of virtually possible worlds,
like the one in which a contingent God to come will accomplish Justice.

What is important to notice here is that the first out-science-fiction that Meillassoux tells us, and which constitutes the condition of possibility of all the others, is the story of the emergence of thought. In order to establish that the laws of nature are contingent, in fact, he has to demonstrate first that thought, or the correlation, is contingent. In other words, the contingency of thought and the contingency of the objects of thought are entangled, and this is clearly stated in *After Finitude*:

> We have to show that the correlationist circle – and what lies at the heart of it, viz., the distinction between the in-itself and the for-us - is only conceivable insofar as it already presupposes an implicit admission of the absoluteness of contingency. More precisely, we must demonstrate how the facticity of the correlation, which provides the basis for the correlationist's disqualification of dogmatic idealism as well as of dogmatic realism, is only conceivable on condition that one admits the absoluteness of the contingency of the given in general.[9]

Thus, it is by accessing the contingency of thought, that Meillassoux can establish the contingency of natural laws since, if thought is in-itself contingent, then any other thing in-itself must be contingent. Thus, in order to claim that thought is a contingent fact, whose conditions cannot be found in nature, he must claim that thought is the result of non-necessary change of these laws. In other words, the appearance of thought is a pure contingency, it cannot be considered as an improbable outcome of the finite possible which is determined by the laws of our actual world, but as an event whose probability is in-itself not calculable, since it depends on the non-totalizable set which is the Hyperchaos.

> We can then challenge both the necessity of the preformation of life within matter itself, and the irrationalism that typically accompanies the affirmation of a novelty irreducible to the elements of the situation within which it occurs, since such an emergence becomes, on the contrary, the correlate of the rational unthinkability of the All. The notion of virtuality permits us, then, to reverse the signs, making of every radical irruption the manifestation, not of a transcendent principle of becoming (a miracle, the sign of a Creator), but of a time that nothing subtends (an emergence, the sign of the non-All). We can then grasp what is signified by the impossibility of tracing a genealogy of novelties directly to a time before their emergence: not the incapacity of reason to discern hidden potentialities, but, quite on the contrary, the capacity of reason to accede to the ineffectivity of an All of potentialities which would pre-exist their emergence. In every radical novelty, time makes manifest that it does not actualize

---

9   Q. MEILLASSOUX, *After Finitude*, p. 90.

a germ of the past, but that it brings forth a virtuality which did not pre-exist in any way, in any totality inaccessible to time, its own advent.[10]

This implies that the genesis of thought cannot be accounted by science, which is the discipline concerned with the possible outcomes of the experienced laws of nature, but only by speculative realist philosophy, which, according to Meillassoux, is concerned with the virtually possible changes of natural laws. So, imagine that we are in the world preceding the emergence of thought and that we know the laws of this world, while writing the story of the future world where there are thinking subjects, we are not making science-fiction, but out-science-fiction, since this event needs a change of the laws as its condition. Meillassoux explanation of the appearance of thought, then, can be considered as an out-science-fiction which narrates the happening of a fact that cannot be predicted according to the laws of our world: it has been determined in an absolutely contingent way. Hence, by claiming that the fact that there is a world of objects is totally independent from the fact there is thought, and by claiming that the fact that there is thought is totally independent from the fact that there are objects, Meillassoux actually succeeds in legitimating scientific knowledge as subject-independent but he asks us to believe that thought has no natural conditions, he asks us to believe in an out-science-fiction.

What is important to notice is that it is actually this out-science-fiction about the genesis of thought that allows to provide a philosophical justification of the possibility of science, since it is the reciprocal exteriority of thought and being which is the condition for subject-independent knowledge. By accessing the absolute beyond the correlation as contingency, in fact, Meillassoux is able to rationally support the thesis that matter is independent from thought and that thought is independent from matter: and this is the condition for non-correlationist knowledge. In fact, correlationism does not consists only in thinking that objects are a consequence of the activity of the subject, but also in thinking that the subject is a consequence of the activity of objects. Indeed, in both these cases, the absolute is the necessary process during which the absolute knows itself by becoming a correlate to itself: the subject becomes its own object of knowledge, or the object becomes the subject of its own knowledge. Thus, by claiming that though is a natural product, a product of the laws of physics (or that nature is a consequence of the activity of determination of the subject) we

---

10   Q. MEILLASSOUX, "Potentiality and Virtuality", in *Collapse II*, Oxford: Urbanomic, March 2007.

are reproducing an absolute circle of correlation. Meillassoux out-science-fiction about the contingent genesis of thought, then, is a non-correlationist alternative to the problem of the genesis of the conditions of knowledge.

However, if we accept Meillassoux solution, where objects can be known in themselves because thought is a product of contingency rather than a natural product, we have also to accept that there is no possibility of thinking our engagement in reality, in other words, we have to accept that philosophy is like out-science-fiction: we cannot think to change this world but we can hope that a better virtually possible world will be actualized, without any necessity, after the end of this one. In other words, while accepting Meillassoux's solution, we avoid any correlationism but we have to believe in out-science-fiction to explain why science is possible and to ground our hopes of a better world to come. The problem is that, following Meillassoux argument, the belief in the reality of out-science-fiction seems to be perfectly rational and the most strange fiction we ever heard seems to be the only true story about the real.

4. We Do Not Have To Believe In Horror Stories But We Can Enjoy Them

While Meillassoux's rationalist speculation becomes a kind of out-science-fiction, Brassier's reasoning reveals that reality is far scarier than a horror story: the will to know is a will for nothing and the will to live is a will for death. What I am going to show here is that Brassier horror story is a consequence of the same problem that originates Meillassoux's out-science-fiction: to provide an explication of the genesis of conditions of scientific knowledge. In other words, it is a matter of accessing the real as what allows the being of objects and the being of thought in such a way to ground the possibility of scientific subject-independent knowledge.

According to *Nihil Unbound*, the Real is the immanent indifferent condition of the differentiation of thought and objects (thought and objects differentiates from *being-nothing* without *being-nothing* differentiates from them in retour). In fact, the condition of thinking is generated within the separation between the inorganic dead matter and the organic living matter, thus in order to grasp its own conditions, thought has to regain the condition which precedes its own being and that allowed its instantiation: dead matter. In this way thought can access the real condition of its being only by aiming to be adequate to death. What is important to notice is that this explication of the real conditions of determination of thought and being is employed by Brassier to provide a philosophical ground to eliminativist cognitive sciences, to which a whole chapter of *Nihil Unbound* is devoted. For Eliminativism, thinking, as a process, can be analyzed by reducing it to the functioning of the brain and this allows to avoid the reference to "folk" notions such as belief, fear, purpose or desire, which are actually the phenomenal appearance of physical determinations. In other words, eliminativism considers the way in which the brain works as science considers any other natural mechanism: without any reference to an underling purpose or meaning. Hence, by explaining that thought differentiates from the inorganic without the inorganic differentiating from thought and that both, objects and thought, are essentially being-nothing, Brassier explains why cognitive science are allowed to consider thought like an object that is naturally determined like any other: in a meaningless and purposeless way.

However, it seems to me, that this sort of naturalization of thought entails the same risk of any other such attempt, which is an absolutization of the correlation. As we saw in the previous paragraph, absolute correlationism is not only implied by the claim that objects are a consequence of the activity of the subject, but also that the subject is a consequence of the activity of the objects, and, it seems to me that, in Brassier transcendental realism, even if objects are not dependent on thought, thought is in a certain way dependent on objects. To support this claim, I am going to consider the article "Concept Object",[11] where Brassier claims that absolute correlationism consists in mistaking the concept of an object, which depend on the subject, with the object in-itself.

> But when I say that Saturn exists un-posited, I am not making a claim about a word or a concept; my claim is rather that the planet which is the referent of the word 'Saturn' existed before we named it and will probably still exist after the beings who named it have ceased to exist, since it is something quite distinct both from the word 'Saturn' and the concept **Saturn** for which the word stands.[12]

Then Brassier's objection against absolute correlationism concerns only the priority of the existence of objects over thought, but is does not concern the original entanglement of objects and thought. Thus, Brassier is not objecting against absolute correlationism that the condition of knowledge is the necessary identity of the subject and of the object, but he is merely claiming that objects must exist before thought,

---

11   R. BRASSIER, "Concept Object", in *Speculative Turn: Continental Materialism and Realism*, Levi Bryant, Nick Srnicek and Graham Harman (eds.), Melbourn: Re.press 2011.

12   R. BRASSIER, "Concept Object", p. 62.

as its condition, and that concepts are different products of the same "nature", i.e. being-nothing. And I would claim that, what makes Brassier blind to the absolute correlation, is the fact that he assumes Laruelle's non-philosophy as a point of departure. In fact, Laruelle's notion of the non-philosophical Real is derived by Fichte's strategy for grounding on a necessary identity the difference of the identity and the non-identity, the difference of thought and objects. Accordingly, Brassier is not objecting to the logical structure that supports the absolute correlation, but he is actually establishing an absolute correlation in the opposite sense: it is not the subject who becomes an object to itself, but the objects differentiates in concepts which are different from the objects, while the objects are not different from thought. Hence, Brassier claims that everything is an objectification or differentiation of death instead of being an objectification of the subject. To Brassier, in fact, being-nothing is the immanent identity of objects and thought, since thought is in-itself a meaningless object which is different from other objects, while, of course, being identical to being-nothing or the zero degree of being. Thus, the condition of thinking in Brassier is the same as in any other absolute correlationism: the identity of being and thought is given as a difference immanent to the indifference of a metaphysical inobjectifiable ground, which is not exhausted by its objectifications. And this allows Brassier to provide eliminativism with a metaphysical idealist justification: conceptual structure can be analyzed to grasp the structure of reality, since the structure of reality is what allows objectifications in thought, while establishing the identity of the identity and the non-identity (concepts are different from objects but objects and thought are identical in being-nothing).

> This is to say that the structure of reality includes but is not exhausted by the structure of discretely individuated objects. Indeed, it is the nature of the epistemological correlation between individuated concepts and individual objects that is currently being investigated by cognitive science. [...] Dualisms such as those of meaning and being, and of knowing and feeling, are not relics of an outmoded metaphysics; they are makeshift but indispensable instruments through which reason begins to be apprized both of its continuity and its discontinuity with regard to what it is still expedient to call 'nature'.[13]

While providing a philosophical justification for scientific knowledge, Brassier is merely claiming that objects are independent from thought, since thought differentiated from inorganic matter which is the condition

---

13   R. BRASSIER, "Concept Object", p. 65.

for its being, but he is considering thought as dependent from objects: concepts are naturally determined according to the real and the real is the condition of objects becoming correlates to themselves (as thought is an object). And this entails that he keeps the same explication of the genesis of the condition of thinking that characterized correlationism while eliminating the narration of the purposefulness of the process to substitute it with a narration of its purposelessness: knowledge is not the purpose and the accomplishment of being, but the purpose of knowledge is to be equal to being as death and to the real as being-nothing. Thus, rather than eliminating the metaphysical narrations where knowledge is the aim of a purposeful being, Brassier merely creates a narration where the aim of knowledge is the purposelessness of being. In fact, it seems clear to me that meaninglessness is a subjective judgment and that nature, for science, is neither meaningful, nor meaningless since any judgment concerning meaning (or its absence) is not objective, thus not scientific. So, to claim, as Brassier does, that nature has no meaning implies the reference to a nihilist narrative that merely inverts the sign of vitalist meaningful narratives without escaping from their correlationist condition.

We could say, then, that Brassier's transcendental realism is actually an horror story, a very convincing one since the arguments are perfectly rational and philosophically relevant. The problem is that he is not establishing any real condition for a non-correlationist knowledge of the real but he is merely claiming that thought is a natural mechanism that, like any other, cannot be objectively accounted as meaningful, even if this does not imply that it can be objectively accounted as meaningless. So we do not have more reason to believe in the purpose of existence than in its purposelessness: both are metaphysical narrations.

Conclusions: the fiction of natural reason or the fiction of unnatural reason?

As seen above, both Meillassoux's and Brassier's speculations tend to approach the disengagement of fiction rather than suggesting a way of being engaged in solving problems according to the interests of life. In fact, for the former, the absolute contingency of anything can only lead to hoping for a virtually possible contingent god to come and for a world that might (or might not) be actualized after the end of our own. For the latter, the objective knowledge of reality does not support our need for meaning, value and purpose, so the only thing that reason suggests to do is to know objects as though we were already dead. However, both the fictional scenarios can be considered as two solutions to the same problem concerning the real conditions of the being of thought and objects. In fact, the real, as Hyperchaos or as being-nothing, is accessed as the condition of existence of two different kind of beings, dead inorganic objects and thought, and it is the particular way in which the real actualizes these beings that renders knowledge possible. On the one hand, the virtual Hyperchaos is responsible for the being of contingent facts (objects and thought) and, according to Meillassoux, only contingent objects can be mathematically described as subject-independent by object-independent contingent subjects: in this way scientific knowledge is legitimated. On the other hand, being-nothing is the metaphysical reason for the existence of a reality that can be scientifically known as purposeless and meaningless by a reason which shares, essentially, this same nature. In other words, in both the cases, the effort consists in rationally accessing the non-experienceable real which is the condition of possibility of scientific knowledge, i.e. of the possibility of organizing the data of experience in an objective way. Hence, what is actually at stake here is a true metaphysical enquiry into the real conditions of existence of knowledge rather than a mere description of the already given subjective transcendental structure. Thus, since it is a matter of grasping the real non-experienceable conditions of experience, we talk of realist *speculation*, that can be defined as the effort of providing the typically post-Kantian problem of the genesis of the transcendental with a solution which is adequate to contemporary scientific knowledge.

With regard to post-Kantianism, then, Meillassoux and Brassier offer two original solutions: the former explains the origin of thought and beings while refusing the idealist idea that knowledge is possible because being is, in-itself, the process during which the object becomes a correlate to itself, i.e. the subject of its own knowledge (or the subject becomes a correlate to himself, i.e. by knowing himself as an object); the latter refuses the idea that knowledge is the purpose of being, the idea that human intelligent life is what express the highest degree of some essential power of the real, such as will, productivity, creativity, etc.

However, only Meillassoux's speculative materialism is able to completely overcome absolute correlationism, since, as I explained before, Brassier's transcendental realism lingers on a form of idealist dialectic that makes of the object and the subject the identity of the identity and the non-identity (objects being different from thought without thought being different from objects, and being-nothing being indifferent to both). Hence the dilemma is the following: if we accept Meillassoux's solution, we avoid any form of correlationism, but we have to believe in a fictional scenario where reason is not a natural product, and this contradicts contemporary scientific credo, according to which thought finds its conditions in nature; conversely, if we accept Brassier's solution, we are allowed to consider thought as a natural product, but we have to believe in a new metaphysical narration, a scary one, where the interests of reason are against the interests of life. It would seem, then, that to provide scientific subject-independent knowledge with a philosophical justification (concerning how thought and being must be in themselves for science to be possible), we have to make a difficult, or even impossible, choice between a non-metaphysical and non-correlationist out-science-fiction where thought appeared without any reason as totally unnatural contingent actualization, and a metaphysical and partially correlationist horror story where thought is an object that, like any other, can be objectively known but as a purposeless and meaningless natural mechanism. This is the serious antinomy which is determining today most of the divergences among the philosophers who are interested in understanding what is the real and how reason can access it.

What do we have to do, then? Do we have to go back to metaphysical narrations where the purpose of being is to know itself by attaining its highest degree of creativity in humans? Or do we have to stop asking this kind of metaphysical questions since they lead to nothing but antinomies? Or, instead, do not we have, to keep on seeking a non-metaphysical and non-correlationist explication of the natural conditions of thought? I think that the latter is the right option: speculative realism's fictions are not mere fictions, they are totally reasonable philosophical efforts to answer a fundamental question, a question that matters today if philosophy wants to have a role in the debate concerning knowledge, rather than culture, if it wants to have the possibility of discussing and grounding, rather than criticizing only, the way in which science is succeeding in describing things as they are, instead of being obsessed by the way in which we see them.

III

CHASE THE RABBIT, OR, LOCATING ABSTRACTION IN NATURE[1]

BEN WOODARD

Those, then, who want to find themselves at the starting point of a truly free philosophy, have to depart even from God. Here the motto is: whoever wants to preserve it will lose it, and whoever abandons it will find it. Only those have reached the ground in themselves and have become aware of the depths of life, who have at one time abandoned everything and have themselves been abandoned by everything, for whom everything has been lost, and who have found themselves alone, face-to-face with the infinite: a decisive step which Plato compared with death. That which Dante saw written on the door of the inferno must be written in a different sense also at the entrance to philosophy: 'Abandon all hope, ye who enter here.' Those who look for true philosophy must be bereft of all hope, all desire, all longing. They must not wish anything, not know anything, must feel completely bare and impoverished, must give everything away in order to gain everything. It is a grim step to take, it is grim to have to depart from the final shore.

Schelling, *On the Nature of Philosophy as a Science*

1. Reconstituting Nature

The dissolution of the always tenuous association of projects clustered under the moniker Speculative Realism has left in its place numerous micro-endeavours which, while even more disparate than before, universally question the future prospects of the human whether it be inhumanly normative, aesthetically speculative, or ontologically prolific. These projects have largely fallen into two poles; either strongly emphasizing epistemological rigor or attempting to replace epistemology with ontological or sensorial apparatuses. In both extremes the naturalistic roots of human sense and human capacities more generally are abstracted: either reduced and

---

1   This text is largely the result of attending the Summer School in Continental Philosophy at Duquesne University in August of 2013 where Iain Grant and Jason Wirth were lecturers. I am also indebted to conversations with G. Anthony Bruno, Daniel Whistler, Deanna Khamis, and Teresa Gillespie.

contained within the permit of scientific discourse alone or obscured in phenomenological or speculative exacerbations. In the following essay I argue for the importance of the work of Iain Hamilton Grant and his elaboration of FWJ von Schelling's expansive naturalism. In such a naturalism the various capacities of thought (reason, imagination, intuition, speculation etc.) become natural forces that do not belong to the human *stricto sensu*, but happen to, and through, the human.

In Grant's articulation, the difficulty arises in locating and identifying how and from where the abstract capacities of the human mind act. In order to extend and modify Grant's account, I argue that the work of various theorists of de-centralized cognition (whether enactivist, embodied mind, geometrical-cognitive and the like) can be utilized to address both the epistemological and the sensorial without over-relying on the normative or the phenomenological at the cost of nature. Grant's approach is not as far afield as it first appears, as he takes inspiration most heavily from Schelling and Post-Kantian thought more generally – the latter being deeply influential on the normative approach of thinkers such as Robert Brandom who in turn serves as a crucial theoretical touchstone for Reza Negarestani, Peter Wolfendale, and others. Brandom's and the Pittsburgh Hegelians' take on German Idealism however is one divested of any concern for nature other than what science defines as the space of nature.[2] Beyond placing an emphasis on nature against those who would read it out of the German Idealist tradition (and, furthermore, who focus more on Fichte and Hegel then on Schelling), Grant's work focuses on a particular reading of the relation between the transcendental methodology of Schelling's project and the maximally expansive naturalistic account which grounds it.

Building on Grant's project but taking quite different paths in regards to contemporary thought, I will argue that the trajectory which Schellingian naturalism takes is one that appears in the continental tradition to combine two quite different forms of analytic thinking: epistemological infinitism and de-centralized theories of cognition. Essentially, I will argue that Schelling's naturalism with a derivative transcendental method combines

---

2   This is following primarily from the work of John McDowell particularly in his well known text *Mind and World*. While McDowell's influence in this regard is largely following from Wilifrid Sellars this is a particularly narrow reading of Sellars as Sellars did not believe questions of science (and questions of nature) should be left to scientists alone. The work of both Ray Brassier and Johanna Seibt for example demonstrate Sellars' concern with nature as constitutive processes informing the way in which we think and act in the world that necessitates rational investigation beyond instrumental testing.

the materiality of embodied cognition while correcting the halting problem of infinite regress in epistemology through embodiment; a notion of embodiment that is not restricted to biological corporeality, but broadened to define a ungrounded dispositional account of nature, one where materiality is the localization of powers' interactions.

2. What is a Location?

> We must of course assume that the Earth is the point of emergence for humanity – why, we do not know, it refers to relations we cannot survey, but humanity is therefore not specifically a product of the Earth – it is a product of the entire process – not the Earth alone, the entire cosmos contributes to humanity, and if of the Earth, as, continuing from the earlier standpoint, he is, then humanity is not exclusively created for the Earth, but for all the stars, since humanity is created as the final goal of the cosmos. If humanity appears to be a local essence, this is not what it originally is, but has become localized.
> Schelling, *Exhibition of the Process of Nature*

In his well-known and remarkable text *All or Nothing*, Paul Franks argues that German Idealism writ large is a response to the Agrippean (or Munchausen) trilemma, of how to sufficiently ground any given knowledge claim while avoiding both unfettered scepticism and rigid dogmatism. The trilemma consists of three equally unsatisfactory options: circularity (or that every consequent leads back to its antecedent), regression (that every step, every consequent requires infinitely more proofs), or axiom (we make a common sense justification to what we are claiming to know as an axiom). But this trilemma is one that centres on the justification theory of *knowledge*, it articulates thought as a disembodied and dematerialized activity. Knowledge and justification are taken only as *within* knowledge, or within the space of reasons that already has autonomy from nature.

Infinitism, the second option, is generally considered the worst choice, yet this is only taking for granted this disembodied version of the thinker regressing. But, as is argued in various recent forms of epistemological infinitism, embracing infinitism does not entail embracing circularity since infinitists do not suggest that a justifcational ground for X can *contain* X. That is to say, circularity eliminates the fact that causal chains have origins (regardless of whether those origins can or cannot be ultimately discovered). Or, perhaps in league with Franks, this epistemological circularity is replaced by infinitism when such circularity is combined with the monist demand i.e. that there is a holism (albeit an indeterminable evolving whole) in which the infinite products affect its shape. The second major claim of infinitist epistemology is that while one rejects circularity one can always demand that a reason for doing something requires a ground that must be provided on pain of arbitrariness. Or, simply put, the general infinitist argument is that causal chains or lines of argumentation have no *ultimate* halting point. But this infinite is augmentative in the procedure of pursuing and does not fall immediately into viciousness.[3] Here we can take the problem of location as an example.

The statement 'all location is relative', while appearing quite obvious, points to a peculiar tension. Anything is where it is in relation to something else or several other things. Because of its fundamental relativity, location must have a stopping or halting point in order to avoid infinite regress. This halting point for the human is generally that of the Earth as global positioning systems frame larger to small nested scales – from land masses down to neighbourhoods, down to in relation to a human or other form of body.

The presumed relativity of a location, however, assumes different means of navigation and/or different material consistencies of the things located relative to one another. Put simply, a map presumes a means of travel (or more abstractly motion) and the means of travel therefore engage with different constraints: the elevation of a mountain peak means something quite different for a plane than it does for a creature scaling it. Thus a location begins to suggest a spectrum of material conditions as any location becomes subject to different natural forces. The relativity of a location is not then just a place relative to another place or another thing, but also becomes a collection of tendencies or powers – forces that tend to circulate and or pass through thereby indicating the kinds of means one utilizes to reach or pass through it. The opening of forces into a location is already pressured by the capacity to locate and reach it – one can survey from a distance with increasingly elaborate technological means or explore by merely moving to and through the space mapping 'as one goes'. These procedures are not mutually exclusive as the surprises of the terrain or unexpected forces require reliance on methods one might not have practiced in advance or predicted, paths sighted as passable may become unbreachable because of the grounds on which they lie or a sighted distance in the desert may, on the course of moving towards it, prove highly inaccurate.

We can then begin to question what the potencies to navigate themselves

---

3   See T. E. Tahko, "Boring Infinite Descent," in *Metaphilosophy*, Vol. 45, No. 2, April 2014. As Ricki Bliss has argued however, circularity may not necessarily lead to viciousness.

rely on or, are relative to. That is, the sighting, guessing, etc. has its roots in more immediate goals: that of biological survival. The potential equation of 'relative to' or 'grounded in' becomes apparently undividable as the means by which we map the relative is grounded in the biological means we trace the most efficient paths of escape, pursuit, concealment and so on. Since our own location as biological entities is always a mobile one, the problem of location and navigation is consequent upon the forms of this mobility – our mobility being the way in which we see ourselves open to external forces as well as productive or contributive of and to them. Furthermore, these natural processes to which we are tied unbind as well as bind us to a place or to a location. Processes restrict us to zones of habitibility as well as to a gravitational body more generally.

Thought appears as that by which we can survey all spaces and places, locate all instances of process, all things – it appears to have dis-located itself from the world in order to grasp it. While thought stems from the mind thought cannot be located once it has left the head. This location of thought is located by thought itself – thought being the ultimate locator but a difficulty arises from the 'us' (the thing that thinks) being in the same 'place' as the process of thought.[4] While thought appears as the infinite locator it fails to locate itself in that, to return to relativity, thought divides itself from itself (mirroring nature but never containing it) thereby producing wherein each production is non-trivial to the extent that it adds to the activity of what it seeks (without ever discovering its origin in space-time). Thought attempting to locate thought divides thought *ad infinitum*, yet this division is incomplete as each instance of thought is only 'separate' from one another in terms of the labour or activity of thought itself being forced here and not there – location begins to become identified with practical or pragmatic focus. Questions of origin and final destination exclude the immediate middle, but this exclusion can be positively (or constructively) viewed (following Gilles Chatelet) as *extainment*. 'Who am I here, what am I doing etc.' are questions which too often are reversed or fast forwarded, while at larger scales the individual that we are becomes immobilized – that is, the locative capacity of thought functions to mobilize the thing that thinks only so that the breadth of its movements confirm its widest capability, but a capability from nowhere in particular.

Schelling's much lauded *Essay on Human Freedom* does not define freedom as a strictly human capacity but attempts to draw out what individuation (as an ontological location) is, or, how the forces in a particular

---

4   See A. BERTHOZ, *The Brain's Sense of Movement*, in which he quotes Gilles Chatelet.

location determine a thing following from the argument that everything is what it is and where it is precisely when it is not everything else.[5] Individuality, or any one thing's specificity, marks a strange alliance between location and existence, location becomes a tension between where and what. The question 'where am I?' and 'what am I' form an identity where they are different only as their bond is stretched but not broken. Hence why Schelling describes individuation in terms of the veil of sadness over all of nature.[6] Since all finite existence requires as its condition particularity, this can only mean that all finite existence and subsequently all finite life must wage war against what opposes it and be worn out by its own activity. Limitation as an ontological location (to be made here by these forces) is the necessary condition of all life that introduces the possibility of navigation, thereby producing the problem of location which is so often papered over by the romanticization of place and belonging.

Location becomes a point of indifference between activity and identity. Like that of reason as a coordinator of thought, location becomes the coordination of space itself, between space as it is and that which populates space the subsequent dimensions of which simultaneously carve out and propagate space. Location then, as already suggested, is that problem which emerges from thought arising where this arising is itself a problem of thought.[7] The most formal approach to location, which very well may be the least satisfactory answer, would be that a location is a point, a point being a determination made by us in increasingly stable (in terms of universally addressable) means. The initial act of determining a point, however, is one of intellectual intuition – an act that is made possible by, and engenders, the coincidence of what we think and what is. While intellectual intuition is one of the most critiqued concepts of Schelling's philosophy (and idealistic philosophy more generally) this is often taken to be because it assumes a degree of temporal immediacy (of knowledge just arriving from nowhere) when, in fact, it is a gesture of spatial immediacy in which time (at least as subjectively grasped) is brought to it.

As Schelling has it, intellectual intuition is the point where the infinite and the finite destroy one another, where it is impossible to distinguish between the doing and thinking the doing (as an act of determination or,

---

5   This is the concluding thought from Iain Grant's "The Construction of Matter and the Deep Field Problem" talk given at Speculations on Anomalous Materials, Fridericianum, Kassel, January 4, 2014.

6   F. W. J. VON SCHELLING, *Philosophical Inquiraries into the Essence of Human Freedom*, trans. James Guttman, (Peru: Open Court, 1986), 79.

7   See I. GRANT, "Movements of the World," *Analecta Hermeneutica*, 3. pp. 1-17, 2011.

in his language, as postulated). Intuition is a producing through which the subject becomes an object to itself[8] with determination being that procedure which finds a place between abolishing and engendering.[9] But an interesting division occurs between the human and the nature which functions as its producer and its (however difficult to determine) ground. While intellectual intuition as determination or postulation allows the thinker to become an object to herself, to say 'here I am', Schelling's definition of thought is that it is nature's attempt to become an object to itself and not only the subject's.[10]

Thought can locate itself while nature cannot and hence the argument arises that thought (at least as it functions for humans) is what locates itself as having no fixed location (as the epigraph above suggests) and yet this is only possible through the abandonment of fixed origins other than as self determined origins, or the genetic view of the human as being capable of producing numerous futures. Nature is the set of potencies that attempts to become an object to itself, but in failing to do so creates everything there is, which in turn fails to be an object to itself. In essence nature produces human thought in order to map itself, but that mapping or modelling capacity over-succeeds in attempting to map the future by using the past as so much genetic material which has the danger of eliminating nature as ground or of forgetting its potencies as unground. Because nature is the space wherein/whereout space is created it has no location but is spread outwards by the dimensional consequences of inorganic, organic, and noetic explorations. Essentially where and what, or location and ontology, become increasingly difficult to separate.

3. What Is Any Thing Apart From Where It Is?

Schelling argues in *The Philosophy of Art* that there is a law of the universe (*weltgesetz*) that decrees 'that everything encompassed by it have its prototype or reflex in something else'[11] and that art and philosophy treat each other as both prototype and reflex.[12] Or, as Schelling articulates it

8   F. W. J. SCHELLING, *tr. Peter Heath, System of Transcendental Idealism*, (Charlottesville: University of Virginia Press, 1978), 28.

9   *Ibid.*, p. 63.

10   *Ibid.*, p. 25.

11   SCHELLING, *The Philosophy of Art*, trans. Douglas Stott, (Minneapolis: University of Minnesota Press, 1989). 5.

12   *Ibid.*, p. 6.

much later in his life, the law of the world is 'that all potentialities self-fulfil and none are suppressed, that all potencies deploy in equal measure.' Or, simply put, nature is that which is as productive as it can be while also being as stable as it can be – this means, of course, that nature is neither endlessly productive nor endlessly stable but its productivity depends upon its stability and its stability upon its productivity. In this sense, and to return to the dependency of antecedent and consequent noted above, any philosophical notion of the absolute is *consequent* for Schelling and any notion of individuality is incomplete. Or as Schelling puts it: 'nothing that we call individual things is real in itself. They are individual because they do not take up the absolute whole into themselves and into their particular form and have separated themselves from that whole; in a reverse fashion, to the extent that they do have it within themselves, they are no longer individual.'[13] An individual then, taking here our thinker-as-Munchausen as example, to be in the world operates by forcing the world to be an outgrowth of it (delimitation), or fuel for it (extraction). In the first case the thinker figure idealizes its ontological constitution and thereby abstractly its location – its capacity to delimit, to cordon off sections of the world, is based upon its purportedly groundless capacity of reason. In the case of extraction the thinker-as-Munchausen enmeshes itself directly into the world in a physicalized sense, so that the thinker is the place from where it acts. The act of extraction becomes one of self-annihilation as the thinker-as-Munchausen has no space to move.

To avoid these extremes, the notion of the world (as opposed to the Earth) and our location in it functions as a conceptual limitation of the sensed world. Nature as such functions as a dotted line as each act that occurs within it has the potentiality of extending past the boundaries that are set and thereby the boundary of nature is an instance of nature as well. Hence Schelling's comment above regarding the relation of the individual and the universal. In the model of delimitation the thinker-as-Munchausen pulls themselves from the swamp as both thinker and world are only functionally or normatively defined, they are collections of rules themselves produced by the purportedly ungrounded nature of thought. At the other end of the spectrum, in terms of extraction, the Munchausen-thinker, in attempting to pull themselves out of the swamp of nature, is hyper-located (all is physicalized) and manages to unground themselves completely, inverting their body, standing in the swamp of matter with nerves and muscles exposed while organs dangle like tree ornaments.

---

13   *Ibid.*, p. 34.

The third way engenders a notion of continuity but one coupled with locative ambiguity, which dislocates the human from the centre of any particular world, though not from the materiality of the earth or, in particular, the swamp. Various forms of thinking cannot escape this predicament of being caught in a continuous horror, but only mobilize processes of nature recognized in and by the human which can be mobilized and repeated by our own activities. The question becomes of how to determine the appropriate safe-distance made possible by, and the formation of materiality between, the shear ideal and the shear physical. To arrive at this middle ground does not entail the *a priori* limiting of the reach of the ideal upwards or the physical downwards but in fact the exacerbation of both in the time to determine the limits of both.

Schelling argues that since human thought is always awash in an excess of thought, the only means of getting to something even resembling objectivity, to be able to make the determination 'x is x or x is y', one requires an excess of ideal activity. It is only by over-thinking, chasing down all the potential roots as well as all the potential consequences of a determined thing, that one is capable of detecting where they are from. Since it is necessary that we isolate in order to think according-to a particular individual (to recognize any one thing's capacity to demonstrate or index consequent absolutes) then it is thought that makes it possible to express a potency of nature for us, to demonstrate something like an absolute or universal – not as something 'out of this world' but within it and constituting it along with other potencies, a potency that cuts across multiple fields of existence. The object so delimited becomes a point of indifference (or a meta-stability) where the absolute (or the broadest concepts) enter the particular, become manifest in a singular determination.[14] Following this the universal or absolute tendency can be extracted, but it order to remain a potency it must be demonstrated (that is reconnected to the world of things). As Schelling writes: 'Everything that is not the absolute is only to the extent that within it, being is not equal to the idea, that is, to the extent that it is itself merely privation and not true being.'[15]

How does one individual identify another individual – is it an operation of delimitation, determination, or extraction? Delimitation suggests a de-localized or disembodied practice, of thought upon a material that has an ambiguous nature. Determination sets itself up as a temporary, and perhaps unsuccessful capture of a selection (such as an image as an object

---

14   *Ibid.*, p. 15.
15   *Ibid.*, p. 25.

of visual perception), whereas extraction presupposes a removal of an individual from its location by seemingly contradictorily over-identifying with the physical. One means of attempting to demonstrate the difference here is to take the concept of the world (as an incomplete whole) in terms of a geological process. Delimitation as a conceptual activity admits no locational aspect – the objects of sense are already available to us (this corresponds to the world of sense being already conceptual laden, or the world being always-already conceptually graspable) and just need to be separated. Delimitation is a surface-level operation, a sifting through the motions on the earth closest-at-hand, but a closeness that is completely ideal in a naïve sense. Or the assigning of value without taking into account how that very assigning is being performed without acknowledging the roots of the agent doing the assigning.

Determination admits a certain location. It admits being physical mediated in the world as well as admitting that the act of determination requires a kind of violence on the materiality of the world, or what appears in the world as being a slower motion than that of thought. Determination is a bordering of the individual but in a way that maintains the weakness of its framing. Determination would be a translation or transformation of one material into another in order to utilize it while keeping in mind the potential costs (both path and future orientated) of committing that act. If delimitation is a panning for gold on the surface of the world, then determination is a geological experiment, a limited digging followed by endless tests and inquiries. Lastly then, extraction recognizes the location, the ground on which to stand, but over-physicalizes the relation and rips out the individuated, the material desired, from its surrounding connections, a kind of open-pit mining of the sensed world. Thus, a parallelism exists between how human-rooted the capacity for abstraction is, and how a human, granted or given such a capacity, relates itself to nature. That is the spectrum of ideal, material, and physical that corresponds to delimitation, determination, and extraction. They all feed into the creation of the human but the subsequent human capacity to divide and individuate leads to abstraction, abstraction being the mobilization of the ideal to stretch or test the extensity of any particular object.

What this means is that the human relation to the world, a relation that is ideal, material, and physical, can be imagined and then abstracted, moved off the world, in such a manner that our relation to individuals purportedly becomes one solely produced by us. In other words, the human and animal capacity to divide up the world, to predict our movements across the earth, to form tools and so on, negates the earth to the degree that abstraction (as the ideal stretching of the physical) is applied to us making us into an image of ourselves and no longer an animal located within material and physical relations. The material, in this case, is the mediation of the ideal and the physical, where the former are the most active capacities of nature, while the latter are its most effective stabilizing elements. As Schelling puts it in the *Philosophy of Art*: 'The first potence of nature is matter to the extent that it is posited within a predominance of affirmed existence or under the form of the informing of ideality into reality.'[16]

Thus for Schelling the ideal is not that which belongs only to human thought, but that which appears to us as the activity of human thought, while ideality more broadly construed is the creative powers of nature which thought *appears* to closely resemble. The material is the continuity between this creativity and its self-inhibition in the formation of the physical, of the individuation of particular things, particular individuals at various scales of organization etc. Locating the human as creative but as a part of this world (i.e. as subject to larger creative forces) can, as demonstrated in the beginning of this paper, lead to an assumption that the human lends itself to the creativity and stability of the world in the phenomenological weight of givenness or the aforementioned immediacy of experience – basically that the material is replaced with the being or existence of the human, i.e. the human becomes the mediator of all in holding the thought and world together.

Essentially our capacity for thought and the consequent capacity for scaling it upwards according to each of the various forms of thinking (concept, intuition, imagination, speculation, abstraction etc.) does not dislocate us from within the world in such a way that the power of thought ontologically or physically de-naturalizes us from the world *tout court*. Thought, in its various forms, and as particularly evident in abstraction as the most extreme instance of cognitive stretching, mobilizes animalistic navigational capacities at various scales, but this mobilization as a material mobilization mediates between the ideal motions of the mind and the physical or embodied roots of that motion, as well as its capacities as a material transmitter between the chemical, the biological and so on. It is only through these uncontrollable complicities with the various strata of nature that the human thinker or the practitioner is even capable of existing having a trajectory, of being tied materially to a location.

If everything is a part of nature, as Schelling seems to mean when he states that 'anything whose conditions cannot be given in nature must be absolutely impossible', then the image of the thinker-as-Munchausen is itself a

---

16   *Ibid.*, p. 27.

part of nature. This in turn suggests that the image as demonstration, denied of its artificiality, cannot be critiqued for the failure of representation to 'capture the experience' since all representation fails necessarily because of the insufficiency of nature. In fact, nature cannot become an object to itself, since the combat between motion and rest is itself constantly between endless motion and a frozen calmness. Thought taken as an ideal activity fails only when it denies the location from which it occurs as well as the fact that the location it indexes, where it points, may be beyond the purview of the instance of the thought issued. If production, whether human or non-human, is a side-effect of nature's productivity, then the difference between forms of production must be taken as various forms of nature's attempt to relate to itself, whereby the image of the thinker-as-Munchausen is the human instance of this attempt at self-mediation or self relation. Only through the recognition of the alienness of, and dependency on, ground can thought and movement lead to an exploration of the objects thought encounters.

4. Why Does Everything Produce Everything Else?

That is, if abstraction is a mobilization of an object's extensity, an object being a cut-out of the field of sense which we take to be the world, than it would appear that the individual entity, or the object, or the work of art in its various modes for example, is a re-physicalization or materialization of that abstraction whether as a fixed-position of a photograph or a physical object, or some other redirection, reallocation of nature towards a perceived end or perceived desire. Thus one could argue that even when the work is mediated in such a way to view itself as a mediation, when something is post-conceptual or even abstract, this never escapes the continuity of production, but attempts to cut itself materially from a particular kind of mediation. Yet it is never non-performing an indexing, even if that indexing is more physical or more ideal; it can never be shorn from its known and unknown antecedents and its possible consequents.

For Schelling, the internal coordination of the living being is what is magnified and exported in the creative process. If this is the case then the danger for humans becomes of overproducing abstraction – of encasing oneself in self-modeling that have no obtainment on mapping the world. Just as nothing can exist without its antecedent conditions, nothing can exist for its own sake as this would be to confuse the ideal with the physical – to deny mediation as the space and time between the two. That is, the place from which one divided the ideal and the physical (or what is for us thought and nature) is itself divided by them. So while the acts we perform are in this middle space where we are uncertain of the material ramifications (of how our acts redirect, block, or accelerate), this can only occur in a certain space of ignorance since we can neither catch up with or contain the productivity of nature in anyone place. There is no place of the human or for the human that can be immobilized or ontologically stabilized by phenomenology or other forms of humanistic buttressing – there is no fundamental isolation from nature. No production of human thought whose conditions cannot be found in nature must be impossible.

Thus the hard limit or halting point of the normative retrojects a pragmatic thesis backwards into nature, thereby eliminating it. While this form of pruning makes sense in the space of making a normative act that is, in terms of making a decision or performing a particular act rather than another, that such an instance of determination is a ground has no basis other than a fear of an unmappable responsibility. All human-'caused' production cannot be inwardly directed due to the fact that all determination requires a pushing aside of both the ideal and the physical aspects of nature. The act of determination then is one that splits an object producing new determinations (whether sheerly ideal or sheerly physical) which forces the thinker to move beyond the initial determination via an examination of the ideal and physical consequences and antecedents from a non-trivial yet mobile perspective. The act of determination would be like the cutting of an object wherein the two halves are larger than the original. To engage with the individual that is the human then – to pull ourselves out of the swamp of matter – does not mean that reason or thought trumps the material nor that thought is tangled in a way that gives us complete control. Rather, it is the act of determination, "of pulling", that is a material instance of the ideal (which we manipulate but that belongs to nature) and the physical (which is essentially a hardened slowed-down concretion of nature's activities), which broadens the continuity to which we belong. The maddening consequence however, is that his belonging is not one of containment but, again following Iain Grant, one of extainment, where natural production is not within nature but creating a temporary within-ness as it pushes every entity, and every entity pushes every other entity.

Nature is thus the name for the equi-primordiality of all things as Schelling denies, against the researches of Goethe and his attempt at finding the primal germ, that there can be a singular origin of all things (whether theological or physical).[17] One could argue that the paranoia of human excep-

---

17   The equiprimordiality of creation lends itself to the image from Buddhist philosophy of Indra's Net.

tionalism is a retroactive injection of the origin problem – the production of origins leading us to be 'forced' to solve it by making ourselves the arbiters of our very own kingdom of ends (as Kant phrased it). That is, the impossibility of finding the ultimate ground gives us 'reason' to make ourselves self-grounding (in the first sheerly ideal model of Munchausen's self-liberation from the muck) or always-already grounded without question in the self-destructive physicalist model.

It is only in embracing the strains of continuity that the human engagement with and as nature that the potencies of nature can be appreciated. Every human addition expands the world as an ideal entity and, potentially, physically as well. Schelling's account of nature, brought into the present moment, ultimately questions contemporary naturalism's break between epistemological and ontological strands in which the former is all too often over-determined by the appearance of current scientific method and not by the production of science as such. In regards to the ontological, Schelling demonstrates the necessity for a pre-conceptual realm of nature albeit one that can only be speculatively formulated from the conceptual realm but that informs even the most pragmatic operations.

IV

PLEROMATICA
OR ELSINORE'S DRUNKENNESS[1]

GABRIEL CATREN

'[...] y en esa noche oscura del fosfeno ver surgir un delfín
iridiscente un arco iris de delfines un delfinado aéreo o irisado
un arqueado delfín'[2]
Nestor Perlongher, *Alabanza y Exaltacion del Padre Mario*

In what follows, I outline a phenoumenodelic scene for conceiving
modern existence, a scene composed of a *suspended stage* (a phantas-
magoric ark '*between the constellations and the sea*'), a *foolhardy task*
('*to vanquish chance*'), and a *patient method* ('*word by word*'). Let's
start with a stubborn fact: we have undergone an exquisite and memo-
rable crisis, a foundational one: the ground has been taken out. Beginning
with the Copernican suspension of the earth and Kant's transcendental
exponentiation of it, we have endured manifold upheavals, a series of
ungroundings that continue to undermine the pre-modern forms of building, dwelling and thinking. The transcendental relativisation of the scientific worldview, the nineteenth century's '*crisis of verse*', the crisis of
foundations in mathematics, the crisis of tonality, the unheimlichization
of the Cartesian subject, the relativistic crisis of the spatiotemporal background, the quantum crisis of (onto-)logic – all of these 'crises' share a
common structure: in each case, a fixed God-given structure, a conjugat-
ed name-of-the-father, a supposed last instance, an aprioristic motionless
Ur-Frame is brought into play, rendered dynamical, naturalized, thrown
into the scene, suspended among a multiplicity of other possible frames.
Far from being an unexpected disaster, this relativizing suspension of Ur-
Grounds is the fine result, refracted into the diverse modes of experience,
of the modern deconstruction of ornitheology, that is – in Mallarmé's

---

1   I would like to thank Dylan Trigg for helpful conversations concerning the
     subjects addressed here and Robin Mackay for reading and making editorial
     suggestions on a first draft of this text.
2   Nestor Perlongher, *Alabanza y Exaltacion del Padre Mario*, in *Chorreo de las
     iluminaciones, Poemas completos* (Buenos Aires: Seix Barral, 1997), p. 335.

terms – of the long and '*terrible struggle with that old and wicked plumage, now crushed, fortunately, God*'.

Now, such a foundational crisis could lead us from bad – the transcendent Father – to Worse – an unrestrained contingency. With the heavens stormed and the earth suspended, it might seem as if there were nothing that could *fix* the bad infinity of chance and sublate the lack of any transcendent orientation for existence and for thinking. Adopting a neo-Karamazovian style, one could argue that, if God does not exist, then necessarily anything can be the case. However, the putative implication from the barred names-of-the-father *qua* Ur-Frames to the consecration of chance is a *non sequitur*. If we refuse to accept the supposed self-evidence of this inference, then the death of God posits a post-critical Elsinorian dilemma that calls for a subjective resolution: we can either accept (or even hypostatize) the sovereignty of chance, or we can interpret the foundational crisis as a determinate negation that opens onto post-critical modes of reason.[3] Let's make a decision: we shall remain faithful to the injunction transmitted by the haunting specters of those who decided, like Mallarmé's *Maître*, and in spite of the lack of any transcendent guarantee or prescription, to carry out eidetic acts, i.e. acts oriented by regulative ideas projected by human reason. Far from sanctioning the irreversible debacle of modern reason, the Maître inferred '*from this conflagration at his feet*'[4] – from the transmutation of the immobile Ur-Ground into an ark continually going under – the coming of '*the one and only Number that cannot be any other*'.[5] In order to avoid any possible misunderstanding regarding the kind of subjective posture that could be attuned to this post-foundational absolute, the Maître bequeathed us, in black and white, an unambiguous maxim: we must try to *vanquish chance word by word*,[6] i.e. we must try to fix the bad infinity of contingency by means of a patient work developed from within the very element affected by this contingency (language, in the situation faced by the Maître). According to this stance, the turmoil unleashed by the modern ungrounding of existence and thinking, the Copernican launching of the

3   A striking development of the first option in relation to Mallarmé's poem *A Dice Throw* was proposed in Q. MEILLASSOUX, *The Number and the Siren*, trans. by Robin Mackay (Falmouth, UK: Urbanomic; New York: Sequence Press, 2012).

4   S. MALLARMÉ, 'A Dice Throw At Any Time Never Will Abolish Chance', in *Collected Poems and Other Verses*, trans. by E.H. and A.M. Blackmore (Oxford: Oxford University Press, 2006), pp. 166-167.

5   *Ibid.*, pp. 166-167.

6   S. MALLARMÉ, 'The Mystery in Letters', in *Divagations*, trans. by Barbara Johnson (Cambridge, MA: Belknap Press of Harvard University Press), p. 236.

Ur-Grounds into orbit, far from being an irrevocable obstruction to the legitimacy of the infinite projects of reason, can be interpreted as an abyssal site in which these projects may be elevated to new, post-foundational modalities. In the particular context provided by the *theoretical* interest of reason, the critical reflection on the transcendental perspectivism of the pre-critical phase of modern science – as well as the consequent relativization of the resulting scientific worldview – would remain a worstward abstract negation, if it did not render possible a post-critical determinate sublation of the transcendental perspectivism expounded by Kant; if it did not permit us to raise the concept of scientificity to new, post-critical powers.

The very possibility of enacting deeds intended to banish chance seems – in the framework provided by the epochal overcoming of the ornitheology – nothing short of pure madness. The Maître, like a good post-Kantian, is conscious that every act accomplished by a human mode of thought, every word uttered by a human mouth, merely '*emits a dice throw*'.[7] Human experience is always already 'transcended' into a *field of impersonal experience* wherein the *abstract* modalities of experience (conceptual, perceptual, imaginary, affective, oneiric, intersubjective, etc.) *concretely* converge.[8] This multiplicity of modes of being always already ahead of itself is necessarily predetermined by the transcendental structure of the corresponding subject. In Kant's jargon, the generic structure of the object in general = X of human experience is contingent upon a transcendental framing, which means that the transcendental apparatus that defines the generic subjective preconditions of a transcendent experience are at the same time the conditions of possibility of the intentional objects of this experience. We could summarize this standpoint by saying that *transcendental transcendence* – i.e. the modes, determined by the subject's transcendental structure, according to which a subject can transcend itself into

---

7   S. MALLARMÉ, 'A Dice Throw At Any Time Never Will Abolish Chance', p. 181.

8   Regarding the notion of an *impersonal* or *anonymous experiential field* (which plays an essential role in what follows) see J. -P. SARTRE, *The transcendence of the ego. An existentialist theory of consciousness*, trans. by Forrest Williams and Robert Kirkpatrick (New York: Hill and Wang, 1960); W. JAMES, *Essays in Radical Empiricism* (Mineola, New York: Dover Publications, Inc., 2003); G. DELEUZE, 'Immanence: A Life', in *Pure Immanence, Essays on A Life*, trans. by Anne Boyman (New York: Urzone Inc., 2001); G. DELEUZE and F. GUATTARI, *What is Philosophy?*, trans. by Hugh Tomlinson and Graham Burchell (New York: Columbia University Press, 1994), Example 3, pp. 44-49; J. -C. GODDARD, *1804-1805. La désubjectivation du transcendantal*, Archives de Philosophie 2009/3, Tome 72, pp. 423-441; and R. BARBARAS, *Dynamique de la manifestation* (Paris: Librairie Philosophique J. Vrin, 2013), Ch. IV.

the impersonal field – is not transcendent enough. In what follows I shall 'naturalize' Kant's stance by assuming that the generic structure defining (what I shall call) the *human transcendental type*, far from being character-ized by some sort of pre-phenoumenal necessity, results from a contingent local subjectivation of the experiential field itself. In other words, we shall assume that the *transcendental a priori* structures of human experience are *a posteriori* products of the *immanental* 'natural' dynamics of the im-personal field.[9] We could say that the excitation of local subjective modes within the experiential field gives rise to *subjective pheno(u)menalizations* of the latter, which can be understood as particular transcendental framings of the field's *impersonal phenoumenalization*. It follows that the human transcendental type defines just one particular mode among others (e.g. vegetable, animal, extraterrestrial) according to which the field of imper-sonal experience locally *umwelts* or frames its narcissistic self-experience. This transcendental conjugation of the thesis according to which '*every thought emits a dice throw*' permits us to set out the task bequeathed by the Maître – that of vanquishing chance – in the following terms: we can un-derstand the infinite projects of reason – such as, for instance, the project of a post-critical science oriented by the regulative idea of truth – as projects of *universalization* intended to bypass the transcendental insularity of hu-man experience, i.e. to enlarge the scope of human experience beyond the limits pre-fixed by its *contingent* transcendental type.

Now, the thesis according to which human experience is framed *a priori* by a contingently determined transcendental structure has elicited a pre-modern counter-revolution that continues to hamper the unfolding of a truly Copernican scenario. This reaction is based on the fallacy according to which the Kantian reflection that brought into focus the transcendental relativity of human experience, far from being the condition of possibility of a post-critical *sublation* of the corresponding limits, entails a juridical *limitation* of human experience. According to this *claustrophobic interpre-tation* of the critical motif, the transcendental structure fixes once and for all the ultimate insurmountable limits of human experience. In particular, the *theoretical* conjugation of this stance amounts to the claim that the scope of scientific rationality is limited *de jure* to the pheno(u)menal *Um-welt* (environing world) determined by the very transcendental structure

---

9   In *Dynamique de la manifestation*, Renaud Barbaras studies in detail the problem of characterizing the 'natural' *a priori* (that I here call *immanental*) that under-pins the '*correlational* [or transcendental] *a priori*' of Husserlian phenomenolo-gy and renders possible the subject-object polarizations, i.e. the very emergence of the correlated poles.

that renders objective science possible – that is, to the *objective nature* defined by the transcendental type of the subject of science. To overcome this limitation, we would have to be able to jump over our own shadows, i.e. to perform transcendental variations enabling us to have phenoumenological experiences of the impersonal field—for instance, experiences 'triangulating' a given phenoumenon from a diversity of transcendental viewpoints. According to the claustrophobic interpretation of the critical motif, such *phenomenological empiricism* is juridically forbidden. Every human thought cannot but emit dice throws, enact experiences predetermined – and ineluctably limited – by the fixed generic structure of its contingent subjective supports. And of course, a dice throw – i.e., a human thought that cannot bypass the contingent structure of its very conditions of possibility – will never abolish chance, will never activate phenoumenological modes of experience capable of overcoming transcendental perspectivism and its concomitant contingency. Now, if we grant that human experience is transcendentally framed, it does not follow that we cannot vary the very transcendental conditions of experience, that we cannot go beyond transcendental transcendence. A critical subject, i.e. a subject capable of performing a critical reflection on its own transcendental structure, can afford the possibility of varying, deforming, or perturbing the very *a priori* structure of its experience. In what follows, I shall call *phenoumenological experience* any experience that involves a shift of the very transcendental structure that renders a transcendent experience possible. A phenoumenological experience entails by definition a *speculative transcendence* that goes 'beyond' transcendental transcendence; a partial trans-(in the sense of *transversal*)-umweltization of experience. The (bio) technological expansion of the scope of human perception and motor functions; the scientific and philosophical reprogramming of the categories of our understanding; literary and philosophical labor on the linguistic *organon*; psychedelic perturbations of neurochemical structure; the possibility of attuning the resolution of sensibility (both perceptive and affective) to different spatial and temporal scales; the perturbation of the very existential structures of being-there (by means of practices such as meditation, isolation, fasting, etc.),[10] are all local operators of transcendental variation giving access to phenoumenological experiences. By definition, a process of speculative transcendence is not an enterprise that could be carried out

---

10   Regarding the conception of these kinds of practices as perturbations of the existentials of the being-there (*Dasein*), see J. -Y. LACOSTE, *Expérience et Absolu* (Paris: Presses Universitaires de France, 1994).

by a subject of a given transcendental type. Even in the particular context
defined by the theoretical interest of reason, the infinite project oriented
by the regulative idea of truth cannot simply proceed by means of acts of
objective knowledge enacted by *the* subject of science: the re-presentation
of nature as something that objectively stands before the subject of science
is nothing but a particular moment of science as such. We might say that a
post-critical science necessarily entails a *spiritual* dimension, in the precise
sense that Foucault gives to this term:

> [...] we could call 'spirituality' the search, practice and experience through
> which the subject carries out the necessary transformations on himself in order
> to have access to the truth. [...] It [spirituality] postulates that for the subject to
> have right of access to the truth he must be changed, transformed, shifted, and
> become, to some extent and up to a certain point, other than himself. The truth
> is only given to the subject at a price that brings the subject's being into play.[11]

The operations of transcendental variation should not be understood as
some sort of definite deliverance of human experience with respect to any
form of transcendental framing, but rather as successful differential trans-
gressions of the limits that apply for each particular occasion. Far from
giving access to a hypothetical noumenal realm absolved from any form
of transcendental overdetermination, these speculative operations merely
loosen the anchoring of experience to a fixed (and contingent) transcendental structure, thereby activating phenoumenological (or transumweltic)
degrees of freedom. What is important here is that the impossibility of
getting rid of the transcendental framing of experience does not entail the
existence of insurmountable barriers to the process of universalizing transumweltization: speculative labor does not claim to purify experience of
its transcendental framings, but rather to endow experience with a speculative mobility with respect to any fixed transcendental structure. If we
were to think that our experience would be 'purer' if we could get rid of
any transcendental framing, then we would be – to *détourne* Kant's words
– like '*the light dove* [that] *in free flight cutting through the air the resistance of which it feels, could get the idea that it could do even better in
airless space.*'[12] Of course, there is no compelling reason to perform such
transcendental variations: the exercise of science, arts, politics and exis-

---

11   M. FOUCAULT, *The Hermeneutics of the Subject, Lectures at the Collège de France,
      1981-82*, trans. by Graham Burchell (New York: Palgrave Macmillan, 2005), p. 15.
12   I. KANT, *Critique of Pure Reason*, trans. by Paul Guyer and Allen W. Wood
      (Cambridge, UK: Cambridge University Press, 1998), A5/B9, p. 129.

tential practices – as well as the exercise of their *concrete* concertation in philosophical thinking – are just existential possibilities among others. But equally, there is no reason whatsoever to limit in an *a priori* and dogmatic manner the scope of such infinite projects, to close off from the outset any possibility of affording transcendental variations.

The very conception of such a phenomenological empiricism presupposes that the transcendental ego is not a pre-phenoumenal entelechy, but rather a structure stemming from a (historico-)natural genesis and subject to both spontaneous and deliberate mutations. The so-called transcendental ego is just a snapshot abstracted from a local process of subjectivation enacted by the experiential field itself. Even the notion of a human transcendental type (which I use just for the sake of convenience) presupposes a coarse-graining that abstracts from cultural, linguistic, historical, gender, social, and ontogenetic variations among the corresponding sub-types. In this way, one of the last avatars of the pre-Copernican Ur-Ground, namely the absolutized transcendental ego conceived of as the ultimate constituting source of experience as such, is also forced to quit its pre-phenoumenal realm and become incarnate, to drift, and to fall through the bottomless and impersonal experiential field. Some might argue that this '*naturalization of the transcendental*' forgets the difference between the empirical and the transcendental – such as, for instance, the difference between the experience of an *objective body* and the *bodily a priori* structure rendering this *objective* experience possible. According to this line of argument, the very transcendental structure that renders objective experience possible cannot, as such, be an object of experience. Now, the thesis according to which the *phenomenological* difference between the empirical and the transcendental – such as the difference between the *objective body* (*Korper*) and the *body-qua-lived-body* (*Leib*) – entails an essential *ontological* difference, is far from self-evident. What do we understand by a transcendental structure framing the subject's experience, if not its perceptive and motor apparatus; its physiological constitution; its cultural, sociological, and historical environments; the categories conveyed by its language; the imaginary schemata by means of which it can categorize sensory data, and so on? As Merleau-Ponty clearly puts it, '*Nature outside of us is revealed by the nature that we are.*'[13] The *transcendental activity* of the transcending subject is always

---

13   Quoted by R. VALLIER, *Être sauvage and the barbaric principle: Merleau-Ponty's reading of Schelling*, in *The Barbarian Principle: Merleau-Ponty, Schelling, and the Question of Nature*, ed. by Jason M. Wirth and Patrick Burke, (New York: State University of New York Press, 2013), p. 133.

underpinned by an *immanental passivity* resulting from the fact that the subject of experience is just a being-there of the same 'nature' as that which is framed by its experience.[14] In the last instance, the *subjective* experience of nature is a narcissistic self-experience *of* nature in the double sense of the genitive. We shall assume, then, that the active subject of the transcendental *constitution* of objective nature is a passive product of a natural *institution*: only the instituted can constitute, only an *incarnated* subject (one endowed with the corresponding transcendental structure) can trigger a local process of umweltic pheno(u)menalization of the field. It is certainly worth emphasizing, nonetheless, that the '*naturalization of the transcendental*' as I understand it here does not rely on a pre-critical scientism: I understand this '*naturalization of the transcendental*' as the other side of the '*speculativization of nature*', i.e. the upgrading of the concept of nature rendered possible by the speculative sublation of its pre-critical concept. In other words, the '*naturalization*' that is at stake here, far from resulting from a pre-critical concept of nature, is correlative to a post-critical concept that is rendered possible by transcendental reflection itself. Therefore, the 'naturalization' of the transcendental should not be understood here as a simple reversal of the transcendental 'idealism' that would place the *objective nature* of pre-critical naturalism – rather than the transcendental ego – in the role of the Ur-Ground (i.e. as a subordination of transcendental philosophy either to science or even to some form of '*philosophy of nature*'). I shall maintain that the theoretical movements addressing the two forms of production – i.e. the transcendental analysis of the *constituted visions* that unfold in the subject's pheno(u)menological *foreground* and the '*ontological psychoanalysis*' (Merleau-Ponty) of the 'unconscious' proto-plasmatic *background* underpinning the *instituted* subjects – define the complementary and interrelated semicircles of a unique speculative theoretical movement. What I shall call *immanental phenoumenology* addresses the *carnal* indivision between the (instituting) *plasma* and the (constituted) *vision*. In Schellingian terms, *transcendental philosophy* (addressing the transcendental constitution of a subject's objective experience) and *philosophy of nature* (addressing the natural institution of the transcendental subject) must be synthesized in an *immanental phenoumenology of identity* in which the cir-

---

14   In Merleau-Ponty's own terms: 'Philosophy has never spoken [...] of the passivity of our activity, as Valéry spoke of a *body of the spirit*: new as our initiatives may be, they come to birth at the heart of being, they are connected onto the times that streams forth in us, supported on the pivots or hinges of our life [...]', M. MERLEAU-PONTY, *The Visible and the Invisible*, trans. by Alphonso Lingis (Evanston: Northwestern University Press, 1968), p. 221.

cular reflections between the speculative promotion of the notion of nature and the naturalization of the transcendental subject raise both the concept of nature and the concept of subject to new post-critical powers. Such an immanental phenoumenology addresses the whole process that envelops the immanental field of impersonal experience as such, the *spermatikos logos* that guarantees its intrinsic rational consistency, the natural processes by means of which local subjects are instituted within the field, the subsequent framings of the latter defined by the subjects' transcendental structures, and the myriad of 'objective natures' (with their pheno(u)menological data and effective natural laws) that govern the structural consistency of the resulting umweltic spheres. Within such an immanental phenoumenology, the congenital idealistic tendencies of *transcendental phenomenology* (foreclosing the natural process of the institution of transcendental subjects) and the possible transcendental naivety of a pre-critical *philosophy of nature* (foreclosing the subjective overdeterminations of the concept of nature) must be mutually counterbalanced. Regarding this circular complementarity between transcendental philosophy and philosophy of nature, it is worth here quoting Merleau-Ponty at length:

> We do not contest the fact that the concepts of Nature, history, and mankind/humanity form a skein, an endless entanglement. But this is precisely why it is impossible to treat Nature as a detail of human history [...]. Every positing of a Nature implies a subjectivity and even an historic intersubjectivity. This does not mean that the sense of natural being is exhausted by its symbolic transcriptions, that there is nothing to think before these transcriptions. It only proves that the being of Nature is to be sought below [*en deçà*] its being posited. If a philosophy of reflection is permitted to treat all philosophy of Nature as a philosophy of spirit and of mankind/humanity in disguise, and to judge it on the basis of the conditions of all possible objects for a spirit or a human, this generalized suspicion, i.e. reflection, cannot exempt itself from investigation. It must turn against itself. And, having measured what we risk losing if we start with Nature, we [must] also account for what we surely lack if we start from subjectivity: the primordial being against which all reflection institutes itself, and without which there is no longer philosophy, for want of an outside against which it has to measure itself.[15]

---

15   M. MERLEAU-PONTY, 'La Nature ou le Monde du silence (pages d'introduction)', in *Maurice Merleau-Ponty*, ed. by Emmanuel de Saint-Aubert (Paris: Hermann Editeurs, 2008), pp. 45-46 (I have used the unofficial translation by D. Meacham and N. Keane). Regarding the relation between Schelling's *Naturphilosophie* and Merleau-Ponty's late philosophy see R. VALLIER, *Être sauvage and the barbaric principle: Merleau-Ponty's reading of Schelling*. See also M. MERLEAU-PONTY, 'The Philosopher and his Shadow', in *Signs*, trans. by Richard McCleary (Evan-

The notion of an *immanental phenoumenology* requires that we re-place the central notions of transcendental philosophy – in particular, the notion of *transcendental subject* and the concomitant notion of *transcendence* – within a new post-critical context. In the first place, a subject open to such variations of the transcendental structure can no longer – by definition – be understood as a particular instantiation of a transcendental type, i.e. of a fixed generic subjective structure. Correlatively, a speculative subject that drifts along gradients of transcendental variation is no longer surrounded by a single environing world: the umweltic bubbles defined by the transcendental types that (s)he can embody merge into a single transumweltic (or non-environmental) *interzone* of experience. In this sense, a speculative subject is '*poorer in world*' than a pre-critical subject, such as for instance a tick or a cactus. We could say that a speculative subject is necessarily a *plastic subject*, i.e. a subject capable of affording 'shamanic' metamorphoses of its very transcendental structure.[16] Only a plastic subject can activate and embody phenoumenological modes of the experiential field, i.e. modes of experience that are not piloted by a unique transcendental type; only a plastic subject can make a foray into the phenoumenodelic pleroma on board of the Transumweltic Express. Secondly, the speculative conception

ston: Northwestern University Press, 1964) and M. MERLEAU-PONTY, *The Visible and the Invisible*. It is also worth noting that William James explicitly links his 'radical empiricism' (or 'philosophy of pure experience') to the post-Kantian 'philosophy of identity': 'Since the acquisition of conscious quality on the part of an experience depends upon a context [a *framing* in our terminology] coming to it, it follows that the sum total of all experiences, having no context, can not strictly be called conscious at all. It is a *that*, an Absolute, a 'pure' experience on an enormous scale, undifferentiated and undifferentiable into thought and thing. This the post-Kantian idealists have always practically acknowledged by calling their doctrine *Identitätsphilosophie*. [...] the philosophy of pure experience being only a more comminuted *Identitätsphilosophie*', W. JAMES, *How Two Minds Can Know One Thing*, in *Essays in Radical Empiricism*, pp. 70-71.

16   In analogous terms, Deleuze argues that the subject of philosophy must necessarily be thought of as a *larval subject*: « In this sense, it is not even clear that thought, in so far as it constitutes the dynamism peculiar to philosophical systems, may be related to a substantial, completed and well-constituted subject, such as the Cartesian Cogito: thought is, rather, one of those terrible movements which can be sustained only under the conditions of a larval subject. » G. DELEUZE, *Difference and Repetition*, trans. by Paul Patton (New York: Columbia University Press, 1994), p. 118. However, the concept of a plastic subject is deprived of the regressive connotation conveyed by the Deleuzian notion of a larval subject: the immanental phenoumenology of spirit as I understand it here unfolds in the sense of an increasing plasticity, which is rendered possible by the post-critical interplay between transcendental reflection and speculative sublation.

of a constituting subject that is itself an instituted natural product requires that we relativise the very characterization of its relation with the experiential field as a form of *transcendence*, i.e. as an act by means of which the subject gains access to a transcendent 'outside' placed before her or him. In the conceptual framework provided by the post-critical naturalization of the transcendental subject, the notion of an individual *thrown into* and *transcended towards* a re-presented world is replaced by that of a subjective enduring fluctuation of the experiential field embodying a particular local form of its self-experience, eliciting a particular process of pheno(u)menalization. As Sartre puts it,

> The transcendent *I* must fall before the stroke of phenomenological reduction. The *Cogito* affirms too much. The certain content of the pseudo-'Cogito' is not '*I* have consciousness of this chair,' but 'There is consciousness of this chair.' This content is sufficient to constitute an infinite and absolute field of investigation for phenomenology.[17]

In this context, an intentional experience is understood as a local polarization of the impersonal field assuming the form of a correlational vector going from a noetic source to a transcendent noematic target. Every *transcendent experience* (i.e. every intentional relation between a local subject and a transcendent object) is always – in the last instance – an *immanent self-experience* of the field itself, an act by means of which the field enriches its internal phenoumenalization. According to Merleau-Ponty, *the subject's vision 'is not a view upon the* outside [...] *The world no longer stands before him through representation; rather, it is* [the subject] *who is born among the things by a sort of concentration or coming-to-itself of the visible'*.[18] Correlatively, the *transcendental conditions* by means of which a subject can have an intentional experience of a *transcendent* object hinge in the last instance on the *immanental conditions* that make possible the *immanent* polarizations of the self-experiencing field itself. Of course, *subjective* experience is necessarily – to a greater or a lesser degree – *local* and *perspectival*, which justifies the characterization of the intentional vectors as gradients of transcendence. It is thanks to this perspectival locality – i.e. to the fact that finite subjects embody empirico-transcendental vantage points entailing new framings of the experiential field – that the latter can

---

17   J. -P. Sartre, *The transcendence of the ego. An existentialist theory of consciousness*, p. 53.
18   M. Merleau-Ponty, 'Eye and Mind', in *The Primacy of Perception*, trans. by Carleton Dallery (Evanston, IL: Northwestern University Press, 1964), pp. 159-190.

deepen its infinite self-experience: *only from the chalice of this realm of finite subjects foams forth within the experiential field its own pleromatic infinitude.*[19] It is worth noting, nonetheless, that even this *subjective* description of experience as a form of transcendence can be the object of a speculative perturbation: the higher the degree of transumweltization associated with the spreading of a plastic subject through different transcendental structures – i.e. the higher the amount of transcendental viewpoints that (s)he can incarnate –, the lower the extent to which its experience is subjectively lived as a form of *transcendence*. In short, the *transumweltization* of a subject's experience goes hand in hand with its *immanentization*. This correlation can be understood as the transcendental version of the fact that multiscopic vision is 'less transcendent', so to speak, than monocular vision. At the limit, the completely transumweltized experience of the field itself – which envelops all transcendental viewpoints that arise in its midst – is an *immanent* self-experience, a no-body's experience of no-thing.

    The effective activation of phenoumenological degrees of freedom requires mobilizing of all the subtleties and resources – as well as the patience – of the corresponding modes of thought. Let's consider the case addressed by the Maître. The Maître not only bequeathed us the task of *vanquishing chance*, but also prescribed specific gestures adapted to his field of operations: such a task must be *patiently* accomplished *word by word* – that is, in the very element of language. Here, language must be understood as a particular example of a *transcendental operator* framing experience. As Kant argued, following Aristotle, language encodes the categorical *a priori* forms of judgmental linkage that structure the human experience of the impersonal field. We could understand language as a symbolic knife tracing *abstract cuts* in the impersonal field, cuts that structure its corresponding umweltic modes of appearing. Now, language is operational: the linguistic abstract cuts of the field – '*the textual work that comes out of the spider's belly*'[20] – interweave a cobweb to trap the intended noematic 'flies'. But language is not like the knife of Chuang-Tzu: its abstract cuts, far from slicing without resistance through the *spermatikos logos* that rationally inseminates the field, render possible a particular coarse-grained experience of the latter. Transcendental reflection makes it explicit that the linguistic cobweb, in order to weave points of impasse for

19   G. W. F. HEGEL, *Phenomenology of Spirit*, trans. by A.V. Miller (Oxford: Oxford University Press, 1977), p. 493.

20   J. LACAN, *On Femenine Sexuality. The Limits of Love and Knowledge*, ed. by Jacques-Allain Miller, trans. by Bruce Fink (New York: W.W. Norton & Company, 1999), p. 93.

the targeted flies, must have its own points of impasse: if the interstices of the lattice were too small, the web would not be invisible to its potential victims, i.e. it would be inefficacious. In this way, every linguistic cobweb is characterized by a given 'power of resolution' that establishes a cut-off demarcating the 'visible' landscape from a background that necessarily remains 'invisible'. The very transcendental operator that allows the spider to grasp the field in an effective manner weaves an umweltic bubble around the spider: every form of pheno(u)menal revealing takes place against a concealed backdrop. The impasses of any particular symbolic cobweb – its invisibles and indiscernibles – are just symptoms of the transumweltic nature of the impersonal field itself, i.e. of the fact that the phenoumenological field as such cannot be idealistically identified with the pheno(u)menal *Umwelt* defined by any possible transcendental structure. In this sense, the impasses of the symbolic order can indeed be understood as symptoms of the phenoumenal 'real'. The sad destiny of Funes the Memorious attests to the fact that finer is not always better. We should not understand a finite resolution as a sort of limitation that could be bypassed merely by increasing the power of resolution, but rather as a particular mode of experience that awakens certain *effective qualities* of the field, qualities that might be invisible *at both higher and lower powers of resolution*. In particular, even low powers of resolution call forth qualities of the field that define legitimate phenomenological data of the experiential flood. In the mode of experience opened up by (what I shall call) *phenoumenodelic suspension*, all the abstract modes of experience (perceptive, affective, conceptual, etc.), all the strata of effective qualities (primary, secondary,..., n-ary), all the *Umwelten* brought forth by the possible transcendental structures, belong to a single experiential field. A given phenomenon P, far from being a hypothetical thing-in-itself existing independently of any pheno(u)menalization, can be understood as a sort of 'functor' assigning to every possible empirico-transcendental structure T what we could call the *T-pheno(u) menalization of P*. This definition has the twofold merit of preserving the ontological scope of the processes of phenoumenalization – thereby upholding the identity between *being* and *appearing* – without succumbing to any form of subjective idealism – thereby banishing from the outset the subjective reduction of the notion of phenomenon. Now, a Kantian spider knows that its cobweb is characterized by a particular power of resolution, that the transcendental grid shaped by the 'evolutionary' process that institutes it as a local arachnid fluctuation of the impersonal field always entails a coarse-graining out of which a particular *Umwelt* arises, endowed with its effective qualities, its spatiotemporal scales, its nomological regularities, its visible flies and its invisible depths. As I argued above, the effectuation of such a transcendental reflection opens up the possibility of activating phenoumenological degrees of freedom: by exploring different stitches, by adjusting the sharpness of the linguistic knife, by increasing or decreasing the grain, a speculative spider can probe the field at different scales and witness how a whole spectrum of sensuoscapes continuously arise and fade as it freely tunes the resolution. The Mallarméan Maître knows better than anyone that we are not constrained to stay within the transcendental limits fixed by a *'universal report'* shaped by the constraints of communication and effective action; that we are not condemned to foreclose the *'real'* points of impasse of the symbolic order, thus limiting the scope of our experience to the transcendental frame defined by the corresponding 'categories'. The Maître's *grimoire* enjoins us to perturb the grammar, thereby *'giving back to the word, which can become viciously stereotyped in us, its mobility'*.[21] According to the Maître, the natural tendency of language to hypostasize its abstract cuts cannot be overcome by means of an ecstatic shot out of a pistol that could tear through the symbolic order and give access to a hypothetical noumenal realm beyond language: only language can patiently – *word by word*, i.e. in the very element of language – transgress its abstract hypostasis. Specifically, we can distinguish two privileged vectors of perturbation of the *'universal report'*: while the poetic treatment of language deforms the grammar, enhances the flux of equivocity, and Joyceanly fosters the *amalgrammation* of the different languages into a single *'*[im]*pure language'* (W. Benjamin), the mathematical-oriented formalization of language reduces equivocity by providing rigorous definitions, abstracts ideal types, and carefully controls the identifications between their tokens. Now, the pleromatic richness of experience is only preserved when language is progressively endowed with the capacity to freely move between the frontiers explored by the different gradients of perturbation of the *'universal report'*, thereby becoming able to grasp both the sensuous (perceptive and affective) *n*-ary qualities and the ideal entities that coalesce within the same experiential field.

Thus far, I have pleaded in favor of a phenoumenodelic extension of the notion of experience. The exploration of the phenoumenodelic field according to the different *abstract* modalities of experience (perceptive, theoretical, etc.) is the task of the corresponding modes of thought (art, science, etc.). In turn, the *systematic* exploration of the field according to the *con-*

---

21   S. MALLARMÉ, 'Notes sur le Langage', in *Igitur, Divagations, Un coup de dès*, ed. by Bertrand Marchal (Paris: Editions Gallimard, 2003), p. 74.

crete ingression of these abstract modalities into a unique synesthetic pleroma defines the proper task of philosophy as I understand it here. Now, even if the Maître acknowledges that the modern ungrounding, rather than entailing the Karamazovian hypostasis of contingency, opens human experience to an absolute phenoumenodelic field absolved from being framed by a unique contingent transcendental structure, there is another compelling objection that fuels its hesitation to carry out eidetic acts: namely, the hypothesis according to which, in the last instance, *'nothing will have taken place'*, not even the place. The *ontic contingency* of the particular transcendental structures of human beings brings forth against the backdrop provided by the *ontological contingency* regarding the very existence of human beings, a contingency that projects backwards towards its origin and forwards towards its fate. In the absence of the ornitheological guarantees and prescriptions of the pre-modern era, the actions prescribed by the eidetic orientations seem to be nothing but follies. Gauged against the background of this contingency, the subjective engagement in the corresponding infinite projects of reason might indeed be understood as nothing but a vain gesticulation of our narcissism, an irreflexive perpetuation of an ancestral madness which is probably – in the last instance – utterly inconsequential. In particular, the infinite project of science as such, performed by *'clever beasts'* condemned to a murky death *'in some out of the way corner of* [the] *universe'*,[22] taking place and time in a cosmos doomed either to the *'lowly splashing'* of a thermodynamical death or to a cosmological collapse after which even space and time will not have taken place—such an act of reason seems to be nothing but a *'frenzied leap'* of nothingness pouring back into nothingness. In the last instance – and without fail – nothing will remain of us, *'nothing will have happened'*[23], we shall exit *time, space, and even number* (V. Hugo), everything – even abysses and epochs – will be dissolved into the original foam of nothingness. This forthcoming dissolution – as well as the correlative contingency of the very emergence of human beings – instills its nihilistic influence in every infinite human project, awakening (what Lyotard called) the *'postmodern affect'*,[24] namely melancholia; and forcing us to halt the automatism of the eidetic drives for a second and seriously ask ourselves *What*

22   F. NIETZSCHE, 'On Truth and Lies in a Nonmoral Sense' in *Philosophy and Truth: Selections from Nietzsche's Notebooks of the Early 1870s*, ed. and trans. by Daniel Breazeale (Atlantic Highlands, New Jersey: Humanities Press, 1979), p. 79.
23   *Ibid.*, p. 79.
24   J.-F. LYOTARD, 'A Postmodern Fable', trans. by Elizabeth Constable and Thomas Cochran, *Yale Journal of Criticism*, 6:1 (1993), p. 237.

for? What good is it to engage in the infinite tasks of reason – rather than just focusing on the administration and the enjoyment of the available resources and the improvement of our life conditions – if in the last instance (only) nothing matters? Why should we follow the injunctions posited by the eidetic regulative poles if we are always already under the influence of the retroactive melancholic wavefront of a cosmic catastrophe to come? In order to face this existential objection to the accomplishment of deeds enacted under the aegis of infinite ideas, let's recall the Holderlinean watchword summoned by Heidegger in order to deal with the (en)framing conveyed by the essence of modern technology: '*where danger is, there the sublating power grows*'. Maybe the nihilistic panorama that I have just depicted did not get deep enough into the heart of the modern abyss; maybe we have to delve further '*where danger is*' and push our situation to a further extreme, an extreme in which the hypothesis of a (scientifically updated) doomsday will assume its true tenor, that of being a 'world picture' subjected to the hyperbolic ungrounding power of modern reason. Firstly, the imaginary hypostasis of every scientific symbolization falls beneath the blows of scientific hypothetization. The very regulative infinite idea of modern science prescribes that we should not transform a successful local symbolization into a hypostatized 'world picture' painted on the vacant surfaces of the umweltic vaults, a constellation in which we could read the tale of our origin and destiny, a new imaginary 'paradigm' giving us the ultimate key to our true situation. The dogmatic conversion of partially successful symbolizations into updated cosmogonical and eschatological certainties also projects a sheltering sky that forecloses the abyssal uncertainty unleashed by modernity: we prefer to embrace the tomb and the certainty of (a cosmic) death rather than facing the pictureless vistas opened by the modern ungrounding. Secondly, the speculative opening of a phenoumenodelic field of experience advances one step further '*where danger is*' by post-critically risking the (environing) world, i.e. by risking the unicity of the very transcendental framing of experience, by absolving subjective existence from being an empirical token of a fixed transcendental type placed at the center of an umweltic sphere. As a result, this transumweltization of experience delivers us from the hypostasis of the eschatological tales inscribed on the underside of sheltering umbrellas: the phenoumenalization of experience '*makes a slit in the* [umweltic] *umbrella*', '*tears open the firmament itself*'[25] and decants cosmodicies into the phenoumenodelic pleroma. In order to remain faithful to the real scope of the modern crisis,

---

25   G. DELEUZE and F. GUATTARI, *What is Philosophy?*, p. 203.

we must resolve ourselves to face the absolute absence of any Ur-frame or world picture that could orient our acts and support our constructions; we must subject ourselves to the imperative that Althusser associated with the term *materialism*, namely '*not to tell ourselves stories*' (or rather, in more accurate terms, not to hypostasize the stories that we can legitimately tell). The generalized suspension of hypostasis – such as the hypostasis of a given tone (e.g. the present, the state of wakefulness, sense-certainty, substantiality) into a fundamental tone, the hypostasis of a given theoretical symbolization into an imaginary world picture, the hypostasis of an umweltic 'story' into a cosmodicy – will be here called *phenoumenodelic epokhé*. In the mode of experience opened up by this suspension, '*everything takes place, by foreshortening, as an hypothesis; we avoid narrative*'.[26] This absolution of experience with respect to the hypostasis of tones, grounds, and narratives gives access to an absolute experiential field in which the different phenoumenodelic data are no longer gauged with respect to any putative motionless Ur-frame, thereby achieving a *general relativization* of the field: '*each utensil, spoon, fork, knife, and plate*' in the Maître's underplasmic ark '*bore on its reverse a letter encircled by a Latin motto:* mobilis in mobili'.[27] In particular, we must admit that, in the last instance, and in spite of our partially successful symbolizations, we do not know what the ultimate nature of the experiential field is, we do not know what is the real scope of our supposed 'freedom' to carry out (or not) eidetic acts, we do not know whether our acts and decisions might have any consequence whatsoever, we do not know whether something will have taken place or not. We just know, since it is a phenoumenodelic datum, that the experiential field manifests itself according to a *concrete* imbrication of the multiple *abstract* modalities of experience (theoretical, affective, perceptive, social, etc.). And we know that the configurations of these modalities that, on each particular occasion, are the case, can be mediated by the different modes of thought (science, arts, existential practices, politics, etc.): we can always understand, thanks to the patient effort of the concept, more than we do at present; we can widen the doors of perception and affect in order to gain access to a whole spectrum of qualitative sensuoscapes; we can perturb the very existentials that frame our existence; we can attune ourselves to the different (cosmological, astrophysical, geological, biologi-

---

26 S. MALLARMÉ, Preface to 'A Dice Throw Will Never Abolish Chance', in *Mallarmé*, ed. Anthony Hartley (Harmondsworth: Penguin Books, 1965), p. 210.

27 J. Verne, *20000 Leagues Under the Sea*, trans. by F.P. Walter (Project Gutenberg Etext), p. 41.

cal, and historical) durations that pulse through the temporal scales characteristic of the 'natural attitude'. Thanks to the *epokhé*, every phenoumenon – captains, sirens, storms – becomes a phenoumenodelic *datum* drifting through the experiential flood: *permeating every garden, infusing every subject, suspending every substance, the plasmic ocean always glitters* (Solaris). Even the sublime *pathos* of an effective catastrophe is forbidden to those who '*by a breath risk more*'; even the ship(wreck) becomes an uncertain phantasmagoria made of the suspended insubstance of the experiential field. Rather than a *reduction* that would allow us to gain a firm and definitive foothold on a hypothetical pre-phenomenal last instance, the *phenoumenodelic epokhé* is a *suspension* of every hypostasis that surpasses the pure impersonal givenness of the phenoumenodelic data. The limitation of the Husserlian *epoché* understood as a *reduction* to the ultimate subjective source of transcendental *constitution* is that the transcendental ego, far from being a pre-phenomenal last instance, is itself an instituted product, a local sentient and expressive fold of the experiential field itself.[28] The *instituted* subject of experience is not the ultimate source of the phenoumenalization, but rather a local subjective vortex – an enduring wave – of an impersonal phenoumenodelic field entailing a new umweltization of the latter. Hence the phenoumenodelic stream cannot be understood here as an ego trip, but rather as the impersonal, ungrounded, and navigable flood upon which any form of transcendental ego must be borne. In his late philosophy, Husserl himself recognized the limits of his idealistic egology.[29] However, the characterization of the pre-subjective stratum that underpins the transcendental constitution of objectivity and envelops the different environing worlds as an Ur-Earth '*which does not move*' – aside from the charm of its provocation regarding the first-order Copernicanism of pre-critical modern science – does foster an unnecessary pre-Copernican (and pre-Einsteinian) regression.[30] Husserl's attempt to overcome the idealism

---

28   Regarding Husserl's phenomenological *epokhé*, see E. HUSSERL, *Cartesian Mediations. An Introduction to Phenomenology*, trans. by Dorion Cairns (The Hague: Martinus Nijhoff Publishers, 1960), §8, pp. 18-21, and § 11, pp. 25-26; and E. HUSSERL, *Ideas Pertaining to a Pure Phenomenology and to a Phenomenological Philosophy. First Book: General Introduction to a Pure Phenomenology*, trans. by F. Kersten (The Hague: Martinus Nijhoff Publishers, 1982), § 49-50, pp. 109-114.

29   Regarding this point, see the commentary proposed by Merleau-Ponty of Husserl's last philosophy in 'The Philosopher and his Shadow', in M. MERLEAU-PONTY, *Signs*.

30   See E. HUSSERL, 'Grundlegende Untersuchungen zum phänmenologischen Ursprung der Räumlichkeit der Natur,' in *Philosophical Essays in Memory of Edmund Husserl*, ed. by Marvin Farber (Cambridge, MA: Harvard University Pr

of a monadic egology is vitiated by the fact that he repeats at the level of the 'lifeworld' the same kind of argument that he uses to forbid any form of naturalization of the transcendental ego: just as the constituting condition of possibility of natural objectivity could not be itself naturalized, the ultimate instance against which every form of motion and rest is gauged must be understood as an Ur-Ground that cannot itself be in motion or at rest.[31] Now, in a post-Copernican and post-Einstenian scenario, the thesis according to which if we *'do not have a representation of a new ground as such, on the basis of which the earth can have [...] sense as a [...] body in motion and at rest [...], to that extent just the earth itself is really the ground and not a body'*[32] is theoretically problematic: we have learned how to conceive motion (even accelerated motion) without requiring a fixed *a priori* kinematic background with respect to which motion and rest would take place.[33]

---

ess, 1940), 305–325; trans. by Fred Kersten and Leonard Lawlor as 'Foundational Investigations of the Phenomenological Origin of the Spatiality of Nature: The Originary Ark, the Earth, Does Not Move,' in *Husserl at the Limits of Phenomenology*, ed. by Leonard Lawlor and Bettina Bergo (Evanston: Northwestern University Press, 2002). For the characterization of the *lifeworld* – understood as the common envelop of the different environing worlds – as an *earth*, see E. Husserl, *Experience and Judgment: Investigations in a Genealogy of Logic*, trans. by James S. Churchill and Karl Ameriks (Evanston: Northwestern University Press, 1973), § 38, p. 163.

31   This point has been clearly recognized by Derrida in the following terms: 'But if an objective science of earthly things is possible, an objective science of the Earth itself, the ground and foundation of these objects, is as radically impossible as that of transcendental subjectivity. The transcendental Earth is not an object and can never become one. And the possibility of a geometry strictly complements the impossibility of what could be called a *'geo-logy,'* the objective science of the Earth itself. [...] There is a science *of* space, insofar as its starting point is not *in* space.', J. Derrida in *Edmund Husserl's Origin of Geometry*, trans. by John P. Leavey, Jr. (Lincoln and London: University of Nebraska Press, 1989), pp. 83-85.

32   E. Husserl, 'Foundational Investigations of the Phenomenological Origin of the Spatiality of Nature: The Originary Ark, the Earth, Does Not Move,' p. 122.

33   A phenomenologist could argue that it is not legitimate to use scientific theories such as the general theory of relativity (which are the result of innumerable mediations that foreclose the pre-objective sedimented layers of that which is immediately given) to argue against phenomenological self-evidence. As Husserl himself puts it in the *Earth* fragment: the phenomenological reduction of the Copernican revolution does *'not even touch upon physics. But [...] we must not forget the pregivenness and constitution belonging to the apodictic Ego or to me, to us, as the source of all actual and possible sense of being, of all possible broadening which can be further constructed in the already constituted world developing historically'*. However, even the claim that every form of motion and rest *appears* as taking place against a motionless background is phenomenologically problemat-

Husserl could go as far as to admit the necessity of embedding the transcendental ego in an intersubjective lifeworld, but he could not definitively
overcome the foundational drive that pervades his overall project, i.e. he
could not resist the pre-modern temptation to understand the lifeworld as a
motionless Ur-Ground. The impossibility of sublating once and for all the
pre-modern foundational motif makes him miss, in spite of the insane sus-
pensive resources of the phenomenological *epokhé*, the immanence of the
phenoumenodelic experiential field. Nonetheless, Husserl's desperate attempt to phenomenologically reduce Copernicanism has the merit of (indirectly) bringing to light the fact that the relation to the ground – whose
canonical model is provided by our dwelling on the empirical Earth –
structures *a priori* (not only our effective experience of physical space, but
also) the *spatial schematization* of the diverse modalities of human experience (such as, for instance – in the particular framework provided by the
theoretical interest of reason – the axiomatic-foundational motifs that per-
vade science and philosophy). In other words, the Copernican revolution
does not by itself entail a suspension of the structuring motif of the Ur-
Ground ubiquitous in all dimensions of human experience. However, this
factice limitation of the scope of the Copernican revolution does not necessarily imply (as Husserl seems to believe) a juridical restriction regarding
the possibility of launching every form of Ur-Ground into orbit, but can be
understood instead as a call for a deepening of the Copernican revolution:
the kernel of transcendental philosophy, as yet undiscovered, is – above
and beyond Husserl – the thesis according to which the Copernicanism can
be raised to a transcendental power, meaning that not only is the Earth as a
physical body in a state of orbital freefall in cosmic space, but every fundamental tone, every possible Ur-Ground of experience (the transcendental
ego, the spatiotemporal background, onto-logic, world pictures painted on
umweltic spheres, etc.), are also instituted phenoumena drifting through an
experiential flood that is turtleless-all-the-way-down. The 'naturalization'

---

ic, i.e. lacking immediate self-evidence: uniform motion and rest are phenomenologically indiscernible. The only type of motion that could possibly be considered
as absolute is accelerated motion. Now, thanks to Einstein, we know that accelerated motion is also relative, that is, relative to the so-called *inertio-gravitational
field* which, far from being absolute, is a dynamical physical entity. Even if this
higher former of relativity is far from being phenomenologically self-evident to us
– human beings – there is no juridical reason to prevent us from conceiving
subjects (or a transcendental variation of our own subjectivity) who, being sensi-
tive enough to the dynamics of the inertio-gravitational field, would experience
the relativity of accelerated motion as phenomenologically evident.

of the transcendental ego must be followed by the relativizing 'naturalization' of the grounds that support egos, of the intersubjective lifeworlds in which they live, of the *Umwelten* that surround them. We shall then assume that every empirico-transcendental support of a subjective process of pheno(u)menalization is not an *arche*, a first principle, a motionless ground, but rather (as Merleau-Ponty suggested) an *ark* carrying local subjective fluctuations of the experiential field through a phenoumenodelic deluge.[34] Here the phenoumenodelic *epokhé* denotes the conversion by means of which supposed Ur-Grounds are experienced and understood as underplasmic arks descending into the Maelstrom. Rather than being conceived of as a *'spaceship earth'* (R. B. Fuller) freefalling through (the transcendental upgraded version of) the Pascalian cosmic spaces, the ark drifts through a pleromatic and impersonal stream of manifestation.

Now, if the environing worlds are *'stopped'* (C. Castaneda), if the world has been *'put out of action'*, *'parenthesized'* (E. Husserl), if *'the world has gone away'* (P. Celan), if even the impersonal phenomenological Ur-Grounds – such as the Husserlian lifeworld – fall before the stroke of the phenoumenodelic *epokhé*, where do we find ourselves, how can we schematize our existential situation? What kind of primordial scene could take the place of the Husserlian pre-modern arche-rooting, the disenchanted Pascalian inter-abyssal site, or the pastoral Heideggerian fourfold (*Geviert*)? Where is the ark – containing the chamber with the *grimoire* prescribing eidetic acts – on board of which the Maître, by *'threatening some destiny and the winds'*, perseveres defiantly in the task of stalking the interzones and grokking the immanental experiential field? How can we schematize the worldless milieu into which the phenoumenodelic *epokhé* launches the Ur-Grounds? What is the characteristic *Stimmung* (affective tonality) distilled by being-thrown into such a milieu? The first thing to note is that the suspension of Ur-Grounds does not necessarily lead to the silent darkness of the infinite spaces and its associated *Stimmung*, namely Pascalian anxiety: the suspension of any form of privileged fundamental tonality opens existence to an atonal milieu full of unheard-of possibilities. We can imagine Pythagoras listening to the skies and wondering *Is Pascal deaf?* The suspended pleroma is pregnant with accords that – by means of a patient work of mediation – can be infinitely unfolded: *'there is no*

---

34 « This « earth » is an ark : it bears the possibility of all-being atop [...] the deluge [...]', M. MERLEAU-PONTY, *L'institution. La passivité. Notes de cours au Collège de France (1954-1955)*, (Paris: Editions Belin, 2003), p. 174.

silence in the universe,[35] only relative thresholds of perceptibility, affect-ability, and understandability. Beyond both the anxiety awoken by being-thrown into *Unzuhause* (not-at-homeness) – which could be understood as the world-picture-independent ontological version of the Pascalian, ontic description of modern existence – and the being-sheltered that results from the bucolic reterritorialization in the paternal homeland, beyond both the modern disenchantment of nature and the reactive mirage of a pastoral homecoming, the speculative *epokhé* can be understood as a *conversion* emplacing us in the midst of a phenoumenodelic pleroma. We could say that the phenoumenodelic *epokhé* opens up – beyond the oscillatory tension between the movements of modern deterritorialization and reactive reterritorializations – the possibility of a solaristic oceanification of existence. The shipwreck, far from denoting any disaster whatsoever, stands for the immersion of the ark in an atonal *daydream* in which every possible tone is a suspended phenoumenodelic *datum* made of the same impersonal hallucinescence. By putting the Maître under the influence of the field, the phenoumenodelic *epokhé* hauntologically smears the hierarchy between a supposedly fundamental tone and the tense tones that are released towards the former, such as for instance the hierarchies between waking and dream states, sense-certainty and hallucinations, living beings and haunting specters, the temporal stances of past, present, and future.[36] Of course, the Maître can navigate through the experiential field by being temporarily attuned to a given tonality – such as for instance the state of wakefulness – which is necessarily haunted by submerged – oneiric – tones. In Benjamin's words:

> As sleep – in a deeper, figurative sense – it [the phenoumenodelic ocean] bears the ship of life on its current, which is accompanied from a distance by the wind and

35   P. VALERY, *Variation sur une* Pensée, in *Variété I et II* (Paris: Editions Gallimard, 1924-1930), p. 118.

36   William James' *'radical empiricism'* also proceeds by flattening perceptual, con-ceptual, imaginary, oneiric, hallucinatory, as well as non-present (past and future) experiences onto a single plane made of the *'primal stuff'* of (impersonal) *'pure experience'* (see W. JAMES, *Does 'Consciousness' exist?*, in *Essays in Radical Empiricism*). It is worth stressing that the flattening onto such a plane of 'pure ex-perience' should not be understood, as James clearly stresses, as a (presup)posi-tion of *'a universal element of which all things are made'* (*Ibid.*, p. 14): the aton-al neutrality of the suspended experiential field means precisely that there is no substantial ground state, no fundamental tone, no motionless Ur-Earth, just a non-hierarchized and ungrounded manifold of phenoumenodelic data.

the stars; as slumber, it arises at night like the tide breaking on the shore of life, on which it leaves dreams lying the next day.[37]

These shifts in regard to the conception of the *site* of existence – from the motionless Ur-Ground to the disenchanted Pascalian abysses and the Heideggerian *Unzuhause*, from the latter to the pleromatic phenoumenodelic draft (*Bezug*) – entails a correlative shift in the characteristic *Stimmung* corresponds to them. In the wake of Heidegger's reading of Rilke, we shall understand the modern ungrounding as a launching that places existence in a worldless medium that, while granting '*none special cover*' in regard to '*being loose into the daring venture*'[38], provides instead a '*safety*'. This safety is created just there, '*outside all caring,* [...] *where the gravity of the pure forces rules*'[39], where the ventured beings no longer resist being drawn along the geodesics of the phenoumenodelic traction. The very conception of such a milieu – which, in the framework of Heidegger's opus, would correspond (if we were forced to choose) to his reactivation of the Greek *physis* – provides an alternative to the tension between the uncanniness and the anxiety elicited by being-thrown into the *Unzuhause* of the first Heidegger and the reactive reterritorialization in the fourfoldian Earth of his last philosophy. Nature as *physis* is at once the Being that '*each time 'gives' particular beings 'over to venture'* '[40] and the very milieu into which they venture, the carnal locale whose fluctuating being-there they are. Since nature ventures the living beings into its own depths, it does not abandon them, they are not expelled out of it: '*As ventured, those who are not protected are nevertheless not abandoned. If they were, they would be just as little ventured as if they were protected. Surrendered only to annihilation, they would no longer hang in the balance.*'[41] Since living beings are just local modes of the phenoumenodelic draft, the dereliction of their being-ventured into its abyssal depths goes hand in hand with the '*safety*' provided by the fact that they are always upheld by the impersonal living flood: '*The venture sets free what is ventured* [...] *Drawing this way, the venture ever and always brings the ventured towards itself in the drawing*'.[42] According to Heidegger, such an unprotected safety '*exists only outside the objectifying turning away from the*

37   W. BENJAMIN, *Nearness and distance (continued)*, in *Selected Writings, Volume 1, 1913-1926*, ed. by Marcus Bullock and Michael W. Jennings (Cambridge, Massachusetts: The Belknap Press of Harvard University Press), p. 399.
38   M. HEIDEGGER, *What are Poets for?*, in *Poetry, Language, Thought*, trans. by A. Hofstadter (New York, Harper & Row Publishers, 1975), p. 101.
39   R. M. RILKE, quoted by Heidegger in *What are Poets for?*, p. 99.
40   M. HEIDEGGER, *What are Poets for?*, p. 101.
41   *Ibid.*, p. 103.
42   *Ibid.*, p. 105.

Open', outside the *re-presentation of* nature as something that *objectively* exists before us; outside – I maintain here – both the reduction of the phenoumenodelic transumweltic openness into a single objectified nature and the concomitant denaturation of the transcendental ego. By risking existence '*by a breath more*' – by risking the fixity of the very system of linguistic categories that frame experience, by perturbing the existentials, by affording the '*poverty in world*' resulting from the speculative transumweltization of experience, by assuming the being-given of the transcendental ego as a local and ephemeral fluctuation of a field of impersonal experience (with the resulting destitution of the egoical narcissism in favor of an impersonal one) – by doing so, beings can venture themselves further into the phenoumenodelic pleroma, thereby gaining an unexpected safety: '*to be secure is to repose safely within the drawing of the whole draft*'[43], to turn '*unshieldedness as such into the Open*'[44], being temporarily upheld by the relentless flood of manifestation.

In order to depict the impersonal stream of manifestation in more carnal terms, I shall abstract two 'elements' out of the '*primal* [or barbarian] *stuff*'[45] of pure experience, namely a connective and cohesive field – which I shall call *vision* – and a shapeless and resilient narcotic – which I shall call *plasma*. Rather than trying to construct an ontology of the experiential field (which is the proper task of the *theoretical* interest of reason), I am here addressing the field from a descriptive phenoumenodelic perspective. We shall therefore resist the monist (Fichtean and Bergsonian) *ontological* temptation to gloriously make beings out of light, and shall (gnostically) distinguish from the outset two distinct *suspended* elements: a *luminescent* one and a *substantial* one. It is worth emphasizing that the recognition of a *substantial* datum within the phenoumenodelic field does not entail an endorsing of a fundamental tone to which the whole field would be referred as to its 'material' presupposition: this substantial datum is itself abstracted from a scene which has been phenoumenodelically suspended.[46] In Sartre's terms, we could say that the phenoumenodelic recognition of this substantial stratum of experience does not '*load down*' the experiential field as such, i.e. it does not make it '*heavy and ponderable*':

---

43   *Ibid.*, p. 120.
44   *Ibid.*, p. 136.
45   W. JAMES, *Does 'Consciousness' exist?*, in *Essays in Radical Empiricism*, p. 2.
46   In an analogous way, Deleuze and Guattari write: 'Immanence does not refer back to the Spinozist substance and modes but, on the contrary, the Spinozist concepts of substance and modes refer back to the plane of immanence as their presupposition.', G. DELEUZE and F. GUATTARI, *What is Philosophy?*, p. 48.

the 'substantial' plasma is also a *suspended* phenoumenodelic datum.[47] In order to open *Lichtungen* (clearings) within the ungrounded depths of the plasma – in order to span local phenoumenodelic horizons rendering possible the bursting forth of manifestation – we shall suppose that the plasma is a *narcotic* element, i.e. an element that can be permeated by the propagation of a vision. Conversely, in order to disseminate unconscious opacities within the luminescent element, i.e. in order to dim the absolute (trans)lucidity and the seamless self-consciousness of the pure vision – which we could associate with a pre-Freudian model of impersonal subjectivity – I shall lachrymally humidify the vision by coupling it to substantial element apt to plasmate the disincarnated apparitions.[48] We shall therefore maintain that the phenoumenodelic suspended scene containing the sinking ark arises from the coalescence of a *connective vision* and *narcotic plasma*: a cohesive element apt to counteract the dispersion of the ungrounded extensions and '*clarify the* [day]*dream where we are*' (Igitur) and an atonal narcotic whose local excitations can reflect – and thereby reveal – the propagating modes of the vision while retaining, embodying, and enduring the resulting vibrations. This coalescence of the elements – the phosphenic enlightening of the plasma – produces a *pneumatic* and *iridescent tissue* that I shall call – taking up Merleau-Ponty's term anew – *flesh*. We could say that *flesh* is a narcotic *plasma* mesmerized by a *vision*, a resilient element which – stoned on its own narcotic virtues – is permeated by the inner propagation of the daydream. The trinity of elements defined by *vision*, *plasma*, and *flesh* can be understood as the constellation that orients the disciplinary correspondences between *transcendental philosophy*, *philosophy of nature*, and what we have called *immanental phenoumenology* (or *philosophy of identity*, in Schelling's terms).

Being atonal, i.e. lacking a ground state toward which its excitations could be released, the plasma is bursting with vibrating and resonating local patterns, reflecting and refracting carnal germs of subjectivation, experience-able and response-able '*waves of a calm narcotic whose vibratory circles*',[49] moving outward and inward, scan the field at different spatial and temporal scales. The

---

47   J. -P. Sartre, *The transcendence of the ego. An existentialist theory of consciousness*, p. 44.

48   A striking description of a lachrymal humidification of a translucid field of self-consciousness supposedly deprived of unconscious opacities can be found in P. Valery, *L'Ange*, in *La Jeune Parque et poèmes en prose* (Paris: Editions Gallimard, 1974), p. 39; trans. as *The Angel* in The Partisan Review, November 1948.

49   S. Mallarmé, *Igitur ou la Folie d'Elbehnon*, in *Igitur, Divagations, Un coup de dès*, ed. by Bertrand Marchal (Paris: Editions Gallimard, 2003), p. 61.

being-made-out-of-flesh of a local subjective fluctuation accounts for both the plasmatic force that – by acting in its bodily background – asserts its impersonal sovereignty on the subject and narcotizes it (i.e. it makes it susceptible to the infusion of the daydream), and for the phenoumenodelic visions thereby unfolded in its foreground. Thanks to the *pneumatic* character of the flesh, its local excitations can contract the iridescent vibrations into perceived qualities (receptive inspiration), embody the resulting rhythmic duration (temporal retention), and send back dehiscent information (expressive expiration). Accordingly, the pneumatic flesh is an autotelic element capable of *locally* enduring the *expressive flow* and the *sentient ebb* of its self-experience: to be there in the midst of the pneumatic flesh is to *breathe*, to undergo the rhythmic conversion between the inner spaces produced by local subjective foldings on the one hand, and objected 'transcendences' on the other.[50]

In this primordial scene – '*far from everything, Nature* [the constellations under the sea] *prepares her Theater*' – the Maître enacts '*the Play par excellence*': methodically '*mad on the outside and flagellated by the contradictory demands of* [eidetic] *duty*'[51] he is inwardly '*the character who, believing in the existence of the sole Absolute, imagines he is everywhere in a* [day]*dream. He acts from the Absolute point of view*'.[52] In particular – and among other visitations – the pneumatic flesh might unfoldd in the form of a siren which – before dissolving back into the liquid sky – immediately evaporates in mist – by means of a slap of her tail – the mirage of an Ur-Ground ('*faux manoir*') capable of imparting an edge to the phenoumenodelic draft. The Maître – local and ephemeral dehiscence of the pneumatic flesh dwelling on an ark that is endlessly shipwrecked – remains faithful to the foolhardy task passed down to him by the haunting specters of his ancestors: that of enduring both the *dereliction* of his *being-flung-loose* into the venture and the *safety* of his *being-upheld* by the impersonal flowing flesh by potentializing the phenoumenodelic degrees of freedom of which he is capable: by living, perceiving, feeling, and understanding the existentials, the percepts, the affects and the concepts he can afford. Ek-sistence is tuning in a state of pneumatic suspension.

---

50 According to (what we could call) James' transcendental principle of pneumatic apperception: '[…] the stream of thinking (which I recognize emphatically as a phenomenon) is only a careless name for what, when scrutinized, reveals itself to consist chiefly of the stream of my breathing. The 'I think' which Kant said must be able to accompany all my objects, is the 'I breathe' which actually does accompany them.', W. JAMES, *Does 'consciousness' exist?*, in *Essays in Radical Empiricism*, p. 19.

51 S. MALLARMÉ, *Hamlet*, in *Igitur, Divagations, Un coup de dès*, ed. by Bertrand Marchal (Paris: Editions Gallimard, 2003), pp. 194-199.

52 S. MALLARMÉ, *Igitur ou la Folie d'Elbehnon*, in *Igitur, Divagations, Un coup de dès*, p. 32.

V

WHAT HAS KANT EVER DONE FOR US?
SPECULATIVE REALISM
AND DYNAMIC KANTIANISM[1]

FABIO GIRONI

[Reason] spreads its wings in vain when seeking to rise above
the world of sense through the mere might of speculation.

I. Kant, *Critique of Pure Reason*

The recent resurgence of realist themes in contemporary continental philosophy has often been accompanied by a more or less explicit critique or rejection of the Kantian heritage. Kant's transcendental critical project, it has been argued, is to be held responsible for curtailing metaphysical ambitions, deflating the notion of objectivity, limiting the scope of philosophy to a self-centered description of our access to the universe, and retrenching human knowledge to the confined sphere of mere appearances, ultimately leading subsequent philosophical developments – in the German idealist tradition first, and in much of twentieth-century continental philosophy later – to forfeit the realist ambition of directly referring to, or even grasping, reality in itself.

While this large-scale historical reconstruction has some truth to it – that is to say, the 'Kantian paradigm'[2] has indeed been adopted and modified by philosophers pursuing a (broadly speaking) anti-realist agenda – I want to argue that perhaps Kant's influence on the last two hundred years of philosophy has been rather unfairly flattened to a 'weak correlationist' position (such is Meillassoux's extremely influential label, applied to the stance which 'proscribes any knowledge of the thing-in-itself (any application of the categories to the supersensible), but maintains the thinkability of the in-itself'). While the label of 'weak correlationist' can be rea-

---

1   I would like to thank Daniel Sacilotto, Carl B. Sachs and Matija Jelaca for their precious comments on a draft of this paper.
2   The term is employed by Lee Braver in his *A Thing of This World: An History of Continental Anti-Realism* (Evanston: Northwestern University Press, 2007).

sonably[3] applied to Kant, the effect of this denunciation has occasionally been that of a wholesale rejection of the transcendental project or, more generally, of the idea that there are epistemological hurdles to overcome before obtaining an access to the real – these cautionary recommendations only seen as an unfortunate symptom of unregenerate anti-realism. Eager to re-inject into philosophy robust metaphysical speculations about reality in itself, we have been (ironically) recommended to say 'Goodbye Kant!',[4] to look with suspicion upon his philosophically disastrous 'Ptolemaic counter-revolution',[5] to reject his pedantic insistence on finitude, in the name of a long-forgotten 'great outdoors, the *absolute* outside of pre-critical thinkers',[6] or to shift his parochial attention from the relationship between rational agents and objects of knowledge to that between objects themselves.[7] Indeed Peter Gratton, in a recent critical survey, tells us how the participants to the 2007 'Speculative Realism' conference in London 'seemingly agree on but one thing: that European philosophy since the time of Kant has stopped talking about reality, since

---

3   But not without controversy: Meillassoux's definition seems to ignore a possible non-metaphysical interpretation of Kantian transcendental idealism, what is today called a 'two-aspects' (as opposed to 'two-worlds'), epistemological reading of the phenomena/noumena distinction, most famously defended by Henry Allison. See H. ALLISON, *Kant's Transcendental Idealism: An Interpretation and Defense* (New Haven and London: Yale University Press, 2004).

4   M. FERRARIS, *Goodbye Kant! What Still Stands of the Critique of Pure Reason* (New York: SUNY Press, 2013). Ferraris' stance towards Kant is more nuanced than the provocative title would suggest. He explains that 'Kant fought, if anything, too successfully against common sense, against a naive view of things, against an immediate relation with the world. And he did so not with the inconclusiveness of a skeptic, but with the constructive desire of an honest philosopher who was also one of the great figures of human thought...The return of realism two hundred years after the Kantian turn is not, then, the result of a tedious pendulum swing, but it is likely to be a sign that that turn has been fully assimilated. A naïve view of the world is possible and even necessary, but the naivete is not given and must be earned' (2013: 103). Nonetheless, I disagree with the emphasis placed on a naïve view of the world, as the naturalized Kantian stance I recommend necessarily presents realism as delivering a non-naïve view of the world, promising such an 'immediate' (non-inferential) commerce with reality in itself only as a never quite grasped regulative ideal.

5   MEILLASSOUX, *After Finitude*, p. 118.

6   MEILLASSOUX, *After Finitude*, p. 7.

7   See G. HARMAN, 'The Current State of Speculative Realism', in *Speculations* IV, (2013), pp. 22-28.

it's stuck thinking about how we *know* reality.'[8]Aiming at a more direct contact with said reality, we have been time and again invited to shed our narcissistic anthropocentrism and with it the excessive preoccupation with conditions for knowledge. Less epistemological navel-gazing, more metaphysical star-gazing.

Yet there is another path for the contemporary realist to take, one keen to preserve the most fundamental insights of the Königsberg philosopher, and concurrently more respectful of our best existing epistemic practices: the natural sciences. It is this Kantian route, I will argue, that leads directly to that corner of contemporary realism where the philosophy of Wilfrid Sellars has been adopted as the best contemporary example of a realist, naturalized Kantianism.[9]A self-appointed realism blind to the contributions to (and conditioning of) empirical inquiry by our conceptual structures, and ready to pay whatever epistemological or metaphysical price in order to finally proceed 'after finitude' is, I contend, not a realism worth fighting for.

---

8   P. GRATTON, *Speculative Realism: Problems and Prospects* (London: Continuum, 2014), p. 4. Of course, Gratton is well aware that this historical observation on the path taken by European post-Kantian philosophy did not lead all four 'speculative realists' to a full-blooded rejection of the Kantian project. Ray Brassier, directly responsible for the introduction of Sellars into this realist debate (and indirectly responsible for my own employment of Sellars in this chapter), never denounced Kant as merely an obstacle to overcome, but tried to marry, with Sellars' help, a realist outlook with a careful assessment of our conceptual means of access to reality. On this topic see R. BRASSIER 'Concepts and Objects' in *The Speculative Turn: Continental Materialism and Realism*, ed. by L. Bryant, N. Srnicek and G. Harman (Melbourne: re.press, 2011). Note that Brassier's critical engagement with Kant's transcendental project (one following a trajectory very similar to the one I'm defending here), dates back to some of his very early work. In a 2001 paper, Brassier endorses Kant's 'basic refusal to have any truck with the homely phenomenological faith in the pre-theoretical experiential immediacy of 'the things themselves'', while highlighting the failure of Kant's complication of transcendental structures of experience with Euclidean geometry and Newtonian dynamics. See R. BRASSIER, 'Behold the Non-Rabbit: Kant, Quine, and Laruelle', in *Pli: The Warwick Journal of Philosophy*, 12 (2001), pp. 50-82 (p. 54).

9   For an excellent analysis, complementing that which I offer here, of how Sellars' work can help resolve problems immanent to 'speculative realism' see Daniel Sacilotto 'Realism and Representation: On the Ontological Turn', in *Speculations* IV, (2013), pp. 53-64.

The Revision of the A Priori

> Therefore, I ask *how do you know* that *a priori* truth is certain,
> exceptionless, and exact? You cannot know it by reasoning. For
> that would be subject to uncertainty and inexactitude. Then, it must
> amount to this that you know it *a priori*; that is, you take *a priori*
> judgments at their own valuation, without criticism or credentials.
> That is barring the gate of inquiry.
> [W]hat has been indubitable one day has often been proved on
> the morrow to be false.
>
> C.S. Peirce, *Collected Papers*

The philosophical tradition concerned with a 'relativization' of the Kantian *a priori* argues that the historically-minded scientific philosopher can and should preserve the Kantian discursive epistemological structure of a conceptually mediated empirical contact with reality, but only where the notion of *a priori* conditions of experience is revised as being (according to various descriptions) 'relativized', 'contextual', 'pragmatic' or 'functional'. I will offer, in what follows, a brief overview of this notion of relativized *a priori* principles, in the work of various philosophers who mobilized this notion, as setting the stage for Sellars' revolutionary synopsis of Kantianism and physicalism.

A first step in this direction can be found within the tradition of 'scientific philosophy' (*wissenschafliche Philosophie*), developed between the latter half of the nineteenth century and the beginning of the twentieth century in Germany, wherein – reacting against the metaphysical excesses of post-Kantian German idealism, particularly that Hegelian/Schellingian form of *Naturphilosophie* holistically fusing, against Kant, concepts and being, life and matter – a 'back to Kant' movement which sought to reconcile the transcendental project with contemporary science.[10] While one of the distinguishing traits of Viennese logical empiricism, particularly under the influence of Moritz Schlick, was the rejection of the Kantian synthetic *a priori*, the history of a 'relativize' form of *a priori* principles can be

---

10   Hermann Helmholtz's 1855 public address *Über das Sehen des Menschen*, offering a physiological account of human sight in accordance with Kant's epistemology, is often considered as the first rallying cry for philosophers keen to pursue this scientific neo-Kantian road. For a far more nuanced account of the historical emergence of neo-Kantianism in German academia, problematizing this somewhat simplistic account of an anti-Idealist backlash, see K. C. Kohnke, *The Rise of Neo-Kantianism: German Academic Philosophy Between Idealism and Positivism* (Cambridge: CUP, 1991).

usefully[11] traced back to the early work of one of its close affiliates: Hans Reichenbach. In some biographical reflections, the Berlin Circle philosopher recounts how it was the encounter with the revolutionary scientific results of his time which led him to a reconsideration of the Kantian project:

> I attended Einstein's lectures at the University of Berlin; at that time, his audience was very small because Einstein's name had not yet become known to a wider public. The theory of relativity impressed me immensely and led me into a conflict with Kant's philosophy. Einstein's critique of the space-time-problem made me realize that Kant's *a priori* concept was indeed untenable. I recorded the result of this profound inner change in a small book entitled *Relativitatstheorie und Erkenntnis Apriori*.[12]

Einsteinian relativity theory, by relying upon a non-Euclidean (Reimannian) geometry and by restricting the validity of the Newtonian laws of motion, threatened to undermine fatally the Kantian system (Euclidean space being the model of the pure form of intuition of space and Newton's laws being considered, by Kant, as empirical exemplifications of pure *a priori* principles of motion).[13] Reichenbach, however, continued to consider Kant as the best philosophical resource for an epistemology of contemporary science (considering such an approach to be more promising than radical forms of empiricism), but detected Kant's crucial mistake in the postulation of a too-straightforward 'agreement between nature and the human ability to know'. On the contrary, he argues, 'there exists the possibility of a contradiction between the human system of concepts and nature. Yet, in such a case, epistemology does not have to fail at all, for *the human being possesses the ability to change his system of concepts and to adapt it to nature*. Just this is what happened with the theory of relativity.'[14]

---

11   The history of conventionalism proper, of course, goes back at least to Poincaré and Mach – looming influences in these debates – but in this paper I try to follow the more explicitly neo-Kantian path, from Reichenbach onwards.

12   M. REICHENBACH and R. S. COHEN, *Hans Reichenbach: Selected Writings, 1909-1953. Volume One* (Dordrecht: Reidel, 1978), p. 2.

13   For a thorough account of which facets of the Kantian notion of synthetic *a priori* can and cannot survive the logico-scientific revolutions of the twentieth century see Chapter 4 of Alan Richardson, *Carnap's construction of the World: The Aufbau and the Emergence of Logical Empiricism* (Cambridge: CUP, 1998).

14   M. REICHENBACH and COHEN, *Selected Writings*, p. 4. Emphasis added. See also M. REICHENBACH and R. S. COHEN, *Hans Reichenbach: Selected Writings, 1909-1953*. Vol. Two (Dordrecht: Reidel, 1978), pp. 37-39.

In his 1920 *Relativity and A Priori Knowledge*,[15] (his *Habilitationsschrift*) one of the first philosophical confrontations with Einstein's new theory, Reichenbach attempts a revision of Kantian epistemology in light of the conceptual revolution brought about by relativity. He crucially distinguishes two meanings of *a priori*: first, Reichenbach argues, *a priori* can be taken to mean 'necessarily true' or 'true for all times'; secondly, it can be interpreted as 'constituting the concept of the object'.[16] It is by rejecting the first characterization while preserving the second that Reichenbach aims to salvage a role for the *a priori*, now conceived as a diachronically contingent but still synchronically necessary principle for the constitution of the meaning of scientific theories. Reichenbach observes that where we discover a contradiction between such arbitrary constitutive principles and empirical (experimental) evidence, the latter forces us to *revise* the former: '[i]t is experience that decides which elements are necessary'[17]. To this extent, Kant's mistake is that 'the system of his *a priori* principles represents merely a canonization of 'common sense', of that naïve affirmation of reason which he himself occasionally rejects with sober incisiveness'.[18] In a synthetic formulation, then, Reichenbach's core thesis is that, contra Kant: "*A priori*' means 'before knowledge', but not 'for all time' and not 'independent of experience".[19] Conceptual frameworks are *a priori* in the sense of being responsible for the organization of our experience but not in the sense of being utterly unrevisable in the face of recalcitrant experience. Against traditional empiricism, then, Reichenbach insists that the study of physical theories demonstrates that there *is* an epistemological difference between *a priori* – in this sense of 'meaning-constituting' – spatio-temporal frameworks ('axioms of coordination', establishing rules of coordination between mathematical representations and empirical reality) and empirical laws ('axioms of connection') presupposing such a framework. As Michael Friedman has shown,[20] however, Reichenbach eventually modified this position after an epistolary exchange with Schlick, essentially abandoning the notion of relativized *a priori* by dissolving the difference between empirical and non-empirical parts of a theory, thus sliding into something like Quinean holism, rejecting the *a priori*/*a posteriori* distinction.

---

15   H. REICHENBACH, *The Theory of Relativity and A Priori Knowledge* (Berkeley and Los Angeles: University of California Press, 1965).
16   REICHENBACH, *The Theory of Relativity*, p. 48.
17   *Ibid.*, p. 88.
18   *Ibid.*, p. 73.
19   *Ibid.*, p 105.
20   See FRIEDMAN, *Reconsidering Logical Positivism* (Cambridge: CUP, 1999), Ch. 3.

Yet Reichenbach has not remained an isolated incident in the history of the revision of the Kantian *a priori*, and Carnap's late discussion of 'linguistic frameworks' can be read in such a relativized Kantian key. In his 1950 paper 'Empiricism Semantics and Ontology', tackling the issue of abstract entities, Carnap introduces the notion of a linguistic framework as a system of linguistic rules (introducing new entities as values of variables), allowing for the formulation of 'internal' questions regarding the domain of entities and the object of the framework in question – questions to be either deflated as analytic (in the case of general questions like 'are there Xs?')[21] or to be answered by empirical investigation. To these internal questions, Carnap opposes 'external' questions (i.e., external to the linguistic framework) – the kind of questions favored by the metaphysician – aimed at deciding general questions of existence, independent from any given framework, or indeed asking to adjudicate between different frameworks in terms of a meta-framework criterion. Carnap takes the latter kind of questions to be intrinsically meaningless, pseudo-questions 'framed in the wrong way',[22] if interpreted as theoretical questions. The choice between the plurality of logical frameworks (between languages within which questions of existence will be legitimately articulated) is seen by Carnap as a purely pragmatic matter, a matter of collective decision, not of empirical justification.[23] Hence Carnap defends his so-called 'Principle of tolerance' according to which '*it is not our busi-*

---

21   So that, as Sellars explains considering Carnap's approach, the assertion 'there are Xs' is, effectively, an explication of the fact that X is a *category* in the framework under consideration. See W. SELLARS 'Empiricism and Abstract Entities', in *The Philosophy of Rudolph Carnap*, ed. by Paul Arthur Schilpp (La Salle: Open Court, 1963), pp. 431-468.

22   R. CARNAP 'Empiricism, Semantics, and Ontology', in A.P. Martinich (ed.), *Analytic Philosophy: An Anthology* (Malden: Blackwell Publishing, 2001), p. 426.

23   Carnap's strict separation of the theoretical from the practical domain, somewhat ironically, resonates with that post-Kantian tradition the positivists were keen to disavow, particularly with the Hegelian revision of Kant according to the principle (as phrased by Brandom, borrowed from Haugeland) that 'all transcendental constitution is social institution'. Yet, unlike Hegel, Carnap ends up *excluding* (scientific) reason from the practical sphere: so Thomas Mormann insightfully questions reconstructions of Carnap as an Enlightenment thinker precisely grounding his objections on Carnap's implicit and 'romantic/Nietzschean' commitment to the dualism of *Geist* and *Leben*, the latter by definition a domain of affect-driven practical action free from rationally motivated decisions, forbidden terrain for the scientific philosopher uninterested in the messy details of the practical world. See T. MORMANN, 'Carnap's *Boundless Ocean of Unlimited Possibilities*: Between Enlightenment and Romanticism', in *Carnap's Ideal of Explication and Naturalism*, ed. by Pierre Wagner (Basingstoke: Palgrave Macmillan, 2012).

ness to set up prohibitions, but to arrive at conventions,'[24] since, '[t]o decree
dogmatic prohibitions of certain linguistic forms instead of testing them by
their success or failure in practical use, is worse than futile; it is positively
harmful because it may obstruct scientific progress'[25]. In other words, different frameworks (i.e., quasi-transcendental logical systems for the constitution of the meaning of scientific statements) can be conventionally adopted
and are to be judged on the grounds of their usefulness for epistemic agents
in the pursuit of scientific knowledge.[26] Coffa sums up this position:

> [t]he 'linguistic' (better, semantic) theory of the *a priori* [...] in the writings
> of [...] Carnap would simply say that all necessity is semantic necessity, that all
> *a priori* truth is truth *ex vi terminorum*, that when a statement is necessary, it is
> because its rejection would be no more than a misleading way of rejecting the
> language (the system of meanings) to which it belongs.[27]

Considering how, in Alan Richardson's words 'the more one engages with
Carnap's thought, the more one finds a sort of open-mindedness and pragmatism right at its very core'[28], it should not be surprising to find philosophers
within the fold of the American pragmatist tradition developing these kinds of
neo-Kantian ideas, and keeping their philosophical focus on those elements of a
scientific theory (or in fact of any process of knowledge whatsoever) that hold a
unique, constitutional epistemological status.[29] So starting with the fundamental

24   R. CARNAP, *Logical Syntax of Language* (London: Routledge, 2000), p. 51.
25   CARNAP, 'Empiricism Semantics and Ontology', p. 433.
26   Carnap's transition from an early 'rational reconstruction' phase, seeking an ulti-
     mate and permanent logical framework for knowledge, to this later pluralistic
     conception of a whole landscape of possible frameworks is best narrated in A.W.
     CARUS, *Carnap and Twentieth-Century Thought: Explication as Enlightenment*
     (Cambridge: CUP, 2007).
27   A. COFFA, *The Semantic Tradition from Kant to Carnap: to the Vienna Station*
     (Cambridge: CUP, 1991), p. 139.
28   A. RICHARDSON 'Carnapian Pragmatism', in R. Creath and M. Friedman (eds.). *The
     Cambridge Companion to Carnap*, (Cambridge: CUP, 2007), p. 296. On the dia-
     logue between Carnap and the Pragmatist tradition in the US see also C. LIMBECK-
     LILENAU, 'Carnap's Encounter with Pragmatism', in *Rudolph Carnap and the Lega-
     cy of Logical Empiricism*, ed. by Richard Creath (Dordrecht: Springer, 2012).
29   All the philosophers connected to pragmatism I will consider here were, in a
     more or less direct fashion, influenced by the work of the great founder of this
     philosophical school, C.S. Peirce. Peirce was an outstandingly rich and complex
     thinker and I whilst I am unable to do justice to his thought in this brief survey,
     I hope readers will take the epigraph of this chapter as signaling that the spirit
     of Peirce's 'Kantian variation' thoroughly permeates my reconstruction of the
     idea of relativized *a priori* principles.

Kantian assumption (shared, in a more or less stringent form, by all the philosophers I herein consider) that '[e]xperience does not categorize itself'[30] since '[w]ithout initial principles by which we guide our attack upon the welter of experience, it would remain forever chaotic and refractory',[31] and yet equally convinced that 'traditional conceptions of the *a priori* have proven untenable',[32] C. I. Lewis gave a *pragmatic* twist to the theory of the *a priori*, arguing that the selection and adoption (or rejection) of such principles is neither intuited nor directly read off experience, but rather dependent on pragmatic considerations and behavioral attitudes, thus responding to human interests and needs:

> while the *a priori* is dictated neither by what is presented in experience nor by any transcendent and eternal factor of human nature, it still answers to criteria of the general type which may be termed pragmatic.[33]
>
> [c]lassifications and their criteria are determined pragmatically, not metaphysically, and even when such criteria have been fixed, there can be nothing which is not classifiable in more than one way. [...]And there can be nothing in the nature of an object which determines the *fundamentum divisionis* by reference to which it shall be classified.[34]

Following a Peircean line, Lewis had a fallibilist understanding of the collective progress of knowledge, holding that the tentative expansion of the boundaries of the known requires – with the aim of increased comprehension of the world in sight – the revision of our rational resources of sense-making, of conceptual frameworks that are to be seen as 'social products, reached in the light of experiences which have much in common, and beaten out, like other pathways, by the coincidence of human purposes and the exigencies of human cooperation'.[35] The *a priori* principles which we adopt as regulative for experience, Lewis holds, are those empirical generalizations we have selected, throughout our cognitive history, as not being susceptible of refutation, and that make further inquiry possible by defining the space of questions to be asked.[36]

---

30 Lewis, *Mind and the World-Order: Outline of a Theory of Knowledge* (New York: Dover, 1956), p. 14.
31 Lewis, *Mind and the World-Order*, p. 254.
32 Lewis, *Collected Papers,* ed. by John D. Goheen and John L. Mothershead (Stanford: Stanford University Press, 1970), p. 231.
33 Lewis, *Mind and the World-Order*, p. 239.
34 Lewis, *An Analysis of Knowledge and Valuation* (La Salle (IL): Open Court, 1946), p. 105.
35 Lewis, *Collected Papers*, p. 239.
36 Chang has recently proposed a Lewis-inspired (but even more praxis-oriented) approach to *a priori* necessity, proposing that 'something is 'necessarily true' if it *needs* to

In a similar vein, and partaking in the same pragmatist tradition of Lewis (yet mostly by way of Dewey's discussion of 'operationally' *a priori* principles), but also more directly influenced by Poincaré's conventionalism, Arthur Pap defended a theory of the *a priori* which rejects the adoption of such principles via transcendental deduction or via a faculty of intellectual intuition: *a priori* principles 'may be called *functional* in so far as the *a priori* is characterized in terms of functions which propositions may perform in existential inquiry, no matter whether they be, on formal grounds, classified as analytic or as synthetic.'[37]

Pap distinguishes between three kinds of *a priori* principles:[38] the formal, the material and the functional *a priori*. All that there is to functional *a priori* statement is *the role it plays* within the system of a physical theory, so that any empirical generalization can, in principle, be selected and 'hardened' into a constitutive role, acquiring a definitional status.[39] So,

> whether a hypothesis functions as *a priori* or not depends on the degree of its generality. It is the most *general* laws that are under all circumstances adhered to as methodological postulates or leading principles, because the very possibility of science depends on their validity.[...]Being undoubtedly synthetic [...] they are not *formally* necessary; their necessity is but functional.[40]

Indeed, Pap insists, '[i]f definitory or analytic statements are of any use in inquiry, if they have, in other words, existential import, and are not idle *nominal* definitions, it is because they are synthetic in origin.'[41]

A few decades later, Hilary Putnam – firmly in the tradition of American pragmatism, but also plausibly influenced by the work of his *Doktorvater*,

---

be *taken* as true for the purpose of some epistemic action', thus construing metaphysical principles as co-varying with the different kinds of epistemic activities we choose to carry out. Hasok Chang, 'Contingent Transcendental Arguments for Metaphysical Principles', *Royal Institute of Philosophy Supplement*, 63 (2008), 113–33 (p. 132). On Lewis's acceptance of some form of non-cognitive (given) element of experience, and his relationship with Sellars see C. B. SACHS, *Intentionality and the Myths of the Given* (London: Pickering and Chatto, forthcoming 2014). On Lewis's understanding of 'the Real', see L. JÄRVILEHTO, 'Concepts and the Real in C. I. Lewis' Epistemology', in *Realism, Science and Pragmatism*, ed. by Kenneth Westphal (London and New York: Routledge, 2014, pp. 243-250.

37   A. PAP, *The A Priori in Physical Theory* (New York: King's Crown Press, 1946), p. viii
38   In his 1944 paper 'Three Different Kinds of a Priori' in *The Limits of Logical Empiricism*, ed. by Alfons Keupnik and Sanford Shieh (Dordrecht: Springer, 2006).
39   For a complete account of Pap's view see D. STUMP, 'Arthur Pap's Functional Theory of the *A Priori*'. *HOPOS: The Journal of the International Society for the History of Philosophy of Science* 1: 273–90.
40   PAP, *The Limits of Logical Empiricism*, p. 73.
41   PAP, *The Limits of Logical Empiricism*, p. 74.

Hans Reichenbach – argued in favor of a weak form of *a priori* principles which he labeled 'contextual apriority', where

> [t]he idea is that we can grant that certain truths, and even, at certain times, certain falsehoods, have a special status, but that we don't have to concede that that status is good old-fashioned apriority. The status these truths and falsehoods have, as long as they have it, is contextual apriority: apriority relative to the body of knowledge. And the thesis that there are no *a priori* truths becomes the thesis that there are no absolutely *a priori* truths.[42]

The relative apriority defended by Putnam, then, refers to the unquestionable character of certain theory-specific (logical or metaphysical) presuppositions, impossible to disconfirm directly (no matter the amount of observational data) from within the conceptual economy of the theory itself, and that 'can only be overthrown by a new theory – sometimes by a revolutionary new theory.[...] Such statements *have* a sort of 'apriority' prior to the invention of the new theory which challenges or replaces them: they are *contextually a priori*'.[43] In other words, while these contextually *a priori* principles furnish the condition of intelligibility of and the basic conceptual framework for the terms of a scientific theory (or any representation of the external world), only a intra-conceptual revolution, a top-down revision of the entire framework, can engender their revision.[44]

This brief survey would not be complete without at least mentioning Thomas Kuhn's theory of scientific revolutions, based on the epochal shift of paradigms – playing the role of sets of *a priori* principles. While Kuhn's stance is too well known to be examined again in detail here, it is worth noting how, in a late pa-

---

42   H. PUTNAM, *Realism and Reason: Philosophical Papers, Volume 3* (Cambridge: CUP, 1983), p. 99.

43   PUTNAM, *Realism and Reason*, p. 95.

44   It is again worth noting that the notion that *a priori* principles can be revised is not identical with Quinean holism to the extent that the latter denies *any* distinction between *a priori* and *a posteriori* statements in a theory. Stump puts it quite clearly when he explains that '[w]hile Quine admits that some elements of empirical theory are much less likely to be revised than others, he underestimates the asymmetric relation between the 'hard core' and the 'periphery'. It is not just that the periphery is more likely to be revised than the hard core, but rather that the statements of the periphery cannot even be stated, let alone tested, without the hard core functioning as an *a priori* in the Kantian sense as a necessary precondition'. David Stump, 'Defending Conventions and Functionally *A Priori* Knowledge', in *Philosophy of Science*, 70:5, (2003), p. 1150. On the difference between Quine and Putnam on this topic, see J. Y. TSOU, 'Putnam's Account of Apriority and Scientific Change: Its Historical and Contemporary Interest', *Synthese* 176 (3), (2009), 429-45.

per, while discussing laws that enter a theory 'stipulatively' and make possible an empirical interpretation of terms, he explicitly states that:

> I do not quite want to call such laws analytic, for experience with nature was essential to their initial formulation. Yet they do have something of the necessity that the label 'analytic' implies. Perhaps 'synthetic *a priori*' comes closer.[45]

Having completed this survey of the idea of a relativized form of *a priori* knowledge, that 'peculiar kind of knowledge that seems necessary and not vacuous, yet at the same time does not quite state any factual claims'[46] (in Coffa's words) and having shown how, in the hands of these philosophers, Kantian principles underwent an historically-motivated modal shift, from necessity to contingency (and back again),[47] I will now focus on one pre-eminent example of such relativization.

---

45   T. KUHN 'Dubbing and Redubbing: The Vulnerability of Rigid Designation', in *Minnesota Studies in the Philosophy of Science*, ed. by Wade Savage, James Conant, and John Haugeland. (Minneapolis: University of Minnesota Press, 1990), p. 306. By 1995 Kuhn claims to 'go round explaining my own position saying I am a Kantian with moveable categories. It's got what is no longer quite a Kantian *a priori*, but that experience [that of giving a presentation on Kant's notion of precondition for knowledge, as a student] surely prepared me for the Kantian synthetic *a priori*'. T. KUHN, *The Road since Structure: Philosophical Essays, 1970-1993, with an Autobiographical Interview*, ed. by James Conant and John Haugeland (Chicago: The University of Chicago Press, 2000), p. 264.

46   COFFA, *The Semantic Tradition from Kant to Carnap*, p. 138.

47   In an insightful paper subtitled 'How the Contingent Becomes Necessary', William Wimsatt offers a *generalized* approach to the process of creation of regulative principles (even though he does not use this terminology) in different contexts. Wimsatt describes the phenomenon of *generative entrenchment*, through which 'initially changeable or dynamical processes can become 'frozen' through use, or freed through disentrenchment. With accumulating dependencies, seemingly arbitrary contingencies can become profoundly necessary, acting as generative structural elements for other contingencies added later' where the structure is question can be 'material, abstract, social, or mental' W. WIMSATT, *Re-Engineering Philosophy for Limited Beings: Piecewise Approximations to Reality* (Cambridge (MA): Harvard University Press, 2007), p. 135. It is interesting to note how Wimsatt's ideas are drawn from the observed behavior of natural systems subject to evolutionary processes, the same kind of scientific background which had such a major influence on those American pragmatists (especially Peirce and Dewey) who profoundly contributed to the idea of relativizing (and in an important sense, *naturalizing*) *a priori* principles.

Friedman's Dynamic Kantianism

> I [...] hope, in the end, to make a transformed – and fundamentally historicized – version of Kantian philosophy more directly relevant to the philosophical, scientific, technological, political, and spiritual predicament of our own times.
>
> M. Friedman, 'Kantian Themes in Contemporary Philosophy'

Michael Friedman has, more than any other contemporary interpreter, exhibited the crucial role that the natural sciences played in the genesis and structure of Kant's philosophy. As he painstakingly demonstrates in a large number of publications on the topic, Kant's primary objective was to engage with and offer a philosophical support to the best science of his days (Newtonian physics). Friedman insists that

> [f]ar from seeing the world-view of modern mathematical-physical science as any kind of threat to his philosophical transcendental argumentation in the Aesthetic and Analytic of the *Critique*, Kant undertakes a key step in that argumentation precisely to secure the philosophical foundations of this world-view once and for all.[48]

Proceeding from the acknowledgment of the contextual imbrication of Kant's philosophy with Newtonian science, Friedman argues that it is however possible to envision the Kantian structure to be flexible enough to accommodate (or evolve with) *new* scientific theories, and that indeed this is what Kant himself intended his philosophical project to be capable of. Through a close examination of Kant's *Metaphysical Foundations of Natural Science* – a crucial, and somewhat underexplored, text in the Kantian canon – Friedman reveals a direct dependency of Kant's general principles of synthetic *a priori* knowledge upon the specific concrete instantiations of these modes of knowledge, as offered by Newtonian physical science (for example, the empirical concept of 'matter' in Newtonian physics directly exemplifying the synthetic *a priori* principle of substance as exposed in the first *Critique*). Friedman's daring thesis, is indeed that

> on the one hand, the more abstract and general synthetic *a priori* principles defended in the first *Critique* are just as subject to refutation by the further progress of empirical natural science as are the more specific and explicitly

---

48   M. FRIEDMAN, *Aristotelian Society Supplementary Volume*, 72 (1), (1998), 111-30, p. 122.

mathematical principles defended in the *Metaphysical Foundations*, and, on the other, it is very hard even to understand Kant's arguments for the still quite rigorous and exacting principles articulated in the former work without giving a central position to the latter.[49]

Making good use of this Kantian interpretation,[50] and arguing that, in the wake of the physical and geometrical revolutions of the late nineteenth and early twentieth century we have 'learned, without a doubt, that [Kantian] conditions of possibility or necessary presuppositions of empirical natural science should not be viewed as rigidly fixed for all time, as forever immune to revision'[51], Friedman starts developing his own variety of neo-Kantian philosophy of science, defending the role of a Reichenbach-inspired notion of a 'dynamical *a priori*' element indispensable for the development of scientific theories. Mobilizing the post-Kuhnian[52] insight that 'our best current historiography of science requires us to draw a fundamental distinction between constitutive principles, on the one side, and properly empirical laws formulated against the background of such principles, on the other.'[53]

Friedman argues that, in order to make sense of the observed historical transition between one set of constitutive principles to another, effectively serving as *movable foundations*[54] for scientific knowledge,

49   M. FRIEDMAN, 'Philosophy and Natural Science', in Paul Guyer (ed). *The Cambridge Companion to Kant and Modern Philosophy* (Cambridge: CUP, 2006), pp. 320-321.

50   See in particular M. FRIEDMAN, *Kant and the Exact Sciences* (Cambridge (MA): Harvard University Press, 1992) and M. FRIEDMAN, *Kant's Construction of Nature: A Reading of the Metaphysical Foundations of Natural Science* (Cambridge: CUP, 2013).

51   M. FRIEDMAN, 'Philosophical Naturalism', in *Proceedings and Addresses of the American Philosophical Association*, 71 (2), (1997), pp. 7-21.

52   See M. FRIEDMAN 'A Post-Kuhnian Approach to the History and Philosophy of Science', in *The Monist* 93 (4), p. 497–517, for an explicit articulation of his dynamic Kantianism as 'developed in response to Thomas Kuhn's theory of scientific revolutions'.

53   M. FRIEDMAN, *Dynamics of Reason* (Stanford: CSLI Publications, 2001), p. 43.

54   Or, attempting a shift of register to Heideggerian parlance, *groundless grounds*. Much more could be said about the history of the Kantian *a priori* condition of experience in a 'continental' context, passing through (at least) Heidegger's historical-phenomenological revision and Foucault's own original elaboration of it. Ian Hacking is an author who, throughout his work, has explored the connection between the Foucauldian attention to history and the post-Kuhnian approach which Friedman intends to revamp. A particularly promising link between the two intellectual traditions, one only briefly highlighted by Friedman himself, is the work of Gaston Bachelard, particularly regarding his insistence on a dialectical rela-

the Kantian conception of the peculiarly 'transcendental' function of philosophy (as a meta-scientific discipline) must [...] be relativized and generalized. The enterprise Kant called 'transcendental philosophy' – the project of articulating and philosophically contextualizing the most basic constitutive principles defining the fundamental spatio-temporal framework of empirical natural science – must be seen as just as dynamical and historically situated as are the mathematical-physical constitutive principles which are its object.[55]

Against the restricted role given to *a priori* philosophical methods by mainstream naturalism, Friedman aims at delimiting a proper role for philosophy to play within our cognitive adventure of inquiry into nature, exploiting the Kant-inspired distinction between a first-order level of inquiry (science proper) and a meta-level of transcendental reflection of the conceptual possibility of such inquiry – thus tracing back to the Kantian influence the birth, out of 'natural philosophy', of the two distinct (yet never fully independent) disciplines of science and philosophy.[56] Proposing a three-tiered picture of knowledge (divided, in order of abstraction, into empirical laws of nature, scientific paradigms, and philosophical meta-paradigms), Friedman holds that what philosophy can and should promote is the

creation and stimulation of new frameworks or paradigms, together with what we might call metaframeworks or meta-paradigms – new conceptions of what a coherent rational understanding of nature might amount to – capable of motivating and sustaining the revolutionary transition to a new first-level or scientific paradigm.[57]

---

tionship between rational-mathematical formulation of principles and empirical experimentation. I am exploring this connection further in my current project.

55   FRIEDMAN, *Dynamics of Reason*, p. 45. Friedman further explains that 'to say that A is a constitutive condition of B rather means that A is a necessary condition, not simply of the truth of B, but of B's meaningfulness or possession of a truth value. It means, in now relatively familiar terminology, that A is a *presupposition* o f B' (*Dynamics of Reason*, p. 74). I wonder if Friedman's choice of word here is an explicit reference to Collingwood's discussion of 'absolute presuppositions' as defining the province of metaphysics, another important – if somewhat underexplored – development of Kantian ideas. See R.G. COLLINGWOOD, *An Essay on Metaphysics* (Oxford: Clarendon Press, 1940).

56   For a more extensive discussion of the history of 'natural philosophy' and the possibility of the reactivation of such synoptic project today, see F. GIRONI 'The Impossible Return of Natural Philosophy: a Speculative Proposal for a Reformed Philosophy (of Science)', forthcoming.

57   FRIEDMAN, *Dynamics of Reason*, p. 23.

To the provocative question I have asked in the title of this paper, then, we could answer, with Friedman, that Kant has (among other things!) given us a still-precious conceptual map to delimit the territory of science and philosophy while maintaining in view the manifold ways in which they *mutually determine* each other's historical evolution: a rather valuable achievement, it seems to me, for any realist philosopher interested in maintaining an informed relationship with science. From the standpoint of the Kantian naturalist, philosophy need not be seen as either 'first philosophy' (echoing Quine's polemical use of the phrase) transcendentally legislating upon what science can or cannot know, nor as 'second philosophy' (as per Maddy's definition)[58] stringently subordinated to science's practices. The proper naturalist position is to conceive of the two on a continuum, but a bidirectional one, where both disciplines offer mutual constraints and create possibility for conceptual creation and empirical discovery.[59]

However, the objection could be formulated that the idea of a relativized *a priori* can appear as incompatible with any robust form of realism: consider indeed Carnap's anti-metaphysical 'neutralism', Putnam's endorsement of 'internal realism' and also Friedman's rather uncommitted position *vis-à-vis* the problem of realism (his thesis of the rationality of the dynamic and progressive revision of constitutive principles, he clarifies 'does not involve a parallel conception of scientific truth – either 'realist' or 'anti-realist'[60]). To talk of a 'free choice', a 'stipulation' or a 'convention', seems to deflate ontological questions and bypass any confrontation with spatio-temporal physical reality.[61] The realist goal, on the contrary,

---

58   P. MADDY, *Second Philosophy: A Naturalistic Method*(Oxford: OUP, 2007).
59   This stance also serves to deflate short-sighted pronunciations denouncing the uselessness of philosophy and promoting scientific autarchy. As Ernan McMullin wrote: '[t]he experience of several centuries has served to eliminate principles that once influenced the course of Science and to give others the sanction of success. One might be tempted to think that regulative principles of a broadly metaphysical kind no longer play a role in the natural sciences. Yet even a moment of reflection about the current debates in elementary particle theory, in quantum-field theory, in cosmology, ought to warn that this is far from the case. True, the principles at issue may not be as overtly metaphysical as they often were in Newton's time; but the distinction is one of degree, not kind'. McMULLIN, *Newton on Matter and Activity* (Notre Dame: University of Notre Dame Press, 1978), p. 127.
60   FRIEDMAN, *Dynamics of Reason*, p. 68, n. 83.
61   To give but one example, Imre Lakatos, another philosopher who can be said to have developed a version of revisable *a priori* principles regulating inquiry, criticized Poincaré precisely for this feature of his conventionalism, explaining that 'our approach differs from Poincaré'sjustificationist conventionalism in the sense that, unlike Poincaré, we maintain that if and when the programme ceases to an-

would be that of preserving a certain pragmatic voluntarism guiding the process of revision of conceptual frameworks (i.e. the free, yet disciplined procedure of guesswork and intra-conceptual hypothesis formulation leading to the adoption of new concepts), without forfeiting the realist commitment to a framework-independent reality we aim to describe with increasing (convergent) approximation. That is to say, the ('speculative', 'new') realist might object that if Kant was guilty of placing reality behind an epistemic-conceptual screen we cannot surpass, all these Kantian revisions are merely relativizing and pluralizing these screens, all the while preserving their unsurpassable nature – essentially what new 'continental' forms of realism accuse the past half century of continental philosophy to have done. But it is worth noting here that the dynamic understanding of *a priori* frameworks is not equivalent to what Meillassoux identified as 'facticity' (an epistemic delimiting principle that post-transcendental philosophy stipulates applies to all human experience) – that same facticity that, from Heidegger's strong correlationism onwards, has trapped us into our epistemic finitude. So Meillassoux claims that 'facticity [...] pertains to those [fixed] structural invariants that supposedly govern the world[...] whose function is in every case to provide the minimal organization of representation [and that] can only be described, not founded', so that facticity 'just consists in not knowing why the correlational structure has to be thus'.[62] The 'dynamic Kantian', conversely, holds that these *a priori* structures are *not* fixed, and that epistemic agents *can* rationally account for their modification, by referring to the experimental (and historical) to and fro with mind-independent physical reality. In explicit reference to Sellars' notion of a 'logical space of reasons', Friedman explains that, in his view,

> a constitutive framework for a mathematical-physical theory gives rise to what we might call an empirical space of reasons: a network of inferential evidential relationships, generated by both logical-mathematical principles and physical coordinating principles, that defines what can count as an empirical reason or justification for any given real possibility.[63]

ticipate novel facts, its hard core might have to be abandoned: that is, our hard core, unlike Poincaré's, may crumble under certain conditions'. LAKATOS, *The Methodology of Scientific Research Programmes: Philosophical Papers, Volume 1* (Cambridge: CUP, 1978). p. 49.

62   MEILLASSOUX, *After Finitude*, p. 39.

63   FRIEDMAN, *Dynamics of Reason*, p. 85.

If conceptual frameworks furnish maps for the navigation of a determinate empirical space of reasons, the rational-philosophical task is that of exploring the meta-level of all possible such configurations of concepts, honing, amending and re-wiring their inferential connections in order to achieve the necessary flexibility to map a complex and dynamic real order. The human ability to *modify our conceptual schemes* is one of the core cognitive skills making scientific inquiry possible, and it is indeed the result of the intrinsically emancipatory and endless labour of reason: formulation, justification and (eventual) revision or repurposing of concepts and beliefs for the improvement of our understanding of the world.[64] For the anti-foundational, fallibilist epistemologist this cognitive flexibility – privileging the *process* of abductive inference over the *result* of a putatively secure foundation for knowledge – is what makes possible the piecemeal approximation, via constant revision, of our concepts to the objects of science. Reasoning, as Peirce put it 'not only corrects its conclusions, it even corrects its premises'.[65]

We are thus required to revise our understanding of both the way *concepts* work (moving away from a static, classical picture of concepts as fixed 'labels' towards an appreciation of the way in which semantic layering and overlap are necessary preconditions for a concept to maintain a grip on objects undergoing continuous contextual variation)[66] and of what *reason* and *reasoning* – of which the mathematical sciences provide one of the most refined exemplars – are (moving from an unmovable, top-down structural paradigm to a collectively realized process of continuous negotiation and re-hauling of commitments).[67] Transcendental structures, then,

---

64 As Lewis put it:'[t]he assumption that our categories are fixed for all time by an original human endowment, is a superstition comparable to the belief of primitive peoples that the general features of their life and culture are immemorial and of supernatural origin', C.I. Lewis, *Mind and the World-Order: Outline of a Theory of Knowledge* (New York: Dover, 1956), p. 234.

65 C.S. Peirce, *Reasoning and the Logic of Things*, ed. by Kenneth Laine Ketner (Cambridge (MA): Harvard University Press, 1992), p. 165.

66 I borrow the term 'classical picture' from Mark Wilson's important critique of this stance, the view that objects and concepts can be, pending sufficient analysis, unambiguously paired off in a once-and-for-all manner (the fixed connection between a predicate an a universal shared by all the objects in question). See M. Wilson, *Wandering Significance: An Essay in Conceptual Behavior* (Oxford: Clarendon, 2006).

67 For an interesting cognitive history of the development of reason as realized by means of mathematical thought see D. Macbeth, *Realizing Reason: A Narrative of Truth and Knowing* (Oxford: OUP, 2014). An excellent account of reasoning as

should be seen as prone to an interminable but progressive process of internal uprooting and updating, *determining* the limits of the thinkable while allowing us to *transcend* them. Importantly, this 'dynamical-structuralist' schema is to be seen as operating in all forms of intellectual inquiry, from the way in which, in mathematics and logic, paradoxes immanently engendered by a given set of axioms (*qua* implicit definitions) can stimulate the production of new logical structures organized around new axioms, to the way in which experimental anomalies, clashing with the background constitutional principles of physical theory, can flag the need for the (philosophico-scientific) development of new *a priori* principles.

Sellars' Kantian Conceptualism and Scientific Realism:

> All classification of objects, however confident and preemptory, is a venture, a venture which at no point finds its justification in a pre-symbolic vision of generic and specific hearts on the sleeves of the objects of experience. Classification resembles the grasping tentacles of an octopus, now tentative, now confident, rather than a salesman's selection of a suit for a customer after a glance at his build.
>
> W. Sellars *Science, Perception, and Reality*

Far from being the rabid scientistic reductionist that ill-informed detractors of the 'Sellarsian turn' within 'speculative realism' allege him to be, Sellars was a thoroughly Kantian thinker, at once firmly committed to the irrevocable primacy of the natural sciences to adjudicate questions of existence *and* to the importance of (Kant-inspired) inferentially articulated structures of conceptual thought, for both the understanding of these scientific results and for the normative explication of our place (*qua* persons, intentional beings) in the universe they describe.[68] The commitment to the priority of science in the dimension of description and explanation of the universe goes, for Sellars, hand in hand with development of the core Kantian insight that concepts are non-descriptive/explanatory rules

---

a *social practice* of responsive engagement with other rational agents is offered in A. S. LADEN, *Reasoning: A Social Picture* (Oxford: OUP, 2012).

68   I will not attempt a thorough exposition of Sellars' often rather complex, systematic philosophy: my modest aim here is to whet the appetite of the realist philosopher, canvassing what his large scale philosophical project aims to achieve, and dispelling some common misconceptions.

of inferential reasoning making description and explanation possible.[69] So, remembering his first encounter with Herbert Feigl (his then-colleague at the University of Iowa), Sellars recalls that

> the seriousness with which I took such ideas as causal necessity, synthetic *a priori* knowledge, intentionality, ethical intuitionism, the problem of universals, etc., etc., must have jarred [Feigl's] empiricist sensibilities. Even when I made it clear that *my aim was to map these structures into a naturalistic, even a materialistic, metaphysics*, he felt, as many have, that I was going around Robin Hood's barn.[70]

It is this synoptic ambition of defending a robustly realist position, while remaining firmly committed to the Kantian tradition (against the sense-data empiricism of his logical positivist contemporaries), which makes Sellars' project palatable for the contemporary realist, keen to take distance from either the return to a pre-Kantian rationalist realism or the possibility of a purely speculative metaphysics, as defended by some 'speculative realists'. Occasional (and singularly conflicting) accusations to the contrary notwithstanding, the Sellarsian realist is *neither* a mad-dog physicalist reductionist *nor* a 'correlationist' once again placing a linguistic/conceptual wall between us and the 'Great Outdoors'. On the contrary, I intend to show in this brief concluding section how the Sellarsian approach to the phenomenon of conceptual revision delivers the best – that is, most epistemically responsible – form of science-informed realism we can currently hope for.

Sellars develops the Kantian idea that our conceptual framework must be understood as a network of rules establishing standards of correctness for judgments, so that the meaning of a concept is evaluated according to the role played within such a framework: 'conceptual status [...] is constituted, *completely* constituted, by syntactical rules',[71] so that 'the conceptual meaning of a descriptive term is constituted by what can be inferred from

---

69   Sellars' dual commitment is often illustrated by referring to two of his most famous maxims: the *'scientia mensura'* passage ('in the dimension of describing and explaining the world, science is the measure of all things, of what is that it is, and of what is not that it is not') and the 'space of reasons' passage ('[t]he essential point is that in characterizing an episode or a state as that of *knowing*, we are not giving an empirical description of that episode or state; we are placing it in the logical space of reasons, of justifying and being able to justify what one says') in EPM §41 and §36 respectively.

70   W. SELLARS 'Autobiographical Reflections', http://www.ditext.com/sellars/ar.html. Emphasis added.

71   W. SELLARS, *Science, Perception, and Reality*, (Atascadero: Ridgeview Publishing Company, 1991), p. 316.

it in accordance with the logical and extra-logical rules of inference of the language (conceptual frame) to which it belongs'.[72] Such functional-role semantics allows him to account for the phenomenon of conceptual change, by conceiving of successor concepts in new scientific theories as functional counterparts of those of the superseded theory – sufficiently similar to play the same functional role within the conceptual economy of the theory, but not necessarily preserving the very same intrinsic character. Experience-organizing concepts, *qua* nodes in an inferential space – establishing logical and material rules for performing inferences – can be modified and preserved (say, 'mass', or 'electron'), or abandoned (say 'ether') where the relevant functional role is not part of the new framework.[73] The kind of synthetic *a priori* proposition Sellars admits, then, is true *ex vi terminorum*, (i.e. an implicit definition), its necessity being relative to the holistic framework of concepts it is embedded into. As Sellars puts it: '[w] hile every conceptual frame involves propositions which, though synthetic, are true *ex vi terminorum*, every conceptual frame is also but one among many which compete for adoption in the market-place of experience.'[74]

What makes Sellars stand apart from all the neo-Kantian variations I've sketched above, however, is his uncompromisingly realist attitude, motivating his idea of *picturing*: a materialist supplement to his theory of truth as an intra-linguistic property of sentences (semantic assertability). Rejecting a theory of meaning based on a problematic semantic 'relation' between a linguistic term and a universal (and offering a nominalist deflation of the problem of abstract entities by reconceiving them as meta-linguistic sortals), Sellars preserves the notion of representation by introducing picturing as a *real relation* (i.e. a relation in the physical order) between, on the one hand, 'natural linguistic object' like phonetic tokens or scriptural marks, or indeed the associated neuro-physiological events (*qua* material patterns) and, on the other, physical 'external' objects, a relation fully specifiable in causal terms. So in the case of 'atomic' matter-of-factual statements, the link between symbols and reality cannot be reduced to yet another convention for it is a causally specified isomorphism outside of the purview of normative (or pragmatic, or conventional) justification: so while '[t]he meaning of a linguistic symbol *as*

---

72 SELLARS, *Science, Perception, and Reality*, p. 317.
73 To adjudicate which concepts to revise and which to abandon in the transition from the conceptual framework of the 'manifest image' of refined common-sense and that of the 'scientific image' of subatomic physics is the principal challenge faced by Sellars' program of a stereoscopic vision.
74 SELLARS, *Science, Perception, and Reality*, p. 320.

a linguistic symbol is entirely constituted by the rules which regulate its use', that is to say, concepts[75] are defined via their inferential role, '[t]he hook-up of a system of rule-regulated symbols with the world is not itself a rule-governed fact',[76] but is a matter of structural uniformities, allowing for an increasingly accurate mapping.

So, the Kantian emphasis on conceptually-mediated nature of perception should not mislead us to assume that we are isolated from the world by means of our conceptual framework. Sellars explains that

> the fact that we tend to think of conceptual acts as having only logical form, as lacking matter-of-factual characteristics, [...] makes it difficult to appreciate that the ultimate point of all the logical powers pertaining to conceptual activity in its epistemic orientation is to generate conceptual structures which as objects in nature stand in certain matter-of-factual relations to other objects in nature.

and continues, in a footnote to this passage, by observing that

> [t]he basic flaw in the Kantian system (as in that of Peirce) is in its inability to do justice to this fact. The insight that logical form belongs only to conceptual acts (i.e., belongs to 'thoughts' rather than to 'things') must be supplemented by the insight that 'thoughts' as well as 'things' must have *empirical* form if they are to mesh with each other in that way which is essential to empirical knowledge.[77]

While a complete unpacking of the ideas that stand in the background of this thesis would require far more space than I can dedicate to it here, these two passages, together with the quotation opening this section, represent one of the most profound and misconceived insight of Sellars' philosophy. *Yes*, our commerce with reality is always conceptually mediated by transcendental concepts having a constitutional role for the way in which we inferentially articulate our knowledge of it. *No*, reality does not possess an intrinsic logico-propositional form we can just 'read off' experience at a glance; on the contrary we bring such concepts to experience *and* must

---

75   Sellars explicitly equates languages and conceptual frameworks.

76   W. SELLARS, *Pure Pragmatics and Possible Worlds* (Atascadero: Ridgeview, 1980), p. 150.

77   W. SELLARS, *Essays on Philosophy and its History* (Dordrecht: Riedel, 1974), p. 52 and p. 61, fn 7.

revise them or propose new ones allowing for a better mapping of reality.[78] And *no*, concepts do not create an ambiguous middle ground between us and reality, for a more or less spirited form of idealism to flourish: concepts are rules functionally expressed by patterns of sign-designs which are ontologically *on par* with the reality they approximate, and as such an immanent part of nature: concepts are functionally/normatively irreducible[79] while ontologically reducible to spatio-temporal physical reality. The grip of concepts upon reality is made possible by a physical-informational isomorphism[80] between one material system and another, so that a conceptual framework's adequacy to describe reality can be rationally (and indeed quantitatively)[81] evaluated in terms of the correct causal mapping of the world. Like Friedman,[82] Sellars conceives of the dynamic progress of conceptual schemes in Peircean terms, as a convergent series asymptotically

---

78   Again, as I noted above when discussing Friedman's position, note how this process of revision and creation is the peculiar meta-scientific role proper of *philosophy*. As Brassier clearly puts it: 'Sellars' rationalistic naturalism grants a decisive role to philosophy. Its task is not only to anatomize the categorial structures proper to the manifest and scientific images respectively but also to propose new categories in light of the obligation to explain the status of conceptual rationality within the natural order. Thus philosophy is not the mere underlaborer of empirical science; it retains an autonomous function as legislator of categorial revision' R. BRASSIER, 'Nominalism, Naturalism and Materialism' in *Contemporary Philosophical Naturalism and Its implications*, ed. by B. Bashour and H.D. Muller (London and New York: Routledge, 2014), p. 112.

79   That is to say, not ontologically irreducible, non-*sui generis*. On this topic, Dionysis Christias argues that, in a Sellarsian light, 'the root error of correlationism, which is not identified as such by Meillassoux, is the construal of the irreducibility of the transcendental to the empirical level in *descriptive/explanatory* terms instead of metalinguistic, practical and normative ones'. Dionysis Christias 'Sellars, Meillassoux, and the Myth of the Categorial Given: A Sellarsian Critique of 'Correlationism' and Meillassoux's 'Speculative Materialism', in *Journal of Philosophical Research*, forthcoming.

80   The isomorphism in question is not to be expected at the morphological or otherwise qualitative level. Sellars defines picturing as a more or less adequate 'relation between two relational structures', *Science and Metaphysics: Variations on Kantian Themes* (London: Routledge and Kegan Paul, 1968), p.135. The 'distant analogy' Sellars employs is that of the relation between the grooves on a vinyl record and the music they produce (in *Science, Perception, and Reality*, p. 53). A more up-to-date example could be that between a string of data (say, a .jpg file) and the image they represent.

81   See J. ROSENBERG, *Wilfrid Sellars: Fusing the Images* (Oxford: OUP, 2007), p. 69, where the Peircean ideal of asymptotic convergence is offered a precise definition in terms of Cauchy convergence to a limit.

82   See FRIEDMAN, *Dynamics of Reason*, p. 64.

approaching a (regulative) ideal of a perfectly adequate match between concepts and reality, so that surely 'our current conceptual structure is both more adequate than its predecessors and less adequate than certain of its potential successors'[83]. Yet, resolving the doubts I raised above regarding the arbitrary nature of relativized *a priori* principles as pragmatically adopted conventions, Sellars criticizes Peirce by noting that *'by not taking into account the dimension of 'picturing'*, he had no Archimedean point outside the series of actual and possible beliefs in terms of which to define the ideal or limit to which members of this series might approximate.'[84]

So, answering my title question once again: Kant gave us the possibility of articulating a proper role for philosophy *vis-à-vis* science as an instrument of transcendental reflection on the *a priori* conceptual structures employed in scientific theorizing. Post-Kantian 'relativizers' of the *a priori* gave us the possibility of preserving a (revised) Kantian structure and make it compatible with the evolution of science. Sellarss naturalized Kantianism[85] bestows upon us a refined picture of how these dynamically and historically changing conceptual schemes are not merely conventional or pragmatic choices, narrowing our epistemic gaze to the phantasmatic realm of phenomena, but should be seen as complex natural structures the construction (and revision) of which depends upon a direct (but never *absolutely secure*) grip on reality itself:

---

83   SELLARS, *Science and Metaphysics*, p. 138. Note, again, that unlike Sellars, Friedman explicitly construes his trans-historical rational convergence towards increasingly accurate frameworks as compatible with Van Fraaseen's constructive empiricism, where the increasing empirical adequacy of a theory does not mean approximation to real entities. See *Dynamics of Reason*, p. 84, n. 16.

84   SELLARS, *Science and Metaphysics*, p. 142.

85   A far more comprehensive analysis of Sellars' naturalistic revision of Kant is offered by James O'Shea, see esp. James O'Shea *Wilfrid Sellars: Naturalism with a Normative Turn* (Malden: Polity, 2007) and James O'Shea 'How to Be a Kantian and a Naturalist about Human Knowledge: Sellars' Middle Way'. *Journal of Philosophical Research* 36, pp. 327-59. O'Shea (successfully, it seems to me) attempts to 'interpret Sellars' synoptic vision as preserving both the substantive neo-Kantian conceptual analyses and the projected ideal scientific explanations' thinks that 'Sellars' stereoscopic vision is precisely a delicate simultaneous combination of those two dimensions, the ongoing scientific-explanatory and the philosophical-analytic, in one coherent view' and argues that while '[i]n an important sense, Sellars rejected Kant's notion of the synthetic *a priori*, ...[he] *also* clearly sought to preserve a pragmatic and framework-relativized version of something akin to the synthetic *a priori*' O'Shea, 'How to be a Kantian...', p. 346. My understanding of Sellars' project is heavily influenced by O'Shea's crystalline exegesis.

a consistent scientific realist must hold that the world of everyday experience is a phenomenal world in the Kantian sense, existing only as the contents of actual and obtainable conceptual representings, the obtainability of which is explained not, as for Kant, by things in themselves known only to God, but by scientific objects about which, barring catastrophe, we shall know more and more as the years go by.[86]

Conclusion

My aim in this paper, pursued through a highly panoramic view of the relativization of *a priori* principles, was ultimately to demonstrate how a 'speculative realism' worthy of this name cannot be construed as free-rein metaphysical speculation, constrained (if at all) only by logical consistency, but should rather be conceived, *very much in the spirit of Kant*, as a transcendental speculative enterprise at the meta-level of conceptual frameworks, facilitating the process of revision of those concepts regulating and systematizing (but not creating) the reality probed by the natural sciences. In order to assuage skeptical objections, doubting that such a project can even be a 'realist' one in a suitably hard-nosed sense of the term, I have offered a glimpse into the profoundly revolutionary project of Wilfrid Sellars, the most illustrious example of a naturalized Kantian – construing norms and concepts as logically irreducible (constitutive of) yet ontologically reducible to (part of) physical reality – that twentieth-century philosophy has to offer. Much more could be said about this project, but I hope, for now, to have convinced the reader that this is a Kantian road well worth travelling.

---

86   SELLARS, *Science and Metaphysics*, p. 173.

VI

BLINDED BY SCIENCE?
SPECULATIVE REALISM
AND SPECULATIVE CONSTRUCTIVISM

MATTHIJS KOUW AND SJOERD VAN TUINEN

Introduction: Speculative Realism and Scientism

Within contemporary philosophy, there is renewed interest in speculative philosophy insofar as it provides an opportunity to deal with the anthropocentric perspective that has held Western philosophy in check since Kant. According to philosophers working under the banner of 'speculative realism', the inseparability of thinking and being, or so-called 'correlationism', prevents thought from considering reality independent of a knowing subject that provides the conditions of possibility and meaning of knowledge.[1] Supposedly, speculative philosophy can only live up to its ideal to explore 'the great outdoors' once the correlate of being and thought is rejected. Even though speculative realists are not a homogenous group, they do collectively argue for the importance of ontological issues and attribute an important role to realism and scientific theories such as materialism.[2]

In what follows, we will formulate some of the reservations we have about this renaissance of ontology as a philosophical practice. While we agree that anthropocentrism has become increasingly problematic both in science and in philosophy (not to mention, in art), the speculative-scientistic faith in rationality does not seem to be an adequate response. In particular, we think that the rationalist fascination with theoretical models puts us at risk of blinding ourselves to their practical sense, even to the point of eliminating the very question of politics. As Gilles Deleuze and Félix Guattari once put it, politics precedes being; as a consequence, even the most theoretical ontological truth ought to be evaluated not from the point of view of truth – let alone that of human subjectivity – but from the point

---

1   Q. MEILLASSOUX, *After Finitude* (London: Continuum, 2006).
2   L. BYANT, N. SRNICEK, Graham Harman (eds.), *The Speculative Turn. Continental Materialism and Realism* (Melbourne: re.press, 2011).

of view of that for which it has real and not just theoretical consequences. Just as what science discovers about the world cannot be separated from the question of how it impinges upon the world, including all other practices that simultaneously exist, speculation should be taken from the calm world of the science of being to the agitated ontology of the world, where its constructions must effectively prove their value.

We will develop this argument by comparing the work of two authors, Manuel DeLanda and Isabelle Stengers, who both find their philosophical mentors in Deleuze and Guattari, yet whose work couldn't be further apart in terms of the extent to which they stake a claim to knowledge of a (presupposed) world 'out there'. DeLanda mobilizes a Deleuzian ontology, to carve out a realism in which the force of computational models is used to produce stable functions, describing morphological relations from which the world emerges. Stengers takes the processes from which knowledge is produced as her starting point, and values scientific knowledge as events in which consensual knowledge about particular phenomena may be established momentarily, only to be unsettled later on. In other words, whereas DeLanda used computational models to establish robust functions and thus seeks to align philosophy with scientific practice, Stengers sees scientific knowledge as established through negotiation and open for contestation. She thus reserves for philosophy a language that serves to (re-)dramatize scientific achievements.

Bootstrapping Ontologies

In *Philosophy and Simulation*, DeLanda refines the conceptual framework developed in his earlier books and proposes a new agenda for science and philosophy. DeLanda wishes to provide scientific explanations of 'emergence': processes where 'novel properties and capacities emerge from a causal interaction'.[3] Whereas science was previously preoccupied with 'simple laws acting as self-evident truths (axioms) from which all causal effects could be deduced as theorems [...] [t]oday a scientific explanation is identified not with some logical operation, but with the more creative endeavor of *elucidating the mechanisms that produce a given effect*.'[4]

DeLanda deploys a conceptual apparatus that describes mecha-

---

3   M. DeLanda, *Philosophy and simulation: the emergence of synthetic reason* (London: Continuum, 2011), p. 1.
4   *Ibid.*, p. 2. Emphasis added.

nisms of emergence: emergent properties, capacities and tendencies. The sharpness of a knife is an example of an *emergent property*. The shape of the cross-section of the knife makes up its sharpness, which requires the knife's metallic atoms to be arranged in such a manner that they form a triangular shape. Sharpness features emergence, since individual metallic atoms cannot produce the required triangular shape. What is more, sharpness provides the knife with the *capacity* to cut things. However, this capacity remains potential without a relational event; in this case, an encounter with something that has the capacity to be cut by the knife. Also, the metallic atoms of the knife must have the capacity to be arranged in such a manner that sharpness emerges. Finally, the knife's blade may have the *tendency* to liquefy if certain conditions change: for instance, in case its environment exceeds a particular temperature. Like capacities, tendencies are closely related to relational events (e.g. rising temperatures) but also to emergent properties, since the metallic atoms of the knife need to interact in such a manner that the blade melts – something individual atoms cannot do.

Whereas tendencies can be enumerated (e.g. the states in which a particular material find itself, such as solid, liquid, or gaseous), capacities are not necessarily finite due to their dependence on being affected and/or affecting innumerable other entities. In such events, DeLanda argues in Deleuzian fashion, capacities and tendencies become 'actual', but 'neither tendencies nor capacities must be actual in order to be real.'[5] Here DeLanda draws upon Deleuze's actual-virtual distinction, where the virtual is not so much a 'possible' lacking reality, but rather something fully real, waiting to be actualized. In Deleuze's ontology, the actual is not the point of departure of change and difference, but that which has been effected by potentiality, or, the virtual.[6]

DeLanda defines the virtual aspects of entities by their emergent properties, capacities and tendencies, which constitute a 'structure of the space of possibilities'[7] that can be explored by means of computer simulations. These exploration proceed in a manner he calls 'bootstrapping': 'a realist ontology may be lifted by its own bootstraps by assuming a minimum of objective knowledge to get the process going and then accounting for the rest.'[8] The structures of spaces of possibilities have an 'objective ex-

---

5   *Ibid.*, p. 5.

6   G. DELEUZE, *Difference and Repetition* (London: Continuum, 2004).

7   M. DELANDA, *Philosophy and simulation: the emergence of synthetic reason, op. cit.*, p. 5.

8   M. DELANDA, 'Ecology and Realist Ontology'. In B. Herzogenrath (Ed.), *Deleuze/ Guattari & Ecology*, (London: Palgrave Macmillan, 2009), pp. 27-28.

istence'[9] that can be investigated mathematically, by the imposition of an arrangement through formalization or 'parametrizing'.[10] Computer simulations enable exploration by allowing experimenters to stage interactions between different entities and investigate the emergent wholes that are the result of these interactions, thereby gaining an understanding of mechanisms of emergence. Philosophy can fulfill the role of synthesizing simulation-enabled insights 'into an emergent materialist world view that finally does justice to the creative powers of matter and energy.'[11]

For DeLanda, science need not neutralize the 'intensive' or differentiating properties of the virtual, much like Deleuze and Guattari argued. In this sense, he has much to offer constructivist debates since his work 'attempts to provide both an ontological and epistemological alternative to philosophies of science based on axiomatic systems, deductive logic, and essentialist typologies, one that is grounded in *creative experiment* rather than theory, in the *multiplication* of models rather than the formulation of universal laws.'[12] However, unlike his mentors, DeLanda grants a particularly authoritative role to science in enabling a rigorous ontology of the virtual.

Eliminativism

In the process of bootstrapping, DeLanda wishes to avoid 'the postulation of general entities (ideal types, eternal laws)', since 'for a realist whose goal is to create a mind-independent ontology, the starting point must be those areas of the world that may be thought of as having existed prior to the emergence of humanity on this planet.'[13] Here DeLanda aligns himself with contemporary critiques of correlationism. By focusing on 'mechanisms of emergence' that produce the subjects studied by various scientific disciplines (such as meteorological phenomena, insect intelligence, and Stone Age economics), science now has the ability to describe '[w]holes the identity of which is determined historically by the processes that initiated and sustain the interactions between their parts.'[14] Concepts

---

9   M. DeLanda, *Philosophy and simulation: the emergence of synthetic reason*, p. 5.

10   *Ibid.*, p. 187.

11   *Ibid.*, p. 6.

12   W. Bogard, Book Review: How The Actual Emerges From The Virtual. *International Journal of Baudrillard Studies*, 2(1). Emphasis added.

13   M. DeLanda, 'Ecology and Realist Ontology', *op. cit.*, p. 28.

14   M. DeLanda, *Philosophy and simulation: the emergence of synthetic reason*, *op. cit.*, p. 3.

which do not elucidate sequences of events that produce emergent effects are considered irrelevant for scientific analyses. Philosophy emerges renewed, banished of reified generalities like 'Life', 'Mind', and 'Deity'.[15] Thus, DeLanda's book on simulations furnishes what we propose to call a 'robust realism': it features both a vigorous commitment to exploration, *and* a boisterous dismissal of knowledge that fails to contribute to what DeLanda hails as an ideal of scientific rationality.

A sense of ontological completion takes root in DeLanda's work over the course of his various publications: from a more speculative alternative history produced by a 'robot historian',[16] via the erudite exploration of the ability of science to engage intensities,[17] to his latest work on simulations that exerts a confidence that readers with more constructivist commitments may find troubling. DeLanda's commitment to intensities and the virtual notwithstanding, he also explicitly claims that knowledge created by means of simulations must abandon 'mystifying entities'.[18] Philosophers are suspected of a 'fear of redundancy', which 'may explain the attachment of philosophers to vague entities as a way of carving out a niche for themselves.'[19] DeLanda's claims come across as a roll call: 'the future of multiagent simulations as models of social reality will depend on how social scientists can affect this technology by deploying it creatively and on how they can be affected by it through the possession of the right social ontology.'[20] Due to the fact that computational power and data storage are becoming cheaper and more abundant, DeLanda argues in a celebratory manner, simulations will become more and more accessible over time.[21] This shows that DeLanda's work is devoid of illustrating the socio-material assemblages in which simulation is carried out, and for whom knowledge produced by means of simulations is relevant.[22]

---

15 *Ibid.*
16 M. DeLanda, *War in the Age of Intelligent Machines* (New York: Zone Books, 1991).
17 M. DeLanda, *Intensive Science and Virtual Philosophy* (London: Continuum, 2002).
18 M. DeLanda, *Philosophy and simulation: the emergence of synthetic reason, op. cit.*, p. 2.
19 *Ibid.*, p. 3.
20 *Ibid.*, p. 183.
21 *Ibid.*, p. 148.
22 E.g. A. MacKenzie *Mechanizing proof : computing, risk, and trust* (Cambridge, Mass.: MIT Press., 2001); G. Gramelsberger, *Computerexperimente: Zum Wandel der Wissenschaft im Zeitalter des Computers* (Bielefeld: Transcript Verlag, 2010); E. Winsberg, *Science in the Age of Computer Simulation* (Chicago: Chicago University Press, 2010).

Cosmopolitics

Proclaiming a privileged role for any scientific enterprise is highly problematic for Stengers, for whom the objectivity attributed to science needs to be seen in the context of historical events, in which science was endowed with the ability to speak on behalf of its subject matter. For example, the Scientific Revolution that began with Galileo Galilei and that conjoined empirical observation with mathematical descriptions, thus furnishing the ideal image of what is still seen as 'true science' today: the ability to explain and predict phenomena, in the objective world 'out there', by means of quantitative methods. In *The Invention of Modern Science*, Stengers characterizes the event of the experimental invention which produced Galilei as its spokesperson as 'the invention of the power to confer upon things the power of conferring on the experimenter the power to speak in their name'.[23] Precisely insofar as these three powers constitute an event in the history of science, it marks not a naturalization of the falling body. On the contrary, it is an unnatural construction because it is based on an abstraction of all friction. It is not a convergence between man and nature, but a divergence, a construction, relating a very specific type of human (the scientist), endorsing very strong obligations, to a very specific kind of phenomena (uniform acceleration), verifying very selective 'disciplinary' requirements. The accomplishments of dynamics are indeed triumphs of scientific imagination and invention, but they are also expressible as physical 'laws' that are bound to the very particular sort of questions addressed: the nature of forces in finite interactions that could be treated mathematically with linear equations. They are hardly applicable to modern economies or the brain.

Thus, the advent of the modern sciences is an event replete with underlying tensions that should not be veiled. This implies a refusal 'to reduce a situation to what the passing of time gives us power to say about it today.'[24] In scientific experiments, objects are witnesses framed in such a way that

---

23   See I. STENGERS, *The Invention of Modern Science* (Minneapolis: University of Minnesota Press, 2000), p. 88; and I. STENGERS, *Power and Invention: Situating Science* (Minneapolis: University of Minnesota Press, 1997), p. 165.

24   I. STENGERS, *Thinking with Whitehead: a free and wild creation of concepts* (Cambridge, Mass.: Harvard University Press, 2011). Quoted in Adrian Mackenzie, Is the Actual World all That Must be Explained? The Sciences and Cultural Theory: Review Essay of Manuel Delanda, *Intensive Science, Virtual Philosophy* (2002) and Isabelle Stengers, *The Invention of Modern Science* (2000). *Journal for Cultural Research*, 9(1), 2005, p. 104.

their behavior confirms the relevance of the aspects of the world mobilized to explain it. But the innate weakness of science is that it tends to turn the entire world into the witness of its own reason and thus immunizes itself against the events of the world. This happens, for example, when Quentin Meillassoux celebrates 'Galileism'[25] or the mathematization of nature as an emancipatory stance (knowledge equals power), whereas he simultaneously realizes it lacks all relevance since nothing real follows from it (the matter of fact that 'anything is possible' is without all concern). By contrast, Galileo's invention is the coming into existence of a new and very particular kind of thinking, not just a matter of a thinker entertaining a new thought. It is a cosmological singularity, not just an epistemological event belonging to the history of science.

Another thinker who has engaged with the power of science to speak on behalf of the world is Bruno Latour, a French anthropologist-sociologist of science, whose work has recently come to be seen in a more ontological light.[26] Like speculative realists and his fellow-traveller Stengers, Latour criticizes anthropocentric worldviews and proposes to replace them by networks composed of human and non-human actors (also called 'actants'). According to Latour, scientific knowledge cannot be based on an objective and accurate representation of a (postulated) outside world, but should rather be seen as a product of scientific research. Research on the structure and status of scientific knowledge can explain how and why scientists take objectivity, accuracy, reliability and truth of scientific knowledge for granted. The work and maintenance that make up scientific knowledge can be explained by an analysis of 'actants' and the ways in which they are brought together and change through a process that Latour describes as 'translation'. The work of the physicist and chemist Boyle can serve as an example. By bringing together air, scientific instruments such as air pumps, and a group of 'independent' spectators, Boyle was able establish his famous law that describes how the pressure of a gas decreases once the volume of a gas increases. Subsequently, the network of actants underlying Boyle's law is hidden from view in a process of 'purification'. As a result, Boyle's law acquires the stature of a representation of fundamental principles of nature. Scientific theories are thus detached from their history and obtain the status of pure representations of nature.[27] Contrary to the modern

25   Q. MEILLASSOUX, *After Finitude*, op. cit., p. 113.
26   G. HARMAN, *Prince of Networks: Bruno Latour and Metaphysics* (Melbourne: re.press, 2009).
27   See B. LATOUR, *Science in Action : How to follow scientists and engineers through society* (Cambridge, Mass.: Harvard University Press, 1987) and B. LATOUR, *We*

ideal of purity, Stengers' use of the concept of power already indicates that the event of the invention of modern science was not neutral, but possessed its own constitutive kind of power. 'The sciences do not depend on the possibility of representing; they invent the possibilities of representing, of constituting a fiction as a legitimate representation of a phenomenon.'[28] The intrinsic connection between power and representation enables Stengers to frame modern science not only as cosmological event, but also as a cosmopolitical invention, without reducing science to power play ('physics is a social practice like any other') or pretending there is a stronghold from which politics can be denounced or judged objectively (*eppure si muove*). The eliminativist tendencies of modern science, including those present in the work of DeLanda and certain other speculative realists, may therefore be contrasted with Stengers' 'diplomatic' criterion as proposed in *L'Invention des sciences modernes* (1993) for 'hard science' no less than 'radical politics', a criterion which she labels 'the Leibnizian constraint'.[29]

As the work of a great mathematician, philosopher, theologian and diplomat, Leibniz's *Monadology* (1714) offers a synoptic perspective before the time of specialization, in which metaphysics constitutes the foundations for such peace. He defined philosophy as a *scientia generalis*, an encyclopedia in which all 'sectarian' forms of knowledge could be included and 'taken further than before'.[30] The only pragmatic constraint was his famous declaration that the various ways of thinking should respect 'established sentiments'. According to Stengers, this was not meant, as is usually thought, in the 'shameful' (Deleuze) sense of the will not to clash with anyone, that is, to establish consensus in the service of Power. Rather, it is a principle of responsibility for the consequences of what one says and does, 'much as a mathematician 'respects' the constraints that give meaning and interest to his problem.' Just as in mathematics, an invention means not the destruction of a past definition and questions, but its conservation as a particular aspect of a transformed definition leading to new questions, '[t]he problem designated by the Leibnizian constraint ties together truth and becoming, and assigns to the statement of what one believes to be true the responsibility not to hinder becoming: not to collide with established sentiments, so as to try to open them to what their established identity led them

       Have Never Been Modern (Cambridge, Mass.: Harvard University Press, 1993).
28   B. LATOUR, 'Foreword. Stengers's Shibboleth', in I. Stengers, *Power and Invention: Situating Science* (Minnesota: University of Minnesota Press, 1997).
29   I. STENGERS, *The Invention of Modern Science*, op. cit., pp. 15-18.
30   G. W. LEIBNIZ, *New Essays on the Human Understanding* (Cambridge: Cambridge University Press, 1982), p. 71.

to refuse, combat, misunderstand.'[31] Put differently, the Leibnizian constraint forces us to distrust words that tempt us either to reduce one practice to another (science is only a social construction) or to reduce differences to an irreducible opposition (science is opposed to politics or religion or to what Meillassoux calls 'fideism'). Yet this doesn't imply some kind of relativism of truth. Rather, it puts its bets on 'truth of the relative'. In terms of Galilei's experiment, Leibniz aims at a 'maximization of friction' and thus at a recovery of what has been obscured by specialized abstraction. This is what makes Leibniz a 'minor key' philosopher for Stengers: a philosopher of recalcitrance[32] who relates the aggressive passion for truth to a 'possible peace, a humor of truth'[33] and who demands us to speculate not about a final conception of the world, but about the collective becoming of practices, in a world full of different and unforeseen events.

At the core of Stengers' work lies the project of an 'ecology of practices', which can be aligned with what Latour has called the 'principle of irreducibility'. This principle indicates that 'nothing is, by itself, either reducible or irreducible to anything else.'[34] As Harman explains: 'In one sense we can never explain religion as the result of social factors, World War I as the result of rail timetables, or the complex motion of bodies as pure examples of Newtonian physics. Yet in another sense we can always attempt such explanations, and sometimes they are fairly convincing. It is always possible to explain anything in terms of anything else—as long as we do the work of showing how one can be transformed into the other, through a chain of equivalences that always has a price and always risks failure.'[35] In this sense, science is 'condemned' to persistent experimentation in the form of producing explanations, by following the 'chains of equivalences'. However, even though science is a matter of experimentation, it is constantly tempted to judge. Judging always happens in the name of something given *a priori* and in relation to which the *a posteriori* can be abstracted. 'The judge is the one who knows, *a priori*, according to what categories it is appropriate to interrogate and understand that with

31 I. Stengers, *The Invention of Modern Science*, op. cit., p. 15.
32 I. Stengers, 'The Cosmopolitical Proposal'. In B. Latour & P. Weibel (Eds.), *Making Things Public: Atmosphere of Democracy* (Cambridge, Mass.: MIT Press, 2005), p. 188.
33 I. Stengers, *Cosmopolitics I*. (Minneapolis: University of Minnesota Press, 2010), p. 4.
34 B. Latour, *The Pasteurization of France* (Cambridge, Mass.: Harvard University Press, 1988), p. 158.
35 G. Harman, *Prince of Networks: Bruno Latour and Metaphysics*, op. cit., pp. 14-15.

which he is dealing.'[36] But judging as such is opposed to construction; the application of principles is opposed to the original event, and the practical discovery of the possibility to submit a phenomenon to experimentation.[37]

According to Latour, the deployment of a completed ontology should be lamented since it implies new ontologies cannot be developed. Instead, Latour favors a pragmatist perspective that emphasizes the need to accurately describe the world and to connect with the practices in which networks of 'actants' are produced and maintained. By characterizing his metaphysics as 'experimental', Latour dissociates himself explicitly from philosophers who want to deliver exhaustive ontologies: ' It's experimental because if we have to begin to agree on the basic furniture of the world [...] then politics is certainly finished, because there is actually no way we will settle these questions'.[38] The experimental nature of metaphysics ensures its alignment with the practices and political aspects of knowledge production. Cosmology is of secondary importance.

As an alternative to the expansion of scientific rationality, cosmopolitics involves a process of 'collective experimentation'.[39] The challenge of cosmopolitics is how to bring about a form of empowerment: to appeal to practitioners (including, but not confined, to scientists) in such a manner that they learn to understand their responsibility for and commitment to understanding the world from their own strength, or from what is relevant to them. In a recent essay, Stengers observes that 'happily equating our understanding with an active elimination of everything about 'us' that cannot be aligned with a so-called 'scientific' conception of matter, is now widely endorsed in the name of scientific rationality.'[40] This so-called 'eliminativism' relegates obstacles to its goals to an epistemological waste bin. Thus, struggle may be omitted from situations that involve conflicts, e.g. by refusing to acknowledge the response of Indian peasants to GMOs. Exceptionalism precludes scientific practitioners taking into account possible becomings of oth-

---

36   I. STENGERS, *Power and Invention: Situating Science*, op. cit., p. 163.

37   *Ibid.*, p. 164.

38   B. LATOUR, G. HARMAN, and P. ERDÉLYI, *The Prince and the Wolf: Latour and Harman at the LSE* (London: Zer0 Books, 2011), p. 46.

39   I. STENGERS, 'Thinking with Deleuze and Whitehead: A Double Test'. In K. Robinson (Ed.), *Deleuze, Whitehead, Bergson: Rhizomatic Connections* (New York: Palgrave Macmillan, 2009).

40   I. STENGERS, 'The Symbiosis Between Experiments and Techniques'. In J. Brouwer, A. Mulder, and L. Spuybroek (Eds.), *The Politics of the Impure* (Rotterdam: NAI Publishers, 2010), p. 368.

ers and forces the production of knowledge to 'mostly follow the landscape of settled interests'.[41]

By staking a claim to rationality, scientific practices and other practices (Stengers provocatively gives the example of tarot-card reading) are seen as a valid and viable claim to knowledge, leaving room for the elimination of those kinds of knowledge that do not contribute to the production of objective knowledge. Stengers argues assessments of the value of different practices should 'refrain from using general judgmental criteria to legitimate their elimination, and to refrain from dreaming about a clean world with no cause to wonder and alarm ... I do not claim we should mimic those practices, but maybe we should accept to seeing them and *wonder*.'[42] It is exactly a sense of wonder or imagination that is important in simulation practice, as indicated in the studies of simulation practice from a STS perspective[43]. Much of DeLanda's work on simulations suggests a similar notion of imagination through exploration in the form of exploration, but is ultimately devoted to formalization in the name of 'purified' science that resolutely distinguishes the objective and the nonsensical. We therefore invite readers of DeLanda's book to ask to what extent it leaves room for imagination. In the light of Stengers' concerns about eliminativism, contemporary notions of scientific relevance, and the perceived appeal of quantitative methods enabled by computational techniques, DeLanda's sweeping claims appear eerily devoid of questions of relevance and socio-political aspects of scientific practice.

Speculative Constructivism

Stengers draws a strict distinction between science as a creative enterprise, a practice of invention and discovery, and science's modernist claim to invalidate all other discourses. She does not have a problem with science's actual, particular positive claims, but rather with its pretensions to universality and the way it is mobilized to deny the validity of all claims and practices other than its own. If there is one criterion according to which

---

41   I. STENGERS, 'Wondering about materialism'. In L. Bryant, G. Harman, N. Srnicek (Eds.), *The Speculative Turn: Continental Materialism and Realism*, op. cit. p. 377.

42   *Ibid.*, p. 379. Emphasis added.

43   O., NAOMI, K. SCHRADER-FRECHETTE, and K. BELITZ. "Verification, Validation, and Confirmation of Numerical Models in the Earth Sciences." Science 263, no. 5147 (1994): 641-46.

we can evaluate scientific practices, it is what Latour has called 'risky construction'.[44] We don't gain access to anything without a construction. As a scientist, Galilei did not pre-exist the invention of the powers through which he came into existence. Even if experimenters may well know in advance what they want to achieve, as was the case with Galilei, a long process of 'tuning' (Andrew Pickering) will nevertheless be needed, within which nothing will be trusted, neither the human hypothesis nor the observations made. What counts is therefore not whether gravity exist as a matter of fact, but the efficacy of this existence. This is the pragmatist constraint: what counts is the ethopoetic transformation an invention is meant to induce. It's the practitioners who take the risk; the speculative philosopher merely learns about their dreams, ambitions and fears.

At the same time, we may wonder what speculation has to add to the world by itself. What does philosophy construct? Besides the 'tender-minded' irenism of Leibniz, Stengers is heir to the empiricist and pragmatist tradition of William James and most of all Alfred North Whitehead, in which she finds the diplomatic project of a 'speculative peace' among contradictory or mutually exclusive visions, ambitions, and methods. Speculative philosophy or cosmology, according to philosopher and mathematician Whitehead, 'is the endeavor to frame a coherent, logical, necessary system of general ideas in terms of which every element of our experience can be interpreted'. Other than a general theory, however, it aims not at the ordered unity of everything that exists, but at the 'engineering' and constant revision of conceptual tools that allow us to move from one particular form of experience to another.[45] Whitehead's main matter of concern was the 'bifurcation of nature' between a causal, objective nature and a free, subjectively perceived nature. Its incoherence is due to a 'fallacy of misplaced concreteness' as an ever renewable source of problems. The question of the naturalization of consciousness, for example, is a false problem, because experience confirms that nature belongs to the mind no less than to the body. The task of speculation is precisely to interpret them together, without opposition, hierarchy or disconnection (which belong to the logic of war) and thus make them more concrete than the abstract representations ('body', 'mind') specialized disciplines create of them. This doesn't mean to play the sad role of rendering thinkable what the bifurcation of

---

44   B. Latour in Isabelle Stengers, *Power and Invention: Situating Science*, op. cit. pp. XIII-XIV.
45   A. North Whitehead, *Process and Reality* (New York: The Free Press, 1979), p. 3-17.

nature has rendered unintelligible – a nature without sound or odor that a mind would hastily clothe with sound and odor – but to create new abstractions that avoid the 'reciprocal capture'[46] between mutually incompatible abstractions. For Whitehead, too, it is therefore not common sense that must be revised, but the power of theoretical abstractions that fixate it into a destructive routine thought.[47]

Stengers gives the example of 'the rather horrifying experience when trying to speak with so-called neo-liberal economists, the stone-blind eye they turn against any argument implying that the market may well be capable of repairing the destructions it causes.'[48] But one can also think of the arrogance with which some neurobiologists or evolutionary psychiatrists speak about psychoanalysis, for example, that it couldn't contrast more with the effective history of sciences: that is, the systematic connection between the production of knowledge and the creation of new practical possibilities, leading to new questions and new ways of belonging. Both cases reveal an obstinate lack of resistance among professionals to their own poisonous abstractions that takes the form of a kind of nasty, even entrepreneurial stupidity (she uses Deleuze's concept of *bêtise*) feeding on the devastating character of its own consequences: 'This stupidity currently organizes a situation in which *homo economicus* warrants an essential coincidence between the law of free competition and what is mathematically defined as progress, in which *homo geneticus* is lending a helping hand, as it adds that we are chained to a past that would make it utopian to escape

---

46   I. STENGERS, *Cosmopolitics I.*, op. cit., pp. 90-91.

47   'This attitude towards common sense or instincts designates Whitehead as a post-Darwinian thinker. What we call common sense is not an anthropological static feature to be opposed to high level speculation, it is maddening, always escaping identifying frames, as it tells of our ability to meaningfully interpret and orientate ourselves in a fluid, ever-changing plurality of situations. For Whitehead, it was the touchstone for any realist doctrine, as it enfolds the bewildering variety of what it means to be both in touch with and touched by 'reality', as it unfolds the dynamics of having things matter and having the way they matter matters. If there must be a speculative creation of concepts, it is thus not to revise common sense but to disarm the power of theoretical abstracts that fix the maddening achievement we call common sense into common sense doctrines, and to contribute continuing the adventure of common sense by unfolding what it demands and having it matter.' (Isabelle Stengers, 'Thinking with Deleuze and Whitehead: A Double Test'. In K. ROBINSON (Ed.), *Deleuze, Whitehead, Bergson: Rhizomatic Connections*, op. cit., 14).

48   I. STENGERS 'Thinking with Deleuze and Whitehead: A Double Test', op. cit., p. 12.

our habits of non-sustainable competition.'[49] In the face of this, Stengers fully subscribes to Whitehead's assignment of the task of philosophy to take care of our 'modes of thought' and 'civilize' our abstractions by enlarging our imagination.[50] What is necessary is a diplomatic practice with its own technical know-how, irreducible to and yet not parasitical on the practices it makes communicate.

Like Leibniz and Whitehead, moreover, Stengers holds that any experience may be transformed, but that it can never be interpreted away in terms of conditions that annihilate what mattered in the first place. This is why the speculative question for her is how to 'think for' (Stengers follows Deleuze here) a possible peace – that is, to bet on it under the test of its virtual presence – and not against it.[51] The ideal of peace cannot be based on a rejection of the ambitions and passions of science, as if speculation was just another attempt to judge over experience according to the modern question of 'what can we know?'. 'The question of what is an object and thus what is an abstraction must belong, if nature is not allowed to bifurcate, to nature and not to knowledge alone'.[52] Hence speculative philosophy is not critical or deconstructivist, as if it would suffice to state that objective knowledge capable of reducing consciousness to a 'state of the central nervous system' requires consciousness as its condition of possibility. Instead, Stengers stresses with Deleuze that it is 'constructivist' and has no foundation but only creative advance as its ultimate. Philosophy constructs conceptual tools capable of 'giving to the situation the power to make us think'.[53] Every matter of fact has a virtual power of thought, but it takes inventiveness to actualize this power and turn it into a matter of concern, i.e. to turn it back into an event. For Whitehead, abstract propositions can act as a 'lure for feeling 'something that matters'', for eliciting interest and setting up a matter of concern.[54] In her own practice, similarly, she seeks to create new

---

49   See I. STENGERS, 'Achieving Coherence. The Importance of Whitehead's 6th Category of Existence.' Presented at The Importance of Process – System and Adventure, the sixth Biosemiotic conference. Salzburg. 2006.

50   WHITEHEAD, *Process and Reality*, p. 17.

51   I. STENGERS, 'The Cosmopolitical Proposal'. In B. Latour & P. Weibel (Eds.), *Making Things Public: Atmosphere of Democracy* (Cambridge, Mass.: MIT Press, 2005), p. 186.

52   I. STENGERS, *Thinking with Whitehead. A Free and Wild Creation of Concepts*, op. cit. p. 95.

53   I. STENGERS, 'The Cosmopolitical Proposal', op. cit., p. 185.

54   Abstraction not as unilateral generalization that ignores empirical specificity (e.g. in logic), but singularization, an operation that exploits the singularirty of what it deals with in constructing new forms of definitions. (see Isabelle Stengers,

'practical identities', new ways for practices to be present, to connect, to become, to belong to something communicated between diverging practices and practitioners, usually at the cost of established contraries.

Thus if scientific reason and politics must be re-associated in a non-hierarchical and non-reductionist way, this is because the vulnerability of each in its separation is proven each time when, in the name of scientific objectivity, problems are defined and redefined that implicate human history. In democratically organized societies, 'politicians' are supposed to be occupied with decisions about how things should be ('prejudiced opinions') whereas 'experts' provide the conditions in terms of how things actually are ('neutral reality'). In practice, Stengers argues, this division of labour between human domain of power and the natural domain of science does not exist, but merely forecloses the possibility of thinking in democratic categories.

In this regard, tensions between speculative realism and speculative constructivism can also be illustrated by a recent debate between Latour and Graham Harman, one of the philosophers often associated with speculative realism (and rather willing to do so himself). Whereas Latour is committed to describing the different relationships of the human and/or non-human elements that make up assemblages, Harman is committed to devising an exhaustive ontological description of the world that precedes such research. Latour finds the deployment of such a completed ontology objectionable, since it problematizes the inclusion of new elements that might come into view over time. Instead, Latour emphasizes the value of a 'pragmatic-anthropological perspective', which delivers elaborate descriptions of knowledge production. According to Latour, this yields an experimental metaphysics through which he wishes to dissociate himself from philosophers who want to exhaustively describe the world prior to engaging with socio-material assemblages. The experimental nature of Latour's metaphysics ensures its alignment with the practices and political aspects that Latour seeks to understand. Ontological descriptions, or cosmologies, are of secondary importance. What really matters according to Latour is cosmopolitics.

Cosmopolitics I., op. cit., p. 196) Abstractions vectorize concrete experience, in the same way as a mathematical circle is not so much abstracted from concrete circular forms as it lures mathematical thought into a new adventure and produces a very concrete mathematical mode of existence. See Isabelle Stengers, 'A Constructivist Reading of *Process and Reality*'. *Theory, Culture & Society* 25 (4), 2008.

Conclusion: Speculative Constructivism And Speculative Realism

The speculative constructivism proposed by Stengers and Latour takes concrete practices and the manner in which they are constructed and maintained as its starting point. This provides a different beginning and nature to philosophical inquiry: instead of thinking about what things are, speculative constructivists are concerned with the question of what politics is possible and necessary, in other words, of what things may become. Today, Stengers is still most famous as a fellow-traveller of, and commentator on, chemistry Nobel prize winner Ilya Prigogine, whose work on far-from-equilibrium systems is also essential to DeLanda's undertaking: *La nouvelle alliance* (1986 [1979]) and *Entre le temps et l'éternité* (1992 [1988]). Yet she constantly emphasizes that her work with Prigogine had nothing to do with her philosophy. Drawing from Deleuze and Guattari's arguments about the respective sufficiency of scientific functions and philosophical concepts, she argues that whereas Prigogine's lifetime work led to 'the creation of a well-defined relation between an irreducibly probabilistic time-asymmetrical mathematical representation and the class of those dynamic systems for which this representation is necessary', philosophy's specific means were of no relevance. [55] In her own work, Prigogine's somewhat romantic idea of a science of time reconciled with the rest of culture in a 'new alliance' therefore features only by allusion. As Bruno Latour writes: 'No matter how time-dependent a science of phenomena far from equilibrium can be, it remains a science, that is, an attempt at stabilizing the world'[56] – such that, ultimately, we could speak of the world as it is 'in itself'. By contrast, isn't speculative philosophy precisely the attempt to destabilize the world, to let in a bit of chaos, and to return existence to the consistency of the event?

---

55   'My own participation in this work was a matter of putting it into historical perspective, of following how the paradoxes and blind generalizations implied in the so-called fundamental laws of nature, acquired their strange, quasi-metaphysical authority. But it was a complete surprise and even a shame to discover the many references in philosophical and cultural studies that were made to Prigogine and Stengers' theory of irreversible time. The very association of our two names was displaying a complete misunderstanding of the demanding character of physical mathematics' own specific means.' (Isabelle Stengers, 'Deleuze and Guattari's Last Enigmatic Message', in: *Angelaki. Journal of Theoretical Humanities*, vol. 10, nr. 2, pp. 151-67).

56   B. LATOUR, 'Foreword. Stengers's Shibboleth', p. x.

VII

TIME DETERMINATION AND HYPER-CHAOS:

The Reformulation of the Principle of Sufficient Reason in Kant and Meillassoux

LIAM SPROD

In his Preface to Quentin Meillassoux's *After Finitude* Alain Badiou observes that Meillassoux 'has opened up a new path in the history of philosophy, hitherto conceived as the history of what it is to know; a path that circumvents Kant's canonical distinction between "dogmatism", "skepticism" and "critique"'.[1] While it is certainly true that Meillassoux sets his own philosophical system of 'speculative materialism' against the transcendental idealism of Kant and the 'correlationist' tradition that develops out of the 'Kantian catastrophe',[2] he nonetheless does not reject Kant wholesale; and, *pace* Badiou, it is precisely through the distinction between 'dogmatism', 'skepticism' and 'critique' that this Kantian inheritance can be understood and indeed be shown to be central to Meillassoux's project. Thus, if Meillassoux's path in philosophy is a new one it nonetheless has the same Kantian starting point as the 'correlationist' one it displaces. However, recognizing this shared starting point of these two paths of philosophy also reveals further parallels between Meillassoux and Kant that are not so readily apparent if the two are simply considered as philosophical antagonists. It is precisely these parallels that this paper will discuss. This discussion will consist of three sections: Firstly the identification of the rejection of the principle of sufficient reason through the challenges of both skepticism and dialectical argument as the shared starting point, and the parallel projects of reconfiguring the possibilities of philosophy after this rejection. Secondly, how both Kant and Meillassoux reconfigure the principle of sufficient reason in terms of time. And, thirdly, how this similarity will allow a dialogue between the two philosophical systems.

---

1 Q. MEILLASSOUX, *After Finitude* (London: Continuum, 2008), p.vii.
2 *Ibid.*, p. 128.

1. The Kantian Inheritance: The rejection of the principle of sufficient reason.

In an essay titled *What Real Progress has Metaphysics Made in Germany Since the Time of Leibniz and Wolff*, written in the years preceding his death but only published posthumously, Kant writes: 'There are therefore three stages which philosophy had to traverse in its approach to metaphysics. The first was the stage of dogmatism; the second that of skepticism; and the third that of the criticism of pure reason.'[3] While the last of these – the criticism of pure reason – is most obviously associated with Kant's own philosophy, what such a quick identification conceals is the way in which he also engaged with, and indeed himself passed through, the preceding stages of dogmatism and skepticism in order to be able to achieve his critical endpoint. These two preceding stages also set the scene for the emergence of Kant's own critical philosophy in the Preface of the A-Edition of the *Critique of Pure Reason*.[4] Here, Kant outlines limitations of reason as is falls into unresolvable contradictions and traces the path of metaphysics from the 'despotic' rule of the dogmatists and the 'anarchy' of the skeptics, to the court of pure reason that 'may secure its [reason's] rightful claims, while dismissing all its groundless pretentions.'[5] The critical project that Kant pursues from this point onwards, and which results in the ongoing development of transcendental idealism, is then an overcoming of the previous dogmatic and skeptical stages of philosophy. The *Critique of Pure Reason* then contains both Kant's criticism of reason itself and thus of the dogmatic metaphysics that it produces – the negative side of the project contained in the Transcendental Dialectic – and his positive response to this, the construction of the system of transcendental idealism, that can provide the legitimate use of reason and thus resist falling prey to the anarchy of skepticism.

Meillassoux in his engagement with the 'Kantian catastrophe' unquestionably rejects the positive element of Kant's project – transcendental ide-

---

3   I. KANT, 'What Real Progress has Metaphysics Made in Germany Since the Time of Leibniz and Wolff' in Henry Allison and Peter Heath (eds.), *Theoretical Philosophy After 1781*. (Cambridge: Cambridge University Press, 2002), p. 20: 264; 365.

4   The A-Edition Preface emphasizes the *critical* element of the book, i.e., the arguments of the Dialectic, much more than that of the B-Edition, which emphasizes how the positive system of transcendental idealism aligns itself with scientific realism and against idealism. This is due to the charge of subjective idealism leveled against Kant after the publication of the A-Edition, which prompted in part the rewriting of the B-Edition.

5   I. KANT, *Critique of Pure Reason* (Cambridge: Cambridge University Press, 1998), A xi.

alism – but he, however, equally unquestionably endorses the negative, truly critical element of Kant's project – the identification of the rejection of dogmatism and the necessity of a response to the challenge of skepticism.[6] Observing that in the current philosophical age, 'we cannot go back to being metaphysicians, just as we cannot go back to being dogmatists', Meillassoux concedes that 'On this point, we cannot but be heirs of Kantianism.'[7] Here Meillassoux shares with Kant at least one of the three stages of philosophy that Badiou claims he circumvents, and indeed like Kant this rejection of dogmatism is the starting point from which Meillassoux recalibrates the possibilities of philosophy and through that builds his own philosophical system. But what exactly does this rejection entail? Meillassoux elaborates: 'to reject dogmatic metaphysics means to reject *all* real necessity, and *a fortiori* to reject the principle of sufficient reason, as well as the ontological argument, which is the keystone that allows the system of real necessity to close in on itself.'[8] There are two important points here: Firstly, that the rejection of dogmatic metaphysics is a rejection of the principle of sufficient reason; and, secondly, that Meillassoux identifies the disproof of the ontological argument as the central move in this rejection.

What is especially interesting about these two points is that while they are certainly there in the *Critique of Pure Reason*, they are also ideas and arguments that Kant had been working through long before his fully developed transcendental idealism appeared. Kant struggles with both the principle of sufficient reason and the ontological argument in one of his earliest texts from 1755, *A New Elucidation on the First Principles of Metaphysical Cognition* (hereafter *New Elucidation*). Returning to this text and recognizing the importance of the rejection of the principle of sufficient reason now can provide a new insight into the system that Kant eventually erects in its place in the *Critique*. Similarly, the fact that Kant rejects the ontological argument so early in his career and yet takes another 26 years and several more reiterations of this disproof suggests that it is not in fact as central a move in the development of transcendental idealism as Meillassoux puts forward.[9]

---

6   The idea that certain elements of Kant's philosophy can be endorsed without a full commitment to transcendental idealism has a long history, perhaps most notably in Peter Strawson's *Bounds of Sense* (1966).

7   MEILLASSOUX, *After Finitude*, p. 29.

8   *Ibid.*, p. 33.

9   This is further suggested by the somewhat peripheral place that Kant gives to this disproof in the *Critique*, it is merely part of the overall destruction of dogmatic metaphysics that takes place in the Dialectic. Furthermore, Kant also

In the *New Elucidation* Kant aims to 'shed light ... on the first principles of our cognition.'[10] In doing so he sets about criticizing some of the most central tenets of rationalist thought specifically with reference to Descartes, Christian Wolff and Leibniz. The text consists of three sections. The first takes issue with the Law of Contradiction, in particular the claim that it alone is the absolutely first, universal principle of all truths. Instead Kant demonstrates that the Law of Contradiction – '*it is impossible that the same thing should simultaneously be and not be*'[11] – must itself rest upon the principle of identity, which must always be expressed in dual manner in positive – '*whatever is, is*' – and negative – '*whatever is not, is not*' – forms.[12] The duality of the principle of identity is necessary to be able to account for both positive and negative truths and provides the underpinning required to be able to move from the purely negative proposition of the Law of Contradiction to be able to assert positive truths through the mediating principle of: '*Everything of which the opposite is false, is true*'[13] The result of this analysis is to undermine the rationalist assumption that there can be a single fundamental principle upon which all metaphysics can be constructed.[14] This duality also contains the seeds of the later dialectical critique of all dogmatic metaphysics.

The second section of the *New Elucidation* is concerned directly with the principle of sufficient reason, which Kant refers to as the principle of determining ground. Although here Kant is fundamentally in favour of the principle, he specifically takes aim at the fact that it has been taken by ra-

---

suggests that the Antinomies, which argue against rational cosmology, were actually much more important to him. In a letter to Christian Garve from September 1798 he recalled that 'it was not the investigation of the existence of God, immortality, and so on, but rather the antinomy of pure reason ... that is what first aroused me from my dogmatic slumber and drove me to the critique of reason itself, in order to resolve the scandal of the ostensible contradiction of reason with itself' (12: 257-8).

The wording here – that they 'aroused him from his dogmatic slumber' – recalls Kant's claim in the *Prolegomena* that it was Hume, and skepticism, that aroused him. This suggests that the stages of dogmatism and skepticism, and the part of the latter in overcoming the former, are closely connected.

10 I. KANT, "New Elucidation," in David Walford and Ralf Meerbote (eds.), *Theoretical Philosophy, 1755-1770* (Cambridge: Cambridge University Press, 1992) 1:387; 5.

11 *Ibid.*, 1:391; 9-10.

12 *Ibid.*, 1:389; 7.

13 *Ibid.*, 1:390-391; 9.

14 M. GRIER, *Kant's Doctrine of Transcendental Illusion* (Cambridge: Cambridge University Press), p. 19.

tionalist philosophers in terms of its complete universality.[15] The line that Kant takes here is similar to his critique of the Law of Contradiction, and consists of showing that what has been taken to be unitary and universal in fact depends upon a multiplicity of assumptions. In this case he distinguishes between an *antecedently* determining ground (the ground of being or becoming) and a *consequentially* determining ground (the ground of knowing).[16] Having drawn this distinction Kant then uses it to criticize Wolff's definition of a ground as 'that by reference to which it is possible to understand why something should rather be than not be.'[17] What becomes more obvious through the earlier distinction between the ground of being and the ground of knowing is that Wolff elides the distinction while at the same time tacitly relying upon it. Simply, to state why a thing *is* rather than *is not* is to state a ground, Wolff asks after the ground of being, but defines it by the ground of knowing. As Kant puts it:

> For if you correctly examine the term [why], you will find that it means the same as *for which ground*. Thus, once the substitution has been duly made, Wolff's definition runs: a ground is that by reference to which it is possible to understand *for which ground* something should be rather than not be.[18]

While the criticism here looks like a charge of circularity, the circle only holds if the distinction between antecedently and consequentially determining grounds is totally elided. The danger of Wolff's definition, now seemingly rendered circular, really arises when the equivocation actually hides the maintenance of the difference. For it is Wolff's conflation of epistemological grounds with metaphysical grounds that erroneously grants causal efficiency to what should in fact be merely epistemological ground: the knowledge of something is taken to be its cause.[19]

It is Kant's careful maintenance of the distinction between the two kinds of ground and avoidance of the error of Wolff's reliance on the principle of sufficient reason in its elusive and equivocal ability to determine the existence of things purely through the ground of knowing, that provides the insight for his critique of the ontological argument as it appears in the *New Elucidation*. The distinction that he has previously established allows Kant to succinctly demolish the argument in one step, he writes: 'Of course,

---

15   *Ibid.*, p. 21.
16   KANT, *New Elucidation*, 1:392; 11.
17   *Ibid.*, 1:393; 13.
18   *Ibid.*
19   GRIER, *Kant's Doctrine of Transcendental Illusion*, p. 22.

I know that appeal is made to the concept itself of God; and the claim is made that the existence of God is determined by that concept. It can, however, easily be seen that this happens ideally, not really.'[20] Although this criticism does not yet have the technical form that it will later take in the *Critique of Pure Reason* – that existence is not a real predicate – the fundamental insight is the same: that any concept can be thought but as such it only has existence as an idea not as reality.

At this point in 1755 Kant is still firmly in his own dogmatic stage and both his alliance to some form of the principle of sufficient reason, now as the principle of determining ground and an argument for the existence of God testify to this dogmatism. He has yet to be awoken from that dogmatic slumber and pass through his own skeptical stage, most notably in 1766's *Dreams of a Spirit-Seer*, before the 'great light' of 1769 alerted him to the distinction between sensibility and understanding and the development of transcendental idealism (Noted in a *Reflexionen* from around 1776-78, 18: 69).[21] First in the proto-form of the *Inaugural Dissertation*, which retained a trace of dogmatism in the ability of the intellect to directly intuit reality; and then in the *Critique*, where in confronting the problems of the Dissertation he purged this dogmatic remainder to fully develop the transcendental philosophy.

2. Time And The Reconfiguration Of The Principle Of Sufficient Reason.

Meillassoux recognizes and reiterates the importance of Hume in motivating Kant's skepticism and his subsequent development of transcendental idealism. Importantly, Meillassoux also connects Kant's Humean 'awakening' to the problems concerning the principle of sufficient reason. In his genealogy of the 'Kantian catastrophe' he points to what he calls the 'Hume event', and outlines it as:

---

20   Kant, *New Elucidation*, 1:394; 15.

21   Arguments that the 'great light' of 1769 was the distinction between sensibility and understanding which was the key to resolving the problem of the Antinomies can be found in Amerkis (1992, 51), Keuhn (1983, 184 n. 37) and is elaborated at length by Beck (1978). Naturally there are other factors that must be considered in Kant's development, such as the distinction between real and ideal existence found in *Negative Magnitudes* (1763) and the analytic/synthetic distinction found in the *Inquiry* (1764).

demonstrating the fallaciousness of all metaphysical forms of rationality, which is to say, by demonstrating the fallaciousness of the absoluteness of the principle of sufficient reason – thought must renounce every form of demonstration intended to establish *a priori* that whatever gives itself as being thus and so must unconditionally be thus and so. The world's being-thus-and-so can only be discovered by way of experience, it cannot be demonstrated by absolute necessity.[22]

Such a connection between Hume and the principle of sufficient reason does not seem immediately obvious. Kant's own identification of the importance of Hume in 'awakening him from his dogmatic slumber' in the *Prolegomena,* and indeed the standard interpretation of the influence of Hume on Kant, concerns Hume's treatment of induction and the problem of causal connection. However, in light of the earlier discussion of the *New Elucidation* and Kant's reformulation of the principle of sufficient reason in terms of antecedently and consequentially determining grounds the connection to Hume's problem of induction becomes clearer as the question of sufficient reason shifts from one of rationality to one of causation. In turn, the careful separation and distinction between reason as the ground of being and the ground of knowing, and the explication of the complicated relation between the two, will not only provide Kant with his solution Hume's problem, but also the key to the Critical project as a whole.

Indeed, on three occasions in the *Critique of Pure Reason* Kant claims to provide a proof for a reformulated principle of sufficient reason, which has been 'often sought, but always in vain.'[23] Given that so much of Kant's argument hinges on the *critique* of reason this claim to have finally provided a proof for the principle of sufficient reason, albeit importantly in a reconfigured form, could be said to be the goal of the *Critique* all along. This will become even more obvious when the details of Kant's reconfiguration are put in context with the other elements of the *Critique*, specifically the 'heart' of the argument, the Transcendental Deduction (this contrast will

---

22   MEILLASSOUX, *After Finitude*, p.125. This quote does call into question the need for Meillassoux to insist on a specifically Kantian inheritance, when there is little difference between what he claims to find in Hume and Kant regarding the principle of sufficient reason. Hume, of course, does not present the same negation of the ontological argument that features strongly in Meillassoux's description of Kant (although it is curiously absent from his genealogical account of the 'catastrophe').

23   KANT, *Critique of Pure* Reason, A 217/B 264-5. The other two points at which he makes this claim are A 201/B246, which will be discussed below in detail, and A 783/B 811, which explicitly claims that this proof was not possible until 'transcendental critique came on the scene'.

also expose a limitation in Meillassoux's consideration of Kant). Before that, it is especially important to note here that Meillassoux's positive philosophical project, his 'speculative materialism', once again parallels that of Kant. In his genealogy of the Kantian catastrophe Meillassoux endorses the philosophical progression he has outlined up until Kant's intervention, valorizing in particular the rejection of the principle of sufficient reason through the intervention of Hume (and presumably Kant, given the earlier discussion about Kant's critique of all forms of rationality and the rejection of the ontological argument in particular). Meillassoux also presents his own position as *'a speculative solution to Hume's problem,'*[24] produced by 'transform[ing] our perspective on unreason.'[25] It is here that Meillassoux avoids the distinction between dogmatism, skepticism and criticism (in the specific sense of Kant's answer to this problem) as he considers each of these solutions to Hume's problem and rejects them in favour of his own. But what he cannot escape, however, it the wider sense in which his project follows this distinction perfectly. So much so that it would not be out of place to suggest that Meillassoux's own solution to Hume's problem is itself actually also 'critical' in that it proceeds through the critique of reason (the rejection of sufficient reason) and erecting in its place another system of reason that has learnt the lessons of this critique. Meillassoux acknowledges this, writing in a passage that is very reminiscent of Kant's Preface to the A-Edition: 'Thus it is essential that a philosophy produces internal mechanisms for regulating its own inferences – signposts and criticisms through which the newly constituted domain is equipped with a set of constraints that provide criteria for distinguishing between licit and illicit claims.' Furthermore, and in even greater echo of Kant, what this alternative critical system produced is once again a form of reason, only now 'a reason emancipated from the principle of reason – *a speculative form of the rational* that would no longer be a *metaphysical reason.*'[26] The parallels do not stop there, for even the solutions provided by Kant and Meillassoux are similar in that both of their reconfigurations of the principle of sufficient reason involve its temporalization.

Kant's reconfiguration of the principle of sufficient reason and his 'solution' or re-solution to Hume's problem takes place in the Second Analogy of Experience.[27] The Analogies of Experience appear after the Deduction

---

24   MEILLASSOUX, *After Finitude*, p. 85. See also p. 127.
25   *Ibid.*, p. 82.
26   MEILLASSOUX, *After Finitude*, p. 77.
27   This is contrary to Meillassoux's claim that Kant resolves Hume's problem in the Transcendental Deduction (88-9). While the arguments of the Analogies certainly

and Schematism, and map out how the different categories play out in possible empirical experience as opposed to operating in purely theoretical terms. The Analogies are concerned with the category of relation and its three modes: Inherence and subsistence, causality and dependence, and, community; and this plays out in terms of the possibility of connecting experience in one time expressed through three modes: persistence, succession and simultaneity. Already this short description pre-empts the answer that Kant will provide, so it is best to provide this from the start and then elaborate upon it. Kant concludes that, 'the principle of sufficient reason is the ground of possible experience, namely the objective cognition of appearances with regard to their relation in a successive series of time.'[28] This is Kant's reconfigured principle of sufficient reason, which now recasts the problem from the *New Elucidation* and takes into account the separation between antecedently and consequentially determining grounds by making itself the *a priori* condition through which the experience of succession is possible, and thus allowing judgments of before and after themselves to be made, that is of both types of 'reasons'.

Kant twists the issue of causation around his reconfiguration of the principle of sufficient reason, and indeed the place of *a priori* reasoning in general. He agrees with Hume's skeptical analysis that 'the concept of cause brings the trait of necessity with it, which no experience can yield.'[29] But following the general reversal of his 'Copernican revolution' this prompts him to instead suggest that the concept of cause must be brought to experience and understanding *a priori* as a condition of its possibility. In the *New Elucidation* Kant criticized Wolff for confusing the ground of being (a cause) with the ground of knowing (understanding) through an equivocation within the principle of sufficient reason. Kant's reconfiguration of the principle of sufficient reason in the *Critique* is a result of his analysis of the possibility of understanding, which is now no longer merely a question of either purely rational argumentation, or analysis of experience, but rather a constitutive element of the possibility of objective experience in the first place, and as such it plays a role in determining how causal judgments, judgments about the ground of being, are even possible.[30] This is because experience is determined in time

---

build upon and extend those of the Deduction, the latter alone does not provide Kant's answer to the specific issue of the problem of induction.

28   KANT, *Critique of Pure Reason*, A 200-1/B 246.
29   *Ibid.*, A 112-13.
30   The connection between the rejection of the principle of sufficient reason in the *New Elucidation* and its reformulation in the *Critique* is examined in by B.

through the application of the categories of relation. As Kant summarizes the argument in the Second Analogy:

> Understanding belongs to all experience and its possibility, and the first thing that it does for this is not to make the representation of the objects distinct, but rather to make the representation of an object possible at all. Now this happens through its conferring temporal order on the appearances and their existence by assigning to each of these, as a consequence, a place in time determined *a priori* in regard to the preceding appearances, without which it would not agree with time itself, which determines the position of all its parts *a priori*.[31]

The very possibility of considering objects of which the question of the ground of being can be asked, already itself has determined those objects in time according to the category of relation. The Analogies of Experience specify that the *a priori* determination of time operates through the category of relation and explicate the three modes of time that reflect that category – simultaneity, succession and co-existence. The principle of sufficient reason, in this reconfigured form, now only applies to the possibility of the time determination of objective experience, which in its most general form provides the idea of the succession of objects and events in time and allows causal thinking across that time.

As such, the Analogies do not show the legitimacy of the application of the category of relation to perception, only how time is actually determined in its three modes. Proof of the legitimacy and the possibility of the connection of the categories to sensations is the task of the Deduction, and the answer that Kant provides there is that this possibility ultimately depends upon the transcendental unity of apperception, by ways of the syntheses of apprehension and imagination. Consequentially, examining the the Analogies in these terms, through their direct engagement with both Hume's problem and the necessity of reconfiguring the principle of sufficient reason after its rejection, they make explicit what is at the core of the positive aspect of the *Critique*: the question of time determination.[32]

LONGUENESSE in the article 'Kant's Deconstruction of the Principle of Sufficient Reason.' (2001).

31   KANT, *Critique of Pure Reason*, A 199/ B 244-5.

32   On the centrality of the issue of time determination in both the *Critique* and also Kant's theory of experience in general, see P. GUYER, *Kant and the Claims of Knowledge*. (Cambridge: Cambridge University Press, 1987). In particular page 62, where Guyer notes that, 'the transcendental theory of experience ... is essentially a theory of time determination.' The complexities around this recognition that Guyer identifies and discusses will be examined in greater detail in §3 of this essay.

Identifying the question of transcendental time determination as the core of Kant's positive project can be set against the temporal element of Meillassoux positive position, which also reconfigures the principle of sufficient reason through time, but in his case as the chaos of time rather than its determination. Meillassoux's response to the rejection of the principle of sufficient reason can also be traced along the distinction made in the *New Elucidation* and once again reveal a parallel between Kant and Meillassoux. Kant uses the equivocation between the ground of being and ground of knowing as a reason to change the nature of understanding itself so that is can encompass both. Meillassoux performs a similar extension across the equivocation but in the opposite direction, locating the proper source of the inability to think necessity not in terms of the ground of knowing but instead in the ground of being. As he puts it:

> *we are going to put back into the thing itself what we mistakenly took to be an incapacity in thought.* In other words, instead of construing the absence of reason inherent in everything as a limit that thought encounters in its search for ultimate reason, we must understand that this absence of reason *is*, and can *only* be the *ultimate* property of the entity.[33]

For Meillassoux the inability of reason to comprehend the world through experience is due to the fact that the world itself is not governed by rationality. This is the lesson to be taken from the Humean and Kantian destruction of rationalist metaphysics; and this is also how Meillassoux find a path back to the absolute, now in the form of absolute unreason, which is his reconfiguration of the principle of sufficient reason. He writes:

> We are no longer upholding a variant of the principle of sufficient reason, according to which there is a necessary reason why everything is the way it is rather than otherwise, but rather the absolute truth of a *principle of unreason*. There is no reason for anything to be or remain the way it is; everything must, without reason, be able to be and/or be able to be other than its is.[34]

The principle of unreason *is* Meillassoux's reconfiguration of the principle of sufficient reason, it is, for him, the only properly rational outcome of reason's realization of its own limitations. It also, and this importantly reinforces Meillassoux's rationalist position, reclaims an absolute after the supposed rejection of the possibility of rationality proving the existence of

---

33 MEILLASSOUX, *After Finitude*, p. 53.
34 *Ibid.*, p. 60.

any absolute. The difference is that the absolute truth of unreason is not a proof of an absolute entity, but rather of the truth of the ground of being itself. This is borne out by the nature of this absolute unreason itself, which negates the possibility of any necessary entity at all by making all entities contingent. This supplies the insight into the nature of being, now reconfigured by the principle of unreason. Meillassoux describes it:

> If we look through the aperture which we have opened up onto the absolute, what we see there is a rather menacing of power – something insensible, and capable of destroying both things and worlds, of bringing forth monstrous absurdities, yet also of never doing anything, of realizing every dream, but also every nightmare, of engendering random and frenetic transformations, or conversely, of producing a universe that remains motionless down to its ultimate recess.

This is what Meillassoux calls 'hyper-chaos' the extension of unreason into being, but he goes on to provide a account of this chaos that is at once both more concrete and more abstract. He continues,

> We see something akin to Time, but a Time that is inconceivable for physics, since it is capable of destroying, without cause or reason, every physical law, just as it is inconceivable for metaphysics, since it is capable of destroying every determinable entity, even a god, even God ... It is a Time capable of destroying even becoming itself by bringing forth, perhaps forever, fixity stasis and death.[35]

Although here Meillassoux is somewhat circumspect, describing hyper-chaos as only 'akin' to time, elsewhere he is more certain on this equation, writing: 'Unreason becomes the attribute of an absolute time able to destroy and create any determined entity,'[36] and 'The answer is *time* – facticity as absolute must be considered as time, *but a very special time*, that I called in *After Finitude* "hyper-chaos."'[37] Hyper-chaos must be time itself, because as an absolute it must be eternal and yet hyper-chaos negates the possibility of any eternal entity including itself as an entity, further to this, even if it is to negate itself, its disappearance must also take place in time, proving the eternality and thus absoluteness of temporality.[38] This identification of hyper-chaos as time is at once more concrete as time is something

---

35   *Ibid.*, p. 64.
36   Q. MEILLASSOUX, "Speculative Realism", *Collapse: Philosophical Research and Development*, vol. 3, p. 431.
37   Q. MEILLASSOUX, 'Time Without Becoming', talk presented at Middlesex University, 8 May 2008, p. 10.
38   MEILLASSOUX, *After Finitude*, p. 62.

that is readily understood and its destructive power or ability to change things is intuitively grasped; however, it is also somewhat more abstract as it is hard to equate this absolute reality of chaotic time with the reality experienced everyday and examined and explained by science.

So far a series of perhaps unexpected parallels between Kant and Meillassoux have been identified. As a result they are left opposed to each other, having diverged from their shared origin in a negative philosophical rejection of dogmatism and a need to respond to the challenge of Humean skepticism. Both proceed in their positive project by reconfiguring the principle of sufficient reason, and both of these reconfigurations can be analyzed in the terms outlined by the young and dogmatic Kant of the *New Elucidation*. His early recognition of the problem hiding in the equivocation of the principle of sufficient reason provides the tools that both he and Meillassoux will eventually use to reconfigure the limitations of both that principle and reason itself, albeit in diametrically opposed ways. In this sense both are critical philosophers, mechanics of reason who through their tinkering not only hope to change what knowledge and experience themselves are, but also hope to reveal something about the fundamental nature of the world and the possibilities of science. And here the ultimate parallel appears as the means through which they both attempt this is through an explication of the nature of time. In Kant's case through the determination of inner sense, a move that seems to reinforce the accusation of correlationism and its catastrophic consequences; and in Meillassoux's case through the insight into the ultimate chaotic and contingent nature of being itself as time. This final parallel also highlights the full extent of the difference between Kant and Meillassoux and thus provides the perfect point of comparison between the two of them.

3. The Problems Of The Temporal Reconfiguration

Highlighting time as the key point of *comparison* between Kant and Meillassoux opens up a new perspective on the *differences* and disputes between them. This is because just as Kant presents time determination as the key problem of the *Critique* and one which he believes that he has overcome with the identification of the transcendental unity of apperception as the key to the transcendental deduction of the categories, time and time determination nonetheless remain a *problematic* element within Kant's system that in fact brings the legitimacy of apperception into question.

This extends the parallel between Kant and Meillassoux, now time is not only the means by which Meillassoux critiques Kant, it is also a disruptive element within Kant, and thus identifying how Kant struggles with this problem will in turn reveal a way for sketching out some of the ways he can interact with Meillassoux's critique, and even pre-empt some of the problems that Meillassoux presents.

Rather than simply returning straight to Kant and examining his theory of time determination and the problematic place it holds within his system, it is instead possible to examine Meillassoux's explicit point of contention with the 'Kantian catastrophe' and reveal how this tacitly engages with the issue of time determination and yet how it also becomes a problematic point for Meillassoux. In turn, the revelation of the problematic question of time determination for Meillassoux also provides a way back to the issue in Kant and how his engagement with it pre-empts problems that Meillassoux also later encounters.

The point of contention that Meillassoux develops with both Kant and the Kantian tradition revolves around his critique of them as 'correlationist', the polemical terms that he coins to denounce the intertwining of subject and object – and, subjectivity and objectivity – that he finds in these philosophies. Meillassoux puts forward the term 'correlationism' in order to sidestep the debates concentrated on idealism that have previously covered similar grounds. He explicitly notes: 'By this term [correlationism] I wanted to avoid the usual 'parade' of transcendental philosophy and phenomenology against the accusation of idealism – I mean answers such as: 'Kantian criticism is not a subjective idealism since there is a refutation of idealism in the *Critique of Pure Reason*.'[39] However, despite this attempted sidestep, his criticism of correlationism nonetheless turns out to be a criticism of idealism, as he uses 'the problem of ancestrality'[40] to show that when confronted with this issue 'every variety of correlationism is exposed as an extreme idealism.'[41]

The problem of ancestrality is introduced with a list of geological and cosmological events ranging from 'the date of the origin of the universe (13.5 billion years ago)' to 'the date of the origin of humankind (*Homo

---

39   MEILLASSOUX, "Speculative Realism", p. 408.
40   MEILLASSOUX, *After Finitude*, p. 128.
41   *Ibid.*, p. 129. Equally, the explicit aim of this evasion, to avoid engaging with the Refutation of Idealism found in the *Critique*, is also a weak point in Meillassoux's method, and identifies a particularly important point of comparison with Kant, as will become apparent below.

habilis, 2 million years ago).'[42] Importantly for Meillassoux, these 'ancestral' events, determined by empirical science from material evidence (the 'ache-fossil'), are anterior to the advent of humanity and thus to all human consciousness. That is, they are *anterior to every form of human relation to the world.*'[43] Meillassoux is not interested in appraising 'the reliability of the techniques employed in order to formulate such statements', but rather in asking *how is correlationism liable to interpret these ancestral statements?*'[44] The challenge that the mere knowledge of these events raises is the question of how the correlationist, who prioritized precisely the relation to the world above the existence of the world alone, can account for the actuality of these events in any meaningful way? The wager that Meillassoux puts forward is that the only possible coherent understanding of the statements of the arche-fossil can be found in taking their meaning in a realist sense, and that on the outcome of this wager rests the proper test of the validity of correlationism as a tenable philosophical position. As he puts it: 'This is what we shall express in terms of the ancestral statement's *irremediable* realism: either this statement has a realist sense, and *only* a realist sense, or it has no sense at all.'[45] The unsaid implication here, that Meillassoux has spelt out immediately before making this statement, is that any sense of the ancestral statement that is not realist, i.e., the correlationist sense, is in fact nonsense, and in particular, the sort of nonsense that is called 'idealism'.

In order to attempt to deal with ancestrality the correlationist must, in Meillassoux's view, locate the meaning of the evidence of the arche-fossil in the present and not in the past, as it is only in the present that there can be a relation between the object of the arche-fossil and human subjectivity. This, for Meillassoux, leads to a counter intuitive claim that the meaning of the fossil comes not from its existence in the past, but must be retrojected from the present, which has implication for the sort of temporality at work in claims about ancestrality. Meillassoux writes that for the correlationist: 'To understand the fossil, it is necessary to proceed from the present to the past, following a logical order, rather than from the past to the present following a chronological order.'[46] The substitution of a retrojective logic for a chronological progression raises problems for Meillassoux when he asks

---

42 MEILLASSOUX, *After Finitude*, p. 9.
43 *Ibid.*, p. 10.
44 *Ibid.* Presumably, this also means that he is not interested in the epistemological issues of how it is possible that these events are known.
45 MEILLASSOUX, *After Finitude*, p. 17.
46 *Ibid.*, p. 16.

about the actual meaning of the 'truth' of the ancestral statement, i.e., what actually happened 13.5 billion years ago when the universe formed, what was it that formed, how can this have any meaning?

This returns to the Galilean-Copernican revolution of science and Meillassoux's characterization of Kant's own 'Copernican revolution' as a 'Ptolemaic counter revolution' against it.[47] The arche-fossil is not only a tool that Meillassoux uses to expose the extreme idealism of all correlationism, he also sees it as revealing something fundamental for empirical science. He writes:

> Closer inspection reveals that the problem of the arche-fossil is not confined to ancestral statements. For it concerns every discourse whose meaning includes a *temporal discrepancy* between thinking and being – thus, not only statements about events occurring prior to the emergence of humans, but also statements about possible events that are *ulterior* to the extinction of the human species.[48]

It is the ability to formulate such statements that concern events anterior or ulterior to *every* human relation to the world that Meillassoux sees as the nature of empirical science. He names the operation of this temporal discrepancy 'dia-chronicity', and this ruptures the necessary synchronicity between thinking and being that is characteristic of correlationism. This reveals the proper importance of the example of the arche-fossil, it is not important that there actually was something there anterior to humanity, but merely that any such statement is meaningful. That is, does not reduce to the 'non-sense' that Meillassoux ascribes to correlationism, i.e., the reduction of chronology to logic.[49] It is not that empirical science provides knowledge of any specific other time that is dia-chronic to humanity, but that makes the very thought of such times as dia-chronic meaningful, and as such it makes the very thought of chronology in general meaningful. The means through which empirical science does this is via the mathematization of nature and the ability to think it as a separate extended substance independent of any sensible qualities; but when coupled with this alternative approach from dia-chronicity they reveal something that is both important and problematic within Meillassoux's philosophical system.

---

47   *Ibid.*, p. 118. It is interesting to note that Paul Guyer also recognizes that Kant's revolution seems 'more Ptolemaic than Copernican', especially with regards to how Kant can treat natural science as an investigation of the objects of the world (Guyer, *Kant and the Claims of Knowledge*, p. 3).

48   *Ibid.*, p. 112.

49   *Ibid.*, p. 16.

The emphasis that Meillassoux puts on dia-chronicity and chronology itself meets up with his earlier-identified assertion that it is the hyper-chaos of *time* that is the absolute reality beyond, and without, any necessary connection to the human subjective point of view, experience or understanding. However, in this conjunction there also appears a contradiction, for it becomes hard to see how the time of hyper-chaos could ever be considered as chronological, even if the flux of hyper-chaos can produce the consistency that Meillassoux deduces through his use of transfinite numbers, then the eternal nature of hyper-chaos, the very feature that lead him to put forwards its absolute nature, precludes it from being determined in any sense like that necessary for chronology. As Peter Gratton notes, there is in Meillassoux's system, 'a heterogeneous relation between the eternal ("time without becoming") and the chronological (that which the eternal can always interrupt via the creation *ex nihilo* of matter, life, thought, and perhaps a world of justice).'[50] Just as he decries correlationism for replacing chronology with logic, Meillassoux provides a much stronger version of the same move; so much stronger that the logical and rational deduction of eternal hyper-chaos does away with any possibility of chronology or time determination in general.[51]

For Meillassoux, the issue of time determination is something that is problematic, but ultimately a problem that he dismisses in favour of the eternal absolute of hyper-chaos. For Kant, time determination is also problematic, however, it is a problem that he aims to resolve, even if his solution remains problematic. Interestingly, Meillassoux himself introduces some of the components that feature in the Kantian maintenance of the problem. As he introduces the problem of ancestrality and the specific examples of arche-fossils in *After Finitude*, he uses a very revealing metaphor, he writes: 'It's just a line. It can have different shades, a little like a spectrum of colours separated by short vertical dashes. Above these are numbers indicating immense quantities.'[52] The numbers are the dates that correspond to the

---

50   P. GRATTON, "Post-Deconstructive Realism: It's About Time," in *Speculations: A journal of Speculative Realism*, IV, p. 88.

51   P. HALLWARD also identifies this inconsistency between the logic of hyper-chaos and the determination of chronology, he writes: 'The idea that the meaning of the statement 'the universe was formed 13.5 billion years ago' might be independent of the mind that thinks it only makes sense if you disregard the quaintly parochial unit of measurement involved (along with the meaning of words like 'ago'...)'. 'Anything is Possible: A Reading of Quentin Meillassoux's *After Finitude*,' in Bryant, Levi, Srnicek, Nick and Harman, Graham, Eds. *The Speculative Turn: Continental Materialism and Realism* (Prahran: re.press, 2011).

52   MEILLASSOUX, *After Finitude*, p. 9.

chronological ordering of how long ago the events detailed – the accretion of the Earth, the emergence of *Homo Sapiens*, etc. – occurred, and the line is a representation of time, stretching back from the now of the present and presumably forwards into the future. Here Meillassoux puts forward the image of chronology that he is using to argue against correlationism, and importantly he defines this time and its determination explicitly through the use of the *spatial* metaphor of a line. In a sense, this spatiality makes sense, in that it is a theme that crops up in several places in *After Finitude*. Meillassoux has already defined his aim as the reclamation of

> the *great outdoors*, the *absolute* outside of pre-critical thinkers: that outside which was not relative to us, and which was given as indifferent to its own givenness to be what it is, existing in itself regardless of whether we are thinking of it or not; that outside which thought could explore with the legitimate feeling of being on foreign territory – of being entirely elsewhere.[53]

Again, it is through the spatial metaphor – with the important addition of a connection with *externality* – that Meillassoux expresses the uncorrelated absolute that he seeks to rehabilitate. This becomes even more explicit when he later aligns it with the world revealed by the sciences of the Galilean-Copernican revolution and defines this as, 'The world of Cartesian extension … a world that acquires the independence of substance.'[54] There is an intuitive correctness to Meillassoux's identification of the absolute with spatiality, because space as simultaneity instead of succession is clearly in a sense eternal, or rather, timeless. The opposition between simultaneity and succession, however, reinforces the impossibility of the former alone determining time, as in a world of pure simultaneity – a pure metaphysics of presence – there is no movement of time to be determined.[55] The spatial metaphor of the straight line as an image of chronology only then works precisely because it is a metaphor, and that time itself is not actually merely

---

53   MEILLASSOUX, *After Finitude*, p. 7.

54   *Ibid.*, p. 115. Although it must be noted that earlier in *After Finitude* he has backed away from completely identifying the absolute with Cartesian extension and pure primary qualities as, 'one cannot imagine an extension which would not be coloured, and hence which would not be associated with a secondary quality' (3). Hence his need to reconfigure the Cartesian aim to know the world absolutely and to know it through reason alone into one that reveals this world as that of hyperchaos and time. Nonetheless, the use of the spatial *metaphor* persists.

55   A diagnosis and critique of Meillassoux's 'speculative materialism' and the wider 'speculative realist' tendency as metaphysics of presence can be found in Peter Gratton's 'Post-Deconstructive Realism: It's About Time' (2013).

a simultaneous straight line stretching backwards and forwards, the very determination of backwards or forwards is impossible by the standards of the line alone. A movement or directionality, precisely the sort of orientation that Meillassoux eliminates from the world of pure extension, is required in order for determination to be both possible and necessary. It is in this interplay between space and time, and within time expressed in the spatial metaphor, that the issue of time determination becomes, and in some sense remains, problematic for Kant. It is through these figures that the Kantian problem of time determination both pre-empts and clarifies the issue as it is troublesome within Meillassoux; and thus, provides the outlines through which the comparison of Meillassoux and Kant can be further traced.

The first step in this line of comparison is to identify how time and time determination are the central problem of the *Critique* and how they remain problematic even when confronted with Kant's supposed answer, through this the connection to space and its importance within Kant's system will be revealed. As argued above, the Analogies of Experience explicate the way in which the category of relation determines time through three specific modes (persistence, succession and simultaneity – the third of these already pointing towards an element of spatiality within the determinations of time) and thus how sensations are determined in a time that is causal, but it is the argument of the Deduction that outlines how it is in general that the categories can relate to sensibility at all, and importantly for Kant this is also a question of time determination. He makes this clear in an important passage at the start of the A-Deduction:

> Wherever our representations may arise, whether through the influence of external things or as the effect of inner causes, whether they have originated *a priori* or empirically as appearances – as modifications of the mind they nevertheless belong to inner sense, and as such all of our cognitions are in the end subjected to the formal condition of inner sense, namely time, as that in which they must all be ordered, connected, and brought into relations. This is the general remark on which one must ground everything that follows.[56]

In setting out the bringing into *relation* of cognitions in time, Kant here prioritizes the category of relation and foreshadows the central role that the Analogies will have in solving central problems within his project. But the question of the Deduction is not concerned with what sort of order of relations actually are made, but with the very possibility of

---

56   KANT, *Critique of Pure Reason*, A 98-9. Paul Guyer calls this section the 'fundamental premise of the Deduction' (Guyer, *Kant and the Claims of Knowledge*, p. 109).

synthesizing disparate representations into a single manifold that can be understood through the categories in general in its unity and totality.

Despite the complete re-write of the Deduction between the two versions of the *Critique* the fundamental answer that Kant provides, is that the synthesis of disparate representations into a single manifold is possible because of the transcendental unity of apperception, which Kant also calls the '*transcendental* unity of self-consciousness'[57] – the '*I think*' that is a intuition of the self that precedes all thinking, and which 'must be able to accompany all my representations,'[58] and as such can provide a transcendental unity across or between all those disparate representations; 'Thus' as Kant puts it, 'all manifold of intuition has a necessary relation to the *I think* in the same subject in which this manifold is to be encountered.'[59] This is the 'subject' that that Meillassoux denounces as the core of correlationism, but instead of following him once again down that path it is more useful to look at how the emphasis on time determination already identified it as problematic for the unity of apperception that is supposed to make it possible.

The problems that the Deduction encounters in its attempt to ground time determination are set out in Paul Guyer's *Kant and the Claims of Knowledge* (1987), a detailed study of the *Critique of Pure Reason* and the *Reflexionen* from silent decade in which it was conceived, developed and written. Guyer's argument does not identify a single fatal flaw in the Deduction that would necessitate its negation, but rather elucidates how the problems within the Deduction also point the way to their eventual overcoming in the later sections of the *Critique*, notably the Schematism, Analogies of Experience and ultimately the Refutation of Idealism.[60] In the Deduction Kant approaches the question of the unity (synthesis) of sensibility and understanding from two sides: the subjective unity and the objective unity, and the movement from one to the other itself constitutes an important step in the shrinking back/ forthcoming resolution at work in the Deduction. In Guyer's reading, the focus on apperception, as the subjective unity of self-consciousness, in the Deduction is incomplete and problematic, but this is because Kant was already pursuing a superior path to the resolution of the fundamental question of the Deduction.[61] The fundamental problem with apperception is the fact that in order to speak of its unity as fundamental that unity must always be both presupposed

57   Kant, *Critique of Pure Reason*, B 132.
58   *Ibid.*, B 131.
59   *Ibid.*, B 132.
60   Guyer, *Kant and the Claims of Knowledge*, p. 150.
61   *Ibid.*, p. 131.

and disavowed. Guyer quotes Kant's assertion that 'Only because I assign all perceptions to a single consciousness (that of original apperception) can I say of all perceptions that I am conscious of them,'[62] and then critiques is by pointing out that it,

> expresses merely a conditional necessity which cannot suffice to support the claim of objective affinity or the guaranteed possibility of an *a priori* synthesis of apperception. For by predicating his argument on the assumption of representations of which I *can say* that I am conscious, Kant restricts it to those representations for which self-consciousness and its concomitant consciousness of a connection are already conceded.[63]

The shift that occurs in the rewriting of the Deduction between the two editions of the *Critique* picks up on precisely this point and this is why the B-Edition attempts to emphasize apperception, presenting at the start of the Deduction rather than at the end as in the A-Edition. Kant is all-too-aware of the limitations of any presupposed self and, as will become explicit in the Refutation, the ultimate emptiness of the representation 'I' (it is no coincidence that that the argument of the Fourth Paralogism against transcendental psychology and its object of a unified and absolute soul from the A-Edition will move to become the basis for the Refutation of Idealism in the B-Edition). These limitations are exposed and reflected in the B-Deduction, where Kant writes, 'The empirical consciousness, which accompanies diverse representations, is in itself scattered and without relation to the identity of the subject.'[64] It is the *a priori* conditions of the synthesis of these diverse representations that will guarantee the unity of self-consciousness as much as the possibility of time-determination. As Guyer, returning to and drawing on earlier insights of the *Reflexionen*, puts it: 'apperception involves an awareness of the temporal succession of representations, and thus ... the conditions for determining such a succession are necessary for the consciousness of apperception itself.'[65] Here is the more original insight, that apperception and the very possibility of the 'I think' depends upon time-determination and does not itself make it possible. Kant, however, does not follow through this insight in its entirety just yet.

This is evident in his attempt to complete the deduction of the categories from the side of objective unity, which also highlights distinctive differ-

---

62   KANT, *Critique of Pure Reason*, A 122.
63   GUYER, *Kant and the Claims of Knowledge*, p. 144.
64   KANT, *Critique of Pure Reason*, B 133.
65   GUYER, *Kant and the Claims of Knowledge*, p. 150.

ences between space and time. Here Kant considers two examples from sensibility and attempts to show how that categories must be at work *a priori* in these perceptions. His first example is the empirical intuition of a house, where the unity of the object must appear from the synthesis of perceptions of the different sides of the house, which itself is only possible through the *a priori* condition of the unity of the form of space – that is, the homogeneity of absolute space within which this orientation to the sides of the house can take place. Kant connects this unity of the form of space to the category of quantity.[66] The second example that Kant considers is the shift, over time, from fluidity to solidity that occurs in the freezing of water and through this he attempts to show the necessity of the unity of the form of time here he runs into more difficulties. For here he cannot resort to homogeneity as in the case of space, for it is precisely the difference or change of time that is in question. Instead Kant calls upon the category of relation and the concept of cause to unite and determine the two different moments in time. However, this seems to merely beg the question, for the concept of cause seems to presuppose the unity of time, not determine it out of differences.

Indeed, Kant recognizes this problem arising from the fundamental difference in change over time and it is for this reason that he puts forward the need for a third thing, somehow homogenous to both concepts and appearance, what he calls a transcendental schema that is capable of mapping a concept onto an object. As what is homogenous to both concepts and appearance is their determination in time, it is precisely through time-determination that this schema will function. As Kant writes: 'Hence an application of the category to appearances becomes possible by means of the transcendental time-determination which, as the schema of the concept of the understanding, mediates the subsumption of the latter under the former.'[67] As has already been observed Kant fundamentally leaves this issue unresolved, instead alluding to the schematism as 'a hidden art in the depths of the human soul'[68] and occluding the issue of time determination once again with a nebulous and elusive subjectivity. However, he does once again relate this question of time-determination back to causation and once again to the category of relation.

Kant's eventual treatment of the issue of causation, and his solutions to Hume's problem of induction and the re-thinking of the principle of sufficient reason, occurs famously in the Second Analogy of Experience, when

---

66   KANT, *Critique of Pure Reason*, B 162.
67   *Ibid.*, A 139/B 178.
68   *Ibid.*, A 141/B 180-1.

he specifically deals with the way in which the category of causality, or succession, determines actual empirical experience. However, what is key to all of the Analogies – that time itself cannot be perceived[69] – also means that the Second Analogy alone does not provide the complete key to the aim of the Deduction. Instead, as is consistent with the aim of the Analogies, it merely shows how the application of the category of relation – in this case of the relation of causality and dependence – results in specific and concrete, yet nonetheless objective, empirical experience. Indeed, it is only in the Refutation of Idealism and with the necessity of objects in *space* outside of the subject, as something that can then be used as a way to present determination in general, that the full condition of the possibility of time-determination in particular is revealed.

The argument of the Refutation is relatively straightforward, but has important implication for the issue of time determination. Essentially it is a *reductio* of Cartesian problematic or sceptical idealism that shows that 'The mere, but empirically determined, consciousness of my own existence proves the existence of objects in space outside me.'[70] The proof that Kant presents of this theorem is that the time determination necessary for empirical self-consciousness, and by extension of the problems it involves, also for apperception, is only possible if there is something permanent and persistent against which the change of time can be gauged. This persistent thing cannot be found within the self or the representations through which the self experiences anything, as those are both only possible through time-determination itself. Therefore, as Kant puts it 'the determination of my existence in time is possible only by means of the existence of actual things that I perceive outside myself.'[71] The properly spatial nature of this perception of outer things is elaborated in the General Note on the System of Principles where Kant writes: 'we need an intuition *in space* (of matter), since space alone persistently determines, while time, however, and thus everything that is inner sense, constantly flows.'[72] The distinction that Kant

---

69   This claim is explicitly repeated in each of the three Analogies, at A181/B225, B233 and B257.

70   KANT, *Critique of Pure Reason*, B 275, The theorem of the Refutation.

71   *Ibid.*, B 275.

72   *Ibid.*, B 291. That time constantly flows is explicitly connected to the impossibility to ground anything determinate in the human subject is explicitly stated in this same argument as it is presented in the A-Edition Fourth Paralogism: 'time ... has in it nothing abiding, and hence gives cognition only a change of determinations, but not the determinable object. For in that which we call the soul [human subjectivity], everything is in continual flux' (A381).

implicitly makes here, between the flow of inner sense and the persistence of space, now specifically also of matter, begins to shift attention away from just the existence of things outside the subject in space, that is the *reductio* of Cartesian scepticism, and to show how Kant's arguments must also affect how the self or subject can be considered. This distinction is also highlighted in the Refutation itself, where Kant writes:

> The consciousness of myself in the representation *I* is no intuition at all, but merely an *intellectual* representation of the self-activity of the thinking subject. And hence this I does not have the least predicate of intuition that, as *persistent* could serve as the correlate for time-determination in inner sense, as, say, *impenetrability* in matter, as *empirical* intuition, does.[73]

The distinction here between the apperceptive self-activity of the thinking subject and the intuitions of inner sense as time-determinations, as two different self consciousnesses highlights the point at which Kant identifies how the possibility of the problem of idealism arises in the first place. It is by confusing these two, by assuming that the intellectual representation of self-activity could by itself be sufficient to provide the empirical intuition of self consciousness as determined in time, that the subject can cut itself off from the necessity of external objects in space as a necessary condition of time-determination, and thus discard the possibility of any proof or even necessity of the external world and slip into idealism and ultimately egoism (see also the note added to the Preface, Bxl-xli, where Kant denounces the need to continually provide arguments against idealism as a 'scandal of philosophy').

In making this distinction between apperception and inner sense the Refutation goes some way towards returning to a difference first set out in the Transcendental Aesthetic, which was, in part, effaced or overcome by the Deduction. Although this distinction will, as it does in the refutation, come down to the issue of the possibility of the spontaneity of self-affection, it actually plays out, again as it does in the Refutation, in terms of the distinction and relation of space and time. In the Aesthetic, Kant distinguishes between space as 'nothing other than merely the form of all appearances of outer sense'[74] and time as 'the form of inner sense, i.e., of the intuition of our self and our inner state.'[75] Importantly, at least at this point in the *Critique*, these two senses are strictly heterogeneous, Kant explicitly specifies

---

73   *Ibid.*, B 278.
74   *Ibid.*, A26/B42.
75   *Ibid.*, A33/B49.

that, 'Time can no more be intuited externally than space can be intuited as something in us.'[76] Kant makes this distinction in the Aesthetic for some of the same reasons as it is implied in the Refutation, that is, to guard against the danger of idealism by pointing to the necessity of *both* inner *and* outer sense, by making it impossible for one to produce the other (i.e., it is not possible to perceive the external world through inner sense alone). This prophylactic function of the distinction is more obvious when it is considered that the argument presented in the Refutation was originally contained in the properly critical section of the *Critique*, the Dialectic, in the form of the Fourth Paralogism. The analysis of sensibility found in the Aesthetic must always be considered in light of the over-arching distinction between sensibility and understanding (the 'two stems'[77] of human knowledge) that is necessary to escape the problems of the Antinomy of pure reason and the danger of transcendental illusion in general (of which rational psychology and its doctrine of the soul is one manifestation).

As has been shown above, the argument of the Deduction in fact proceeds by attempting to *overcome* the heterogeneity set out in the Aesthetic through a preference and prioritization of time and inner sense and the eventual replacement of the self-consciousness of inner sense with that of apperception, which also encompasses and includes the sensations of outer sense through their determination in time as appearances. While the Aesthetic appears to be clear about the heterogeneity of inner and outer sense, it is not quite so simple as even there Kant ascribes a certain priority to inner sense, he writes: 'Time is the *a priori* formal condition of all appearances in general. Space, as the pure form of all outer intuitions, is limited as an *a priori* condition merely to outer images.'[78] This statement pre-empts the 'fundamental premise' of the Deduction from A99, which sets out its main question as one of time determination. The Aesthetic, however, is not totally committed to this position, in addition to the general statement of heterogeneity, Kant also identifies the indeterminate nature of time itself, he writes:

> For time cannot be a determination of outer appearances; it belongs neither to a shape or a position, etc., but on the contrary determines the relation of representations in our inner state. And just because this inner intuition yields no shape we also attempt to remedy this through analogies, and represent the temporal sequence through a line progressing to infinity.[79]

---

76   *Ibid.*
77   *Ibid.*, A15/B29.
78   *Ibid.*, A34/B50.
79   *Ibid.*, A33/B50.

This section pre-empts and prefigures the conclusions of the Refutation and highlights a tension in the Aesthetic that plays out across the rest of the *Critique* as well as the rest of Kant's writings (see especially the *Leningrad Fragment* – 'On Inner Sense', R6316 (18:621-3) from around 1790-1[80] – and the *Opus Postumum*). Ultimately, this tension between time determination, apperception, the inner and outer senses and spatiality remains unresolved and problematic despite the work of Kant and his numerous interpreters.[81] However, in pinpointing this *as* a central tension of Kant's critical philosophy also provides a set of figures and figurations through which Meillassoux's criticism of Kant and the correlationist tradition, as well as Meillassoux's own positive philosophical system, can be examined.

The tension of self-consciousness as the distinction and sometime identity or confusion of inner sense and apperception is the central issue around which both Kant's entire system and his criticism of idealism and dogmatism revolve. Recognizing this and the fact that this tension is never resolved but remains problematic within Kant's philosophy also can be used as a key to unlock and explain Meillassoux's criticism of Kant as correlationist. Both Kant and Meillassoux commence with a rejection of the principle of sufficient reason, and both replace this principle with a reformulation of time and temporality; for Kant it is through the recognition of the importance transcendental time determination as being able to sequence disparate times into a single unity, while for Meillassoux it is through the hyper-chaos of his principle of unreason. Meillassoux criticizes Kant as being correlationist because of how

---

80   On the importance of this *Reflexion* see H. ROBINSON, 'A New Fragment of Immanuel Kant: "On Inner Sense"' H. ROBINSON, 'Inner Sense and the Leningrad Reflexion', G. ZOELLER, 'Making Sense out of Inner Sense', M. BAUM, 'Kant on Cosmological Apperception', all in *International Philosophical Quarterly* 29: 3 (1989); as well as H. ROBINSON, 'The Priority of Inner Sense,' *Kant Studien* 79 (1988), pp. 165-182.

81   R. PIPPIN refers to Kant's doctrine of inner sense as a 'dark theory' (*Kant's Theory of Form: An Essay on the Critique of Pure Reason*. New Haven: Yale University Press, 1982, p. 173); P. STRAWSON similarly identifies it as 'one of the obscurest points of all' (*Bounds of Sense: An Essay on Kant's Critique of Pure Reason*. London: Methuen & Co Ltd., 1966, p. 247) and distinguishes the distinction of the inner and the outer as one of the 'Four great dualities [that] dominate Kant's theory of the nature of human experience ... All [of which] appear in ... the Transcendental Aesthetic' (p. 47); H. ALLISON speaks about the 'inherently paradoxical' and 'exceedingly fragmented' nature of Kant's discussion of inner sense (*Kant's Transcendental Idealism: An Interpretation and Defense Revised and enlarged edition*. New Haven: Yale University Press, 2004, p. 276); and, G. W. GREEN, in his book of the same title, examines the entirety of the Critique in terms of what he calls 'the aporia of inner sense' (The Aporia of Inner Sense: The Self-Knowledge of Reason and the Critique of Metaphysics in Kant. Leiden: Koninklijke Brill, 2010).

this issue of time determination, and in turn possibility of all objective experience and knowledge, seems to rest entirely upon the subject. Meillassoux locates the argument that Kant puts forward for this entirely in the Transcendental Deduction. While it is certainly true that the argument of the Deduction focuses on subjectivity and the importance of self-consciousness through the unity of apperception (and thus is susceptible to the charge of correlationism), to focus on this exclusively and at the expense of any consideration of the rest of the *Critique* fatally curtails Kant's argument. The argument presented in the Deduction, with its excessive, almost myopic focus on apperception, is incomplete, even by Kant's own standards (a simple proof of this is the fact that it alone cannot resolve Hume's problem of induction, and must be supplemented by the Analogies at least). It is here that the tension identified begins to appear, for as the argument presented in the Deduction must be readdressed through the Analogies, Schematism and ultimately the B-Edition's Refutation of Idealism, the centrality of apperception is challenged and changed. This problematization of the centrality of dominance of apperception and subjectivity, and indeed the assertion and its arguments in general, casts doubt on Meillassoux's assertion that Kant definitely grounds his entire system in the subjectivity of apperception and endorses or inaugurates correlationism. By focusing entirely on the Deduction and meaningfully ignoring the Refutation, Meilassoux misses some of the subtlety, and, it must be admitted problems, of Kant's position and his attempts to work through it.

Setting aside the undeniable arguments for realism and materialism that it provides, the Refutation of Idealism also calls into question the emphasis that has been placed on the spontaneity and sufficiency of self-consciousness as apperception in the Deduction. Here Kant returns to the doctrine of inner sense as it was presented in the Aesthetic and through a reiteration of the argument that time can have no determinate objects, stresses the necessity of outer sense of objects in space for any time determination. The Refutation, thus, at most reverses the priority of time over space that appeared to operate in the Deduction, and at least disrupts any potential relationship between space and inner sense, reinforcing without entirely endorsing the heterogeneity between inner and outer sense given in the Aesthetic. Either way, space and outer sense now becomes vital, if somewhat disruptive, elements within Kant's system. This identification of the importance of spatiality casts new light on Meillassoux's criticism of Kant (and correlationism) as well as his own positive philosophy.

Just as spatiality is indispensible yet disruptive element within Kant's system, it can now be seen as performing a somewhat similar role within that of Meillassoux. The characterization of the objective world (in his case disconnected entirely from any subjectivity) as *external*, repeats the connection that Kant's Refutation of Idealism makes between objectivity and spatiality.[82] This alone should be enough to complicate Meillassoux's own prioritization of temporality as hyper-chaos, but the interference of spatiality goes deeper within his system. For it reveals an equivocation within the temporality that Meillassoux proposes, on the one hand time is the indeterminacy – yet regularity it must be noted – of hyper-chaos, and on the other it is the determined pastness of ancestrality. While Meillassoux pointedly does not engage with the issue of time determination as a question, he nonetheless implicitly provides an answer to it with his own use of the spatial metaphor to determine the pastness of the ancestral realm. Even if it is not explicitly engage with spatiality, just as he does not engage with the Refutation of Idealism, the (interconnected) arguments associated with both of them reflect back upon Meillassoux's philosophy and disrupt it in advance as well as open up a new path of enquiry with which it must deal.

Despite his polemical attempts to distance himself from Kant, closer inspection reveals that the path of philosophy that Meillassoux attempts to tread around Kant in fact commences from the same point (the rejection of the principle of sufficient reason), follows some of the same steps (its reconfiguration through temporality), and encounters some of the same difficulties (the disruptions involved in thinking time through the spatial metaphor). The aim of this comparison and its emphasis on continuities between the two thinkers rather than their antagonisms has been to attempt to sidestep the polemical nature of their engagement, and avoid simply endorsing one at the expense of the other. In setting aside the question of the opposition between Kant and Meillassoux, this comparison is able to expose how both are dealing with a similar set of problems, the objective determination of time and the question of time in general, and how both encounter a similar problem, the relation of time to space and spatiality as something disruptive. In turn this provides an alternative schema for the investigation of the set of problems that surround transcendental idealism, correlationism and speculative materialism, as well as the examination of the historical movements and developments associated with this set of philosophies.

---

82   In *Individuals: An Essay in Descriptive Metaphysics*, P. Strawson notes the connection between spatiality and objectivity and explicitly traces it back to Kant (London: Routledge, 1996, p. 62).

VIII

BRUNO LATOUR AND THE MIRACULOUS PRESENT OF ENUNCIATION

Erik Bordeleau

> So, there exists a form of original utterance that speaks of the present, of definitive presence, of completion, of the fulfilment of time, and which, because it speaks of it in the present, must always be brought forward to compensate for the inevitable backsliding of the instant towards the past
>
> Bruno Latour, *Rejoicing or the Torments of Religious Speech*

> "Science" only gives the impression of existing by turning its existence into permanent miracle.
>
> Bruno Latour, *The Pasteurization of France*

A drama of presence[1]

'In their flight toward the future, the Moderns are absent to themselves'. Bruno Latour uttered this sentence during the "Speculative Gestures" colloquium organized by Isabelle Stengers and Didier Debaise at Cerisy-la-Salle in July 2013. He had first given an inspiring talk on how *not* to deanimate scientific descriptions, as part of a larger reflection on storytelling and "Agency at the Time of the Anthropocene", which was later published in *New literary History[2]*, alongside an article by the archaeologist Ian Hodder on the entanglement of humans and things, and a reply to both of them by the philosopher Graham Harman.

The presence of Harman as a commentator in this context comes as no surprise. His object-oriented philosophy has been deeply influenced by Latour's metaphysical treaty *Irreductions*. Harman's crusade against po-

---

1   I would like to thank François Lemieux and Heather Davis for their invaluable presence by my side during the Cerisy conference. This text owes a lot to them both.

2   B. Latour, "Agency at the Time of the Anthropocene", in *New literary History,* Vol. 45, N° 1.

tentiality and for the affirmation of the primacy of actuality has found a decisive impulse in the idea that we need to go 'from the vertigo of power to
the simple and banal positivity of forces'.[3] Reciprocally, Latour's James-
ian attempt at cultivating a *'stubbornly realist attitude'*[4] in order to stay
close to the *pragmata* (the Greek word for thing) found in Harman's work
a source of inspiration. In 2004, Latour dedicated an important article to
exposing his views on matters of concern to Harman ("Why has Critique
Run out of Steam? From Matters of Fact to Matters of Concern") and
since then, on until 2008 or so, he repeatedly insisted on the importance of
adopting an object-oriented attitude with regards to inquiry and politics,
promoting the ideas of a Parliament of things and of an 'object-oriented
democracy'.[5] Nonetheless, during the 2008 debate at the London School
of Economics, published three years later under the title *The Prince and
the Wolf*,[6] Latour unexpectedly criticized the actualism depicted in *Irreductions* that Harman is so fond of. If *Irreductions* was a necessary book in
order to solve the problem of the humans/non-humans opposition, Latour
said, it now appeared to be 'a flawed, a completely flawed philosophy' that
was mainly useful for polemical reasons, precisely because it obliterates
the question of virtuality or potentiality.[7]

For Latour, the deployment of networks depicted in *Irreductions* leads to
a flat ontology that doesn't pay enough attention to the notion of trajectory,
thus painting everything in grey; it doesn't allow one to properly capture the
different modes of existence of things and beings – 'the key in which things
are sent, so to speak.'[8] Latour then explained that only three years after the
publication of *Irreductions*, he embarked on a multifaceted exploration of
regimes of enunciation that, more than 15 years later, culminated in a book
that appears as Latour's *opus magnum*: *An Inquiry into Modes of Existence*.[9]
Latour's interest in the inner narrativity of things that I will explore further
in this article exemplifies the ultimate consequences of this radical turn-over.

---

3   B. LATOUR, "Préface de la nouvelle édition", in *Irreductions* (Paris : La découverte,
     2001), p. 8 (my translation).
4   B. LATOUR, "Why critique has run out of steam", in *Critical Inquiry*, Special issue
     on the Future of Critique, Vol 30 n° 2, p. 231.
5   B. LATOUR, "From Realpolitik to Dingpolitik or How to Make Things Public",
     Bruno Latour and Peter Weibel (eds.), *Making Things Public: Atmosphere of
     Democracy* (Cambridge: MIT Press, 2005), p. 16.
6   B. LATOUR and G. HARMAN, *The prince and the Wolf* (Washington: Zero Books, 2011).
7   *Ibid.*, p. 46.
8   *Ibid.*, p. 48.
9   B. LATOUR, *An Inquiry into Modes of Existence* (Cambridge MA: Harvard
     University Press 2013).

Let's come back to Latour's presentation at Cerisy. There he showed how, in scientific texts, performances precede competencies and are therefore inherently 'animated'. 'There is no other way, Latour maintains, to define the characters of the agents they [the scientific accounts] mobilize but via the *actions* through which they have to be slowly captured'.[10] It is in this sense that, insofar as it is composed of meaningful and active agents – '*as long as they act, agents have meaning*'[11] – the world for Latour is inherently *dramatic*. It is this ontological proposition that I would like to explore more at length in the following pages.

After his talk, Latour found himself in a heated debate with the discussant and friend Donna Haraway. The discussion was moderated by Isabelle Stengers and concerned the modes of figuration of Gaia. Haraway opened the discussion with an eco-feminist critique of the epic and its totalizing and universalizing account of coming catastrophes. Against the generalizing and paralysing effect attributed to apocalyptic narratives, she argued for localized, speculative fabulations that multiply human and non-human viewpoints so as to transform our relation with mobilization and question our ways of responding to the ecological crisis. It is along this line of thought that Haraway somehow provocatively came to suggest that our modes of existence should enter into a process of 'detumescence'. Was that term at least partly referring to Latour's rather pastoral rhetoric, magnanimous demeanours and predilection for all-encompassing 'charitable fiction' (as he describes his AIME project)? Was her abrasive depiction including Latour, a thinker so skilful at occupying the stage and unabashedly at ease at staging modernity 'at large'? The tone of Haraway's intervention was passionate and polemical, yet friendly. It was unquestionably an amazing moment of thought. She was certainly pushing Latour to his very limits, but she was doing it as someone who enjoyed Latour's trust. In fact, although the theme was never fully disclosed, there was little doubt that underpinning the discussion between them was the issue of what to do with the Christian tradition and its world-making modes of narration.

It is no secret that Latour is a practicing Catholic and that his rather idiosyncratic conception of religion plays an overarching role in his system of thought, especially in relation to the possibility of being absent – and, most importantly, present – to oneself and the world. Haraway's response to Latour seemed to garner spontaneous approval among the audience.

---

10   B. LATOUR, "Agency at the Time of the Anthropocene", in *New literary History* Vol.45 N. 1 (2014), p. 11.
11   *Ibid.*, p. 12.

Her fierce anti-monotheistic stance and praise for multi-species muddling seemed to be in tune with the general orientation of the week-long encounter. Although the organizers put forth no exclusive definition, they had presented the speculative gestures as 'situated virtualities' and ways to engage with 'a possible'. The conference's focus on the situatedness of knowledge production practices is, no surprise here, heavily influenced by Haraway's work. It echoed most directly with her presentation at Cerisy, in which she spoke of the mediality of worlding processes and how we cannot think but through apparatuses of thinking. She illustrated her point with these sharp and thought-provoking formulas inspired by Marilyn Strathern's seminal book *Reproducing the Future*: 'It matters what thoughts think thoughts; what knowledges know knowledge; what relations relate relations; what worlds world worlds; what stories tell stories.' Celebrating the 'partial takes' and 'continuous weaving' involved in the arts of storytelling, she promoted an ethics of 'staying with the trouble', stressing the fact that 'response-ability is almost never a matter of choice, but of dealing with the hand that was imparted to us.'

Latour's approach to the question of the modes of figuration of Gaia or to the kind of arts of narration to be fostered in the age of the Anthropocene is closely related to that of Haraway. They both tend to put emphasis on the eventfulness of the act of storytelling. In fact, as Latour puts it, they think of narrativity not as 'a feature of the language *about* the world' but as '*a property of the world itself*'.[12] In his criticism of how, in the 'scientific worldview', 'the agency of all the entities making up the world has been made to vanish',[13] Latour does indeed side with Haraway: 'The great paradox of the "scientific worldview" is to have succeeded in *withdrawing historicity* from the world. And with it, of course, the inner *narrativity* that is part and parcel of being in the world – or, as Donna Haraway prefers to say, "with the world"'.[14]

Why then was Latour so manifestly put on the defensive by Haraway during their challenging dialogue? What could be so passionately at stake in their discussion, considering that they share a common understanding of how inner narrativity or 'storytelling is not just a property of language, but one of the many consequences of being thrown in a world that is, by itself, fully articulated and active'?[15] If Latour agrees with Haraway

---

12   *Ibid.*
13   *Ibid.*, p. 13.
14   *Ibid.*, p. 13.
15   *Ibid.*, p. 14.

on the need 'to *distribute* agency as far and in as *differentiated* a way as possible',[16] he nonetheless holds a very different position on the sense and role of apocalypse, a structuring idea of the Christian art of storytelling and activating presence if there is one.

Latour's act of enunciation in response to Haraway's sustained critical fire is worth describing in detail, as it constitutes a sort of embodied and performative hint at how science and religion intersect in his thought. Around the end of the discussion, Latour responded to a question coming from the audience about Foucault and his treatment of conversion or *metanoia* in antiquity. It was at that moment that he said, in a careful and somehow prospective way: 'In their flight toward the future, the Moderns are absent to themselves'. This was but the first trait of a lively gesture of thought, the inauguration of a *remise en présence*[17] that couldn't but emanate, I daresay, from his soul, as it is of 'the near, the origin, the present my [his] soul longs for.'[18] The heavily charged and rather enigmatic sentence – what does Latour allude to exactly when he suggest that Moderns are absent to themselves? – hovered up in the air, suspended, as no interlocutor seemed to take account of it. So then, a few minutes later, Latour reasserted his point. He gazed upwards, threw his arms up and then energetically brought them back towards him, as if invoking some greater force or gathering his strength in order to establish a new point of departure in the exchange. And then, against all odds, he defended the idea of apocalypse. He made it resonate with clarity and technical distinction, bringing it back in the discussion in spite of the fashionable disregard it was subjected to up until then. Latour basically said that we shouldn't deprive ourselves of the resources of apocalypse, for they allow us to pose the problem of our presence in the world, of *how to be present* to the challenges we are now facing. And just then, the bell announcing lunchtime rang. The debate stopped suddenly. While the participants slowly dispersed, I stayed there, immobile, with a friend who was just as struck as myself by what had just happened, and we started to collect our thoughts about this unexpected turn of events, trying to wrap our minds around it. More than a year later, I guess I'm still at it.

The questions of presence and of the activating relation to the future are crucial to Latour's work. For Latour, apocalypse ties in closely with how

---

16   *Ibid.*, p. 15.
17   This key formulation is quite hard to translate in English. Literally, we could say "put back in presence"; but the translator of *Rejoicing* has preferred another solution that privileges the relation to spatial proximity: "made close again".
18   B. LATOUR, *Rejoicing or the Torments of Religious Speech*, p. 98.

post-human Gaians or, to use Latour's preferred formulation, the 'Earth-bound', envisage the future and inhabit the present. It is an essential histori-cal ingredient that, he suggests, should not be left aside in our attempt to weave 'the various threads of geostory' in new ways.[19] Latour's realist dra-ma of presence[20] includes the notion of apocalypse within a complex and, at least at first sight, paradoxical understanding of how 'in the real world time flows from the future to the present.'[21] In this passage, Latour refers polemically to the reductionist version of an objective 'natural world' that is conceived of as inherently drama-free and should remain so, insofar as sci-entific rigour precisely consists in resisting the temptation of anthropomor-phizing it. The speculative image of thought Latour elaborates against the idea of inert and deanimated matter can only be fully understood, I would argue, if we bring to the picture how he conceives of the fabrication of pres-ent persons within the realm or mode of existence of religion. In both cases, to put it more succinctly, what is at stake is the affirmation of a regime of enunciation that resists the 'inevitable backsliding of the instant towards the past' and coincides with a form of temporality that, radiating from a 'mi-raculous' present, challenges common definitions of causality. Therein lies, I would argue, the crux of Latour's renewed political theology.

"Apocalypse is our chance"

A few weeks after the Cerisy debate, Latour gave an interview to the French newspaper *Le monde* in which he extrapolated his conception of apocalypse and how it could affect positively our perception of the current situation. Questioned about the discrepancy between the gravity of the ecological crisis and our ability to react appropriately to it, Latour suggest-ed that we are witnessing a movement of 'understandable withdrawal in

---

19   B. LATOUR, "Agency at the Time of the Anthropocene", p. 15.

20   I'm referring here to Ernesto de Martino's concept. In his study on the magical world, the Italian anthropologist described how presence in the world is constant-ly at risk of dissolution and needs to be collectively reinstituted through different existential techniques. '[The sorcerer] transforms the critical moments of being-in-the-world in a courageous and dramatic decision, that of situating oneself in the world.' E. DE MARTINO, *Le monde magique* (Paris: Institut d'édition Sanofi-Syn-thélabo, 2003), p. 126. This approach to the consolidation of a being-there bears close parallels with what Latour calls in *Rejoicing* 'the making of individuals made close again' [la fabrication des personnes remises en présence], p. 155.

21   B. LATOUR, "Agency at the Time of the Anthropocene", p. 13.

front of the coming apocalypse.'[22] With his typical enthusiasm and acting out as some sort of great motivator and decipherer of the French people, Latour expressed his admiration for the 'marvellous association between the trust in science, republican spirit and modernization'[23] that permeated the formation of French institutions. The tone and tenor of Latour's public address bears great importance with regard to the type of political intervention he concretely envisages and performs in his speeches and writings. For Latour, the solution to the global ecological crisis inevitably passes through an in-depth reform and revitalization of our institutions, primarily that of the State – which makes him rather unpopular among a great part of the left intelligentsia. In this regard (and the same applies to his long-term friend Peter Sloterdijk, to whom he dedicated his Gifford Lectures entitled *Facing Gaia: Six Lectures on the Political Theology of Nature*) Latour can be thought of as some sort of creative and megalopathic adviser of the Anthropocenic Prince.

Latour's reference to the notion of apocalypse is enmeshed in a description of our current state of affairs that involves the State as an unavoidable collective actor. In fact, although he states that 'we are assuredly in a situation of revolution',[24] it is one of such a novel kind that the revolutionary and anti-capitalist traditions appear to be, in his opinion, largely irrelevant. Indeed, facing the great challenges of our times requires equipping the State with more accurate and perceptive tools so that it can better 'palpate', 'experiment and produce the general will'.[25] I won't comment further on Latour's pragmatist and optimistic views about the State as an instrument of collective representation and as a 'great machine to distillate general will'[26]. What I'm interested in here is to show how Latour's characterization of apocalypse as an opportunity is a key element in his system of thought, elucidating both his conception of semio-ontological dramaticity and the eulogical and evangelical tenor of his political mode of address. The latter must be understood in a generous and expanded Nietzschean way, as suggested by Sloterdijk in his *The Competition of Good news: Nietzsche Evangelist* in which he presents his own account of modern disenchantment and path to overcome it: 'And if the contemporary is

---

22   B. LATOUR, "L'apocalypse est notre chance", *Le monde*, September 20th, 2013, available online here: http://www.lemonde.fr/idees/article/2013/09/20/bruno-latour-l-apocalypse-est-notre-chance_3481862_3232.html (my translation).

23   *Ibid.*

24   *Ibid.*

25   *Ibid.*

26   *Ibid.*

not capable of praise anymore, isn't it precisely because it was forced to allow primacy to the irremediable?'[27]

Latour proposes a practical definition of apocalypse that rejects its common assimilation with the idea of catastrophe, bringing forth its original meaning as 'revelation' without mentioning it explicitly:

> Apocalypse signifies the certitude that the future has changed shape, and that we can do something. It's as if the form of time had changed and that, therefore, we could now at last do something. It is a thought for action against stupor and panic. (...) apocalypse is the understanding that something is happening and that we must make ourselves worthy of what is coming to us. It is, in fact, a revolutionary situation. [28]

This passage could allow for an extended theological exegesis. I will try to stay as brief as possible, focusing on how Latour envisages the idea of apocalypse in relation to a transformed – activating – relation to the future. Latour's definition of apocalypse is technical and generic enough to be extended to any moment whatsoever. In this example it works in relation to the massive advent of the Anthropocene, but nothing prevents it from applying, with most interesting results, to our way of characterizing agency in scientific narratives. In this sense, while he insists on the importance of being object-oriented, Latour's reference to apocalypse is essentially concerned with getting our subjectivity right, that is, with favouring a politically informed and active stance in time. In the interview he mobilized the dramatic and historical resources of apocalypse in a rather conventional way, so as to reveal the present-informed-by-the-future as an opportunity to be seized. But in fact for Latour, following Whitehead's conception of the atomicity of becoming, it is the fabric of the world itself that is made of a myriad of *actual occasions* to be acknowledged and 'revealed' as such.

The certitude of which Latour talks with regard to the change affecting present time bears surprising similarity with how Christianity conceives of faith as *what makes the future present* in the subject who believes. For example, in his encyclical letter about hope, Cardinal Ratzinger explains how 'eternal life' is but a vibrant relation to a future that is already there:

> Faith draws the future into the present, so that it is no longer simply a 'not yet'. The fact that this future exists changes the present; the present is touched

---

27   P. SLOTERDIJK, *La compétition des Bonnes Nouvelles: Nietzsche évangéliste*, Trans. By Olivier Mannoni (Paris: Mille et une nuits, 2002), p. 55 (my translation).

28   B. LATOUR, "L'apocalypse est notre chance".

by the future reality, and thus the things of the future spill over into those of the present and those of the present into those of the future.[29]

Even though he talks about certainty in his own account of apocalypse, Latour would most certainly contest a definition of faith that involves a dimension of belief. 'Faith and belief have nothing to say to one another'[30] Latour vehemently sustains. As is well known, an essential component of his work aims at debunking the notion of belief. His book *On the Modern Cult of the Factish Gods* is fully dedicated to show that 'a Modern is someone who believes that others believe.'[31] He posits that we should do without a category producing an undesirable distinction between interiority and exteriority, passivity and activity, theory and practice. And indeed, belief is just too reductive and subjective a category when it comes to giving a proper – that is, fantastic, ambitious and, in the end, realist enough – account of how the world as we experience and discover it is composed of indivisible events irreducible to a strict subject/object division.

Latour doesn't mobilize the resources of apocalypse in the name of religion understood as some sort of *supplement d'âme* for a desolated 'material' world. He doesn't want to spiritualize or re-enchant the world – presenting things in this way would mean that one has already lost the (ever-enchanted) world in the first place. On the contrary, as he nicely puts it, 'The symbolic is the magic of those who have lost the world. It is the only way they have found to maintain "in addition" to "objective things" the "spiritual atmosphere" without which things would "only" be natural.'[32] If anything, Latour wants to bring our attention to the dimension of (real)

---

29 BENEDICTUS XVI, *Spe Salvi* (Vatican, Libreria Editrice Vaticana, 2007), available online here: http://www.vatican.va/holy_father/benedict_xvi/encyclicals/documents/hf_ben-xvi_enc_20071130_spe-salvi_en.html.

30 B. LATOUR, "'Thou Shalt Not Take the Lord's Name in Vain': Being a Sort of Sermon on the Hesitations in Religious Speech" *RES: Anthropology and Aesthetics*, N.39 (Spring 2001), pp. 215-234 (p. 231).

31 B. LATOUR, *On the Modern Cult of the Factish Gods*, Trans. by Catherine Porter and Heather MacLean (Durham and London: Duke University Press, 2010), p. 2

32 B. LATOUR "Irreductions", in *The Pasteurization of France*, Trans. by Alan Sheridan and John Law (Cambridge: Harvard University Press ,1993), p. 187. One can also think of this famous passage from *We have never been Modern*: 'They [the antimoderns] take on the courageous task of saving what can be saved: souls, minds, emotions, interpersonal relations, the symbolic dimension, human warmth, local specificities, hermeneutics, that margins and the peripheries. An a dmirable mission, but one that would be more admirable still if all those sacred vessels were actually threatened.' B. LATOUR, *We have never been Modern*, trans. by Catherine Porter (Cambridge: Harvard University Press, 1993), p. 123.

futurity inherent in every present. In this sense, faith is about nourishing a
noble and speculative disposition towards the future, one that participates
decisively in the plural arts of immanent attention.[33]

Adam S. Miller's remarkable *Speculative Grace: Bruno Latour and
Object-Oriented Theology* underlines how, for Latour, religion is an ethical
exercise in immanent attention aimed at staying with the historical trouble
– a training to live by and speak *from things*. '*Religion*, he says, *is what
breaks our will to go away*.'[34] Against the grain of the usual association
of religion with the other-wordly, Latour affirms that 'it is religion that
attempts to access the this-worldly in its most radical presence (...)'.[35] Inversely, he can't seem to have harsh enough words for any form of escap-
ism: 'The dream of going to another world is just that: a dream, and probably also a deep sin.'[36]

The heart of Latour's realism thus stands, paradoxically as it would appear at first glance, in his conception of religion. Or, to be more precise: La-

---

33   In *The Present Feeling: Contemporary Art and the Question of Time*, a collective
text that will be published in the catalogue of the 2014 Montreal Biennale, the
SenseLab explores the question of futurity in a way that is different from, but not
incompatible with, the narrative art of immanent attention suggested by Latour.
For the SenseLab, 'to respond ably with the world in the making is to align
oneself eventfully with the futurity in the present.' In contrast with Latour's insistence on the way in which the future is made present, the SenseLab thinks of
the responsibility towards what is coming in terms of an aesthetic of potential
responsiveness, promoting an enhanced sensibility to the enmeshed temporalities forming the contemporary. 'Think of the contemporary as the commingling
of all these temporalities: the *con*-temporary as the textured "*with*ness" of times.
Feel the textures inherent to this conjecture of experience. Feel how immanent *a
future* is in this moment, feel how far, how close, how *else* it is to yourself, how
topologically intimate it is to itself. *Now*, imagine the future as *anything that
could come out of the mix*, as the potential of all that vibrates and comes together in witness. What could come is always still in the mix. This potential
– *futurity* – can only be felt. In the present.' The SenseLab's focus on futurity as
potential diverges significantly from the agents' inner historicity as highlighted
in Latour's approach. It is more prone to celebrate the burstability of *a* life and
the creative involution inherent to becoming-animal.

34   Adam S. Miller, *Speculative Grace: Bruno Latour and Object-Oriented Theology* (New York: Fordham University Press, 2013) p. 145.

35   B. Latour, "Will Non-Humans Be Saved? An Argument in Ecotheology",
Journal of the Royal Anthropological Institute, Vol 15 (2009) pp. 459-475 (p.
464), cited in Adam S. Miller *Speculative Grace: Bruno Latour and Object-
Oriented Theology*, p. 157.

36   B. Latour, "Will Non-Humans Be Saved? An Argument in Ecotheology", p. 473,
cited in *Speculative Grace: Bruno Latour and Object-Oriented Theology*, p. 156.

tour draws the ultimate consequences of the most singular feature of Judeo-Christianity, namely its thoroughly historical perspective. In a move similar to those readers of Leibniz who cancel God from his system and keep the thus liberated and anarchic monads, he subtracts the idea of an unearthly Providence in order to emphasize the Christian sense of *historical contingency*.[37] In the wake of Martin Rudwick's work on geohistory, from whom he retains that 'when geohistory began to "burst the limits of time" it was not to escape from the narrow prison of the Church's teachings,'[38] Latour takes the Bible as a model of historically grounded narrative. He thus obtains a rather counter-intuitive yet convincing way of resisting the Modernist or rationalist divide between science and religion. In his Gifford lecture, this operation culminates in his presentation of Gaia as a fully secularized, realist and contingent historical figure. The keyword here is history, as it brings together narrativity and contingent factuality. As suggested earlier, Latour's realism is anchored in a strong conception of narration:

> I use the word 'narrative' to designate the specific ontology of events that might have unfolded otherwise, events that had no plan, that are not lead by any Providence, journeys that succeed or fail depending on constant retelling and continual re-evaluation that modifies, once again, their contingent meaning.[39]

Gaia is the name of a radically secularized and immanent *geohistory*. If Latour sides with Lovelock and his contested choice of term, it is not because the concept of Gaia might suggest a touchy-feely 'sentient being', but because it 'captures the distributed intentionality of all the agents that are modifying their surroundings to suit themselves better.'[40]As Latour

---

37   I would suggest that Latour's realist stance takes its full significance when conceived in relation to the idea that Christianity favours a sense of *active personality*. Latour's dramatic realism is indeed thoroughly personalist. Or to put it in other words: the last and fully differentiated word of Latour's radical narrativism is that of (a) *person*. I cannot argue this point more in details here. It would require discussing in details how his philosophy draws from and resonates with William James' conception of the relation between theism and action, and with Whitehead's remarks on actuality and the question of evil. For a preliminary attempt at elucidating this question, see Erik Bordeleau, "La méthode de dramatisation et la question 'Qui?'", *Inflexions* N°8, 2015.

38   B. LATOUR "The puzzling face of a secular Gaia", *Facing Gaia: Six lectures on the political theology of nature*, Gifford Lectures on Natural Religion, Edinburgh, 18th-28th of February 2013, p. 73. The lectures are available online here: http://www.bruno-latour.fr/sites/default/files/downloads/GIFFORD-SIX-LECTURES_1.pdf.

39   B. LATOUR, "The puzzling face of a secular Gaia", p. 72.

40   *Ibid.*, p. 67.

explains against the idea of natural actors 'playing on the planks of an inanimate stage':[41]

> every organism that is taken as the point of departure of a biochemical reaction should be seen not as thriving 'in' an environment, but as *curbing* the environment to accommodate its need to thrive better into it. In that sense, every organism intentionally manipulates its surroundings to its own benefit.[42]

Gaia thus gives a name to the all-encompassing and rather cruel game of inter-capture between a myriad of agents pursuing 'their interest all the way to the bitter end.'[43] When conceived as such,

> the Blue Planet suddenly stands out as what is made of a long concatenation of historical, local, hazardous, specific and contingent events as if it were the temporary outcome of a 'geohistory' as attached to specific places and dates as the Biblical narrative, that is, exactly what was not to be taken into account when considered simply as a falling body among all the others.[44]

We now have all the elements required to give a concluding, if not entirely satisfactory, account of how Latour conceives of the headlong rush of the Moderns. Moderns are damned insofar as they believe that the truly rationalist way to be in the world is to flatten futurity. In this perspective, materialism is the ultimate idealism. Matter is the illusory substance that supposedly flows purely *'from past to present'*,[45] the other-worldly thing in which 'the consequences are *already there* in the cause', and for which therefore there is 'no suspense to expect, no sudden transformation, no metamorphosis, no ambiguity.'[46] Alongside their fetish matter, Moderns too would like to simply flow from past to present. Their conception of deanimated matter conflates with the most insane ascesis, that of becoming a pure and unreal flow of information without transformation. Inversely, and against all odds, Latour maintains that 'in the real world time flows from the future to the present'. Life is but a zone of contingent, metamorphic and always somehow miraculous encounters. Acting as some sort of secular prophet of the puzzling Gaia, Latour exposes us to a civilizational choice. He calls us to stand up to the challenge posed by an animated and

---

41 *Ibid.*
42 *Ibid.*
43 *Ibid.*, p. 69.
44 *Ibid.*, p. 55.
45 B. Latour, "Agency at the Time of the Anthropocene", p. 10.
46 *Ibid.*

inherently dramatic *materiality*, one that is produced by a constant and active re-addressing of time that commands 'a realist definition of the many *occasions* through which agencies are being discovered.'[47] And there opens a realist drama of presence, in which things are thrown into the risky business of existing and organisms-that-person proliferate joyfully.

*

Contrary to what they often say of themselves, Modernists are not forward-looking, but almost exclusively *backward*-looking creatures. This is why the irruption of Gaia surprises them so much. Since they have no eyes in the back of their head, they *deny* it is coming at them at all, as if they were too busy fleeing the horrors of the times of old. It seems that their vision of the future had blinded them to where they were going; or rather, as if what they meant by the future was entirely made of their rejected past without any realistic content about 'things to come.' (French usefully distinguishes between 'le futur' and 'l'avenir.')[48]

47   B. Latour, "Agency at the Time of the Anthropocene", p. 14.
48   B. Latour, "War of the Worlds: Humans against Earthbound", *Facing Gaia: Six lectures on the political theology of nature*, p. 106.

IX

PHENOMENOLOGICAL ONTOLOGY AND PRACTICAL REASON

A Response to Meillassoux's After Finitude

ANDREA ZHOK

1. What is at Stake?

In the contemporary philosophical landscape scientific realism, especially in the form of an overt support to naturalistic approaches, is arguably the most widespread theoretical approach worldwide. Curiously enough, Quentin Meillassoux (henceforth shortened as M.) in his recent work *After Finitude* (*Après la finitude*)[1] regards realism as a minority view among contemporary philosophers, while he considers approaches like Husserl's phenomenology, Wittgenstein's language analysis and their manifold heritage to represent the dominant theoretical attitude in contemporary thought[2]. Whatever one may think of this evaluation (which I seriously doubt), it does have a positive implication: M.'s critical analysis shows an unusual degree of care and discernment in tackling his polemical object. I especially appreciate that with regard to *phenomenology*, which is a theoretical approach I mostly endorse, since most criticisms of the phenomenological approach inspired by scientific realism are often embarrassingly shallow.[3] On the contrary, M. devises a radical attack to some of the core tenets of phenomenology, while showing a good understanding of them.

Let us briefly recall here the outlines of M.'s work. *After Finitude* is articulated in five chapters. Roughly, the first two mainly have a critical character (*pars destruens*), while the remaining three try to provide elements for a renewed approach to realism (*pars construens*). In Ch. 1, M. introduces

---

1   Q. MEILLASSOUX, *After Finitude. An Essay on the Necessity of Contingency* (London: Continuum 2008). Original edition *Après la finitude. Essai sur la nécessité de la contingence* (Paris: Seuil 2006)].

2   MEILLASSOUX, *After Finitude*, p. 6 ff.

3   Cf. D. DENNETT, *Consciousness Explained* (Boston: Back Bay Books 1991), p. 57 ff.

his polemical target, which is labelled 'correlationism'. Correlationism is a term of art that embraces a very comprehensive philosophical framework, including some of the most influential meditations of twentieth Century, from Husserlian phenomenology to Wittgensteinian language analysis. What such diverse approaches share, their 'correlationist' core, would be the thesis that it is dogmatic and naïve to entertain the possibility to talk about any object (inclusive of any *real* object) without implying simultaneous reference to a subjective dimension (consciousness, language).

Correlationism is deemed to be essentially incompatible with any kind of realism. The 'correlationist' philosopher would position herself in a sort of 'transparent cage',[4] which forbids her access to the *'great outdoors'* where classical philosophy dared to venture: under correlationist premises we would never be in a position to sensibly talk about reality in itself, about the Absolute, about ontology in any substantive sense.

For M., philosophy is forcefully called to question correlationism in the wake of a simple remark, and precisely that '[e]mpirical science is today capable of producing statements about events anterior to the advent of life as well as consciousness'.[5] Philosophy is required to take a radical stance towards natural science insofar as scientific assertions posit both life and consciousness as *relative and local events in a reality that subsists regardless of life and consciousness*. These assertions seem straightforwardly incompatible with the correlationist thesis, according to which it makes no sense to speak of *being* before and irrespective of *being given to a consciousness*.[6]

M. calls *'ancestral'* events all those events that are set by scientific accounts as subsistent before life and consciousness existed anywhere in the universe. The crucial stance that the philosopher is required to take concerns the ontological status of ancestral events (e.g., the Big Bang, the emergence of life on Earth, etc.). M. thinks that the correlationist is forced to a paradoxical stance, such that scientific accounts of ancestral statements must be regarded both as *true* and *inconceivable*: '*[T]he ancestral statement is a true statement, in that it is objective, but one whose referent cannot possibly have actually existed in the way this truth describes it*'.[7] According to M. the correlationist, even in the most refined form of transcendental idealism (Kant, Husserl), should realize that his position is straightforwardly incompatible with scientific realism; therefore, the cor-

---

4   MEILLASSOUX, *After Finitude*, p. 7.
5   *Ibid.*, p. 9.
6   *Ibid.*, p. 14.
7   *Ibid.*, p. 16.

relationist should take the courage to say that all scientific statements about the 'thing-in-itself' (as in ancestral assertions) are *illusory*.[8] From this point of view Husserl's transcendental idealism, Berkeley's subjective idealism or Hegel's absolute idealism would be indistinguishable.[9]

In Ch. 2, M. completes his criticism of correlationism by arguing that correlationism turns out to be a paradoxical ally of fideism and irrationalism. The reason for that involuntary alliance would be that correlationism outlaws the possibility to rationally delegitimize '*irrational* discourses about the absolute on the pretext of their irrationality'.[10] Since correlationism is not in a position to make rational assertion on absolute reality, it would actually clear the way for fideistic claims.

In Ch. 3, M. begins to provide some positive arguments that should finally lead him to gain a kind of novel Cartesian access to the absolute. He argues for the validity of a first unshakable ontological truth: the absoluteness and necessity of contingency.[11] From this first notion a second strong thesis is obtained, that is, the absolute validity of non-contradiction at an ontological level.[12] These theses should allow M. to revive the Cartesian idea of primary qualities, which are properties that are mathematizable and are posited as real independently of any human subjectivity. Primary qualities can then be used in scientific accounts of reality in itself.

In Ch. 4, M. takes up again and radicalizes Hume's idea of contingency, by rejecting all arguments that assume that we could exclude absolute contingency on the basis of our experience of regularity.

In Ch. 5, he states that modern science as mathematical science for the first time enables a meaningful discussion of ancestral events, i.e., of reality before consciousness and thought.[13] '[S]cience's dia-chronic statements assume that the 'question of the witness' has become irrelevant to knowledge of the event'.[14] He argues that the mathematization of science gives access to a realm of pure possibilities, which need no reference to any kind of subjectivity.[15]

The book comes somehow abruptly to an end by acknowledging that

---

8.   Meillassoux, *After Finitude*, p. 17.
9   *Ibid.*, p. 18.
10   *Ibid.*, p. 41.
11   *Ibid.*, p. 59.
12   *Ibid.*, p. 67.
13   *Ibid.*, p. 113.
14   *Ibid.*, p. 116.
15   *Ibid.*, p. 117.

the possibility of empirical science in realistic terms requires a proof of the stability of laws of nature, proof that M. is unable to provide.

M.'s text seems much more convincing in its *pars destruens* than in its *pars construens*, and since there would be anyway no room for a systematic confrontation, I will propose a discussion just of the critical theses that apply to the phenomenological perspective. In fact, I happen to share most of the 'correlationist' theses stigmatized by M., while at the same time supporting realism of a kind,[16] thus it seems that if M. is right I must be badly wrong.

Thus, in the following, I will focus on three crucial passages in M.'s text, from whose interpretation and plausibility depends the overall tenability of M.'s criticism. While I do believe that most of M.'s arguments can be successfully countered by specific analyses belonging to the phenomenological tradition, I think that a reply centered on philological qualifications and exegetic illustrations would be scarcely fruitful. A preferable strategy would be to take the opportunity of M.'s criticisms in order to outline a phenomenologically inspired vision that could make room for some of M.'s theoretical aspirations, while providing a more comprehensive ground for them. This would ideally be our aim. In the present limits this strategy can be pursued only in a restricted way, still, I hope at least to provide some productive suggestion to be further developed.

Let us come to the core of the matter. I think that there are three strategic theses on which the *pars destruens* of the text hinges: 1) the idea that correlationism, inclusive of Husserl's phenomenology, equates *being with being given to consciousness*; 2) the idea that correlationism is forced to an *anti-realist stance when it comes to deal with 'ancestral' events*; 3) the idea that the time of science can be considered a *condition for the taking place of the transcendental*. We will deal in turn with each of these theses.

2. Do We Really Know What We Mean By 'Real'?

From now on, since 'correlationism' includes 'phenomenology' and I am going to defend phenomenological positions, I will mostly substitute the second term for the first.

16   The philosophical term 'realism' is notoriously far from univocal. In their most general sense all 'realisms' support the idea that there are mind-independent entities. *What* these entities are, how the mind can *account for* them, and how to conceive the relevant *mind*, are the crucial qualifications whose variance generates all genres of 'realism'.

In the first pages of the text M. outlines the general position of 'correlationists', inclusive of phenomenologists. According to M., phenomenologists 'will maintain that it is naïve to think we are able to think *something* (...) while abstracting from the fact that it is invariably we who are thinking that something'.[17] He holds that phenomenologists consider an absurdity to believe both that 'being is not coextensive with manifestation' and that '*manifestation* is not the *givenness of a world*, but rather an intra-worldly occurrence'.[18]

This is the primal core of M.'s criticism and at first sight it may seem a justified statement. Indeed, Husserl considers that any object is an intentional object and that, if something exists for us, it must somehow affect our mind. This thesis can be expanded by saying that *objective* existence demands subjective experience. The point is that whenever we claim that something has objective validity, we are claiming that an indefinite plurality of subjects could agree on it.[19] Thus, potential intersubjective agreement is the phenomenological equivalent of *objectivity*. Yet, any *intersubjectively shared* content must primarily be content for *first-person subjects*. Whenever we meaningfully talk about a shared content, the conditions that confer meaningfulness to that content must already belong to each subject. This implies that the sphere of what we can intersubjectively agree on must be a *subset of the sphere of what each of us can apprehend in the first person*. Therefore, objectivity is introduced as a *restriction* on the range of first-person validities, and this means that phenomena (i.e., what can be experienced and apprehended in the first person) are *the most comprehensive field of meanings that can be made available*.

In order to explore this field of meanings (phenomena), Husserl introduces the methodological procedure known as *Epoché*. *Epoché* requires the subject to *systematically avoid any reference to the ontological status* of the relevant contents: when I describe X I must abstain from (tacitly or overtly) implying that X is true or illusory, that it belongs to my mind or to the world in itself, that it is to be reduced to a deeper underlying reality or not, etc.[20] *Epoché* opens up the field of *phenomena*, which is just the whole of what is subjectively available.[21]

---

17   MEILLASSOUX, *After Finitude*, p. 4.
18   *Ibid.*, p. 14.
19   E. HUSSERL, *Cartesianische Meditationen und Pariser Vorträge*, Husserliana I, S. Strasser (ed.), (L'Aia: Martinus Nijhoff 1973), p. 127. [Quoted as *Hua I*].
20   E. HUSSERL, *Zur phänomenologischen Reduktion. Texte aus dem Nachlass* (1926-1935), S. Luft (ed.), Husserliana XXXIV, (Dordrecht: Kluwer Academic Publishers 2002), p. 130. [Quoted as Hua XXXIV].
21   *Ibid.*, p. 204.

What is the aim of this operation? For the present purposes, we can say that it accounts for the process that *leads to truthful, essential and/ or intersubjectively shared contents by exploring their first-person conditions*. We could express it less formally as follows: each of us was born, learned a language, grasped opinions and prejudices, was trained in scientific procedures, acquired criteria of truthfulness and verification, etc. Yet, as adult, well-informed and knowledgeable men and women, we often discover that notions and ideas, whose meaning we were sure to command, turn out to bear enigmatic implications and to be verbally shared without true reciprocal understanding. This is one of the oldest philosophical intuitions, dating back at least to Socrates: we may competently use words for ourselves and for others without fully grasping what their implications are; this inner misunderstanding may lead to many sorts of false beliefs. Husserl's phenomenology, as much as Wittgenstein's analysis of language games or Kant's criticism of metaphysics, are reflections dominated by this problem: they are explorations of the *meanings* we handle, in order to determine the reach of our *truths*, since any truth is a meaning which also passed a meaningful criterion of intersubjective validity (confirmation, verification, corroboration, etc.). Our truths cannot be better than our meanings, and meaningless expressions lead to merely apparent truths (metaphysics in Kantian and Wittgensteinian acceptation).

It must be noticed in passing that M. appears to be remarkably refractory to this philosophical worry: the question of what is and *can be* meant by some words seems to be irrelevant for his vindication of realism. This is visible in quite a few daring passages, especially in the third chapter, where he seems to be over-confident that the words he uses have a univocal meaning and an obvious referent. But what is especially remarkable for a text that wants to propose a new approach to *realism* is that no question is made about what is meant by 'reality'.

Quite to the contrary, this is a crucial issue in Husserlian phenomenology, and is an issue whose solution has many implications for an approach like M.'s one. As we said, the phenomenological method implies an initial suspension of all beliefs and interpretations concerning the *ontological* status of what is described. This step allows tackling the realm of meaning in the most comprehensive way, since no appearance is initially disqualified as illusion, epiphenomenon and the like. This, therefore, also enables to explore how all notions of ontological bearing, like *reality* and *cause*, are apprehended and what their scope is.

The meaning of reality, as the meaning of all words and concepts that Husserl, as well as M., uses, is something that can subsist only in relation to the subject that entertains them: meanings do not fall from the sky or grow from trees. Does this mean that we are forbidden to meaningfully *talk about reality in itself*? This is not the case, as we will see. Yet, does this mean that we can *describe* reality in itself without taking into account the meanings by which we describe it? This cannot be the case either. If we did, our attitude would be entirely naïve and pre-philosophical, and would be constitutively conducive to dogmatic stances.

In the space between these two positions lies the theoretical ground that does or does not legitimate M.'s approach.

In order to better understand this point we will briefly introduce Husserl's strategic notion of *transcendence*. By transcendence Husserl means *what appears to consciousness as existing beyond consciousness*. Whenever we experience events or situations where something affects us without us being in control of what happens, we experience something 'transcendent'.[22] The primal sphere of transcendence is *sensuous transcendence*, which names the *self-givenness* within perceptual acts: anything in perception that is irreducible to the activity of the subject signals sensuous transcendence.[23]

The notion of transcendence is the phenomenological homologue of the Kantian 'thing-in-itself'. The crucial feature of the notion of transcendence is its borderline character: it is no dogmatic assumption concerning what could *be* beyond any possible conscious access, but it is neither the self-enclosure of subjectivity in the 'transparent cage' of settled meanings. The sphere of transcendence (i.e., the phenomenological 'reality-in-itself') enters subjective life and the sphere of meanings in two ways: it produces *affections* that call for appropriate practical reactions and it may induce *changes* in our settled meanings. Far from being 'nothing', the sphere of transcendence is crucial for all our 'practical and theoretical attitudes', although the meanings that we entertain grasp and preserve only our (practical and theoretical) reactions to the transcendent sphere and can *never resolve the otherness of transcendence*. In a sense transcendence is constitutively *contingent*, although this does not mean that it must be inconstant, haphazard, messy, or the like.

If we go back to M.'s claims, we can see that his idea that according to phenomenologists 'being is coextensive with manifestation' and that this

---

22   E. Husserl, *Die Idee der Phanomenologie. Funf Vorlesungen*, Husserliana II, W. Biemel (ed.), (L'Aia: Martinus Nijhoff 1973), p. 72. [Quoted as *Hua II*].
23   E. Husserl, *Spate Texte über Zeitkonstitution (1929-1934). Die C-Manuskripte*, Husserliana Materialien VIII, D. Lohmar (ed.), (Dordrecht: Springer 2006), p. 52-110. [Quoted as *Hua Mat VIII*].

amounts to locking oneself in a 'transparent cage' is misleading, because it communicates the wrong impression that manifestation (or consciousness) is a kind of container without doors and windows. But consciousness is not just self-consciousness, and we are continuously conscious of something *other* than consciousness (for instance, in each perceptual act).

Still, M. could reply that what he contests is that phenomenologists are losing the 'great outdoors' of reality because they deem the 'thing-in-itself' (i.e., the transcendent sphere) to be unknowable. But this is again unclear: if the claims of cognoscibility are taken to imply that the *object* of knowledge can be *reduced* to the *knowledge* of object, this would be absolute idealism and no Husserlian phenomenology. If cognoscibility means the possibility of complete, exhaustive or absolute knowledge of reality, indeed, phenomenology does not endorse this view, but, for that matter, neither does modern science. But, then, we are quite uncertain about what M. may really mean. Does he mean that since phenomenology holds that transcendent reality can be never resolved into its knowledge, then reality is regarded as unknowable and therefore irrelevant for consciousness? But this would be entirely absurd. The whole sphere of perception, which in phenomenological terms is the first source of all knowledge, is a steady confrontation with sensuous transcendence. What phenomenology says is just that consciousness, its meanings and laws, can be never bypassed by dogmatic assumptions about real objects, which do not (or cannot) explain how such objects could be approached and recognized. The attitude that makes room for real objects, regardless of the way they are apprehended, is called *objectivism* (*Objektivismus*).[24] If M. wants to vindicate that the 'external world' or the 'principle of contradiction' *are* what they are regardless of being *thought*, well, this is precisely what phenomenologists *think* of them. If he wants to go further and claim that then we can provide *qualifications* of the 'external world' or the 'principle of contradiction' without involving consciousness, this is sheer objectivism and I declare myself unable to make sense of what he might properly mean.

Thus, when M. wants to be free to state that 'manifestation is not the *givenness of a world*, but rather an intra-worldly occurrence', inevitably, it is *he* who is stating it. Therefore, the whole content that he wants to communicate is meant *by* a consciousness and exists *for* that consciousness (and other ones). If you want to call 'manifestation' whatever is given

---

24   E. Husserl, *Die Krisis der Europäischen Wissenschaften und die transzendentale Phänomenologie*, Husserliana VI, W. Biemel (ed.), (L'Aia: Martinus Nijhoff 1954), pp. 338, 342. [Quoted as *Hua VI*].

to a consciousness, then naturally the above mentioned sentence is itself a manifestation. This is no obnoxious 'codicil of modernity',[25] it is plain evidence. Yet, the crucial point is that a manifestation is not *limited* by its settled meanings, but can refer to something else and can also *refer to the unknown*. Therefore, the *world* that consciousness refers to is not somehow included in the 'transparent cage' of thought, but is meant as other than thought *by motivated thought*. And if anybody wants to protest against the latter clause, I would invite her to show by what else could be meant.

The only plausible matter of contention that I envisage concerns the status of scientific explanation, which somebody could consider methodologically adequate in the absence of any reflection on its practical and theoretical presuppositions, while somebody else (among which phenomenologists, but in good company) could think that the layers of conceptual presuppositions of scientific explanations must be brought to light in order to have a proper grasp of the scope of scientific statements. This would be a praiseworthy discussion, but it seems that M. is neither committed to, nor interested in it.

3. What Is The Reality Of 'Temporality'?

The second charge that we have to deal with is the idea that correlationism (or phenomenology) would be forced to an *anti-realist stance when it has to deal with 'ancestral' events*. Why should correlationism and scientific realism be regarded as incompatible? Because the correlationist (phenomenologist) does not think that the 'literal sense' of scientific statements is also their ultimate sense.[26] Up to this point there is no matter of contention: indeed, phenomenology (as well as all philosophical attitudes that reflect on the *meaning* of scientific statements) does not take the prima facie value of scientific statements for their ultimate sense.

But according to M. here lurks a serious difficulty for 'correlationism'. He thinks that the correlationist (phenomenologist) is forced to grant that

> the ancestral statement is a true statement, in that it is objective, but one whose referent cannot possibly have actually existed in the way this truth describes it. It is a true statement, but what it describes as real is an impossible event; it is an 'objective' statement, but it has no conceivable object.[27]

25 MEILLASSOUX, *After Finitude*, p. 13.
26 *Ibid.*, p. 17.
27 *Ibid.*, p. 16.

This is a strange charge. In fact, neither thesis would be actually supported from a phenomenological point of view.

First, ancestral statements are at most statements on which there *currently* is intersubjective agreement, which is not objectivity yet. Intersubjective agreement *de facto* is neither objectivity nor truth yet, since what is established as criterion of truth is an *ideal* intersubjective agreement, which represents the horizon of *all* the potentially most *detailed and comprehensive* views on the relevant matter. If merely *actual* intersubjective agreement would amount to truth, we could just determine truth through a nice democratic vote, which is too silly an option to be dwelt on.

Secondly, M. has repeatedly complained that the correlationist deprives herself of an access to reality in itself, precisely because of her proneness to declare it unknown and incognoscible. As we have seen this is not quite true, but let us assume M.'s thesis. Now, if this were the case, it is hard to see how the correlationist would be also taken to state that the real referent 'cannot possibly have existed' in a certain way. How could she claim that it was an 'impossible event'? If she, by assumption, does not know how things have been, how could she say that things had *not* been so as presently described? M's charge does not rest on any concrete instantiation of such claim, and theoretically this is no claim that could be inferred from phenomenological stances. Thus, the alleged difficulty is wholly insubstantial.

What the 'correlationist' could indeed say is that the current scientific description cannot claim to be either ultimate or exhaustive. But frankly I think that only very poor scientists would claim of any scientific truth, and especially an 'ancestral' one, that it be ultimate and exhaustive.

Surely, what a phenomenologist would say is more ambitious than that. She would add that her own account of the same event may be *more comprehensive* than the scientific one, to the extent (and only to the extent) that it is able to show what the theoretical and practical presuppositions of the relevant scientific truth are. M. puts the realist meaning and the phenomenological meaning in opposition, as if one would exclude the other.[28] But this is true only in a very peculiar sense: if the realist meaning assumes that the event that is meant is *univocally and ultimately* so as it is described now, then, indeed, it would exclude the very idea of different accounts of the same event. In this sense the opposition would be authentic and irredeemable. I am very doubtful that this highly dogmatic attitude would be an acceptable description of scientific truth for many thinkers, even naturalistically oriented ones. In all other cases, scientific and phenomenologi-

---

28   *Ibid.*, p. 14.

cal accounts would not be in opposition; although, admittedly, the phenomenologist would claim a more *comprehensive* view (while granting that her own position is parasitic on path-breaking scientific operations).

The fact that phenomenological and scientific accounts are not logically incompatible, of course, does not mean that they raise the same claims. This point can be treated by looking more closely to the question of the 'ancestral events', with special reference to the nature of temporal reality. In this framework, M. raises two core objections to a phenomenological perspective. The first one asks how can the phenomenologist '*conceive of a time in which the given as such passes from non-being into being*';[29] the second one questions the distinction between transcendental and empirical level.[30]

The first objection repeats in a different context the same mistake that we examined above: M. thinks that the idea that consciousness emerges in time is challenging for phenomenological theses. Since he believes that for the phenomenologist being and the consciousness of being are the same, then the very thought of the temporal emergence of consciousness would prove self-contradictory. But to the phenomenologist this is no more problematic than the thought that her own parents existed before she was born: there is no paradox whatsoever because consciousness *refers* also to what is not 'inside' consciousness (transcendent being). In fact, consciousness is not a bag (in non-phenomenological terms, it is more like a '*function*') and therefore to conceive of it as something whose borders cannot be trespassed is deeply misleading.

What is true is that, for the Husserlian phenomenologist, objective time and in general the time used by natural sciences is to be regarded as a (well-grounded) concept that *rests on some fundamental features of consciousness*. This does not mean that time is 'merely subjective' in the sense of 'illusory'; it just means that time cannot be considered a brute fact, since all facts take place in time. We cannot here significantly dwell on the rich Husserlian analyses of temporality, however a few reminders are appropriate.

Time is primarily given to consciousness at the level of perceptual activity in the form of 'retentions' and 'protentions'.[31] Retentions can be exemplified as follows: the tenth tone of a melody we hear is more than an instantaneous sound, since it receives its musical meaning by the sequence of previous tones, empty intervals and specific durations. This shows that the experiencing consciousness retains experiences (even empty ones) with

---

29   *Ibid.*, p. 21.
30   *Ibid.*, pp. 24-25.
31   HUSSERL, *Hua Mat VIII*, pp. 8ff.

specific order and internal proportions, without which no actual percept would be what we ordinarily recognize as percept:[32] this is the core of any temporal ordering and of the constitution of what we call past. Protentions are tacit expectations, which can also be empty of any specific content: I would be badly 'surprised' if my next breath would be hindered, but this does not mean that I usually have any clear-cut expectation about my next breathing act; in fact, the same 'surprise' would be experienced even if I had been altogether unable to produce reflective acts with possible pre-figurations. Thus, protentions are immediate non-thematic expectations that shape the forward-looking dimension of experience, which is the primal apprehension of what we call future. Retentions and protentions provide the primal form of all temporal ordering: they are 'acts' of consciousness, insofar as they require a living and receptive consciousness in order to unfold; but they are not *active* in the sense of being subject to the will or belonging to the sphere of conscious activity.

The Husserlian analysis of temporal constitution does not concern the mere appearance of a 'psychological time', while universal (real) time would lie somewhere else, untouched by consciousness. What is claimed is that *universal time is shaped by our primal experience of retentions and protentions*, and that no temporal judgments of ours have meaning without involving these fundamental properties of consciousness. This thesis, it must be stressed, does not imply that 'factual change' is produced by consciousness, which would amount to idealism, but states that the *ordering* factor that defines changes as temporal depends on consciousness. Let us try to clarify the features of temporal constitution.

First, one may be inclined to read the time of consciousness through the psychological categories of *memory*. When this happens, experienced temporality is understood as an event *in* time. This is certainly the vision that M. and most realists would endorse. But while a phenomenologist may perfectly grant that each individual experience of time can be positioned in *objective time*, she would not grant that objective time 'exists' somewhere regardless of consciousness. There is something fatally wrong in 'psychologizing' experienced temporality. When we *psychologize* an experience X we implicitly *reduce* the status of X to a different ontological level, that is, we implicitly say that X could be explained away by a different order of events, and precisely the ones taking place in a *human brain*. That is, we assume that

---

32   Cf. E. Husserl, *Vorlesungen zur Phänomenologie des inneren Zeitbewusstseins* (1893-1917), Husserliana X, R. Böhm (ed.), (L'Aia: Martinus Nijhoff 1966), p. 24f. [Quoted as *Hua* X].

we can operate a reduction of X to the *explanatory resources* occurring in the description of a human being interpreted as an object in the world. With reference to time this could mean, for instance, that experienced time can be reduced to some events in the brain, for instance to the psycho-physiological facts of memory. But how could this happen? Let us first think of what M. calls an *arche-fossil*:[33] for example, a sample of sedimentary rock. What we actually have is a present 'thing', which can be used to unfold a plausible series of geological events. This process is doubtlessly '*a retrojection of the past on the basis of the present*', as M. correctly says. Actually, I do not think that anybody would deny that all our scientific statements about ancestral events have the form of 'verified' (or at least 'corroborated') hypotheses. The past is not waiting for us anywhere to be inspected, but its ordering can be reconstructed by the rational use of hypotheses; and such hypotheses are corroborated (or falsified) by what belongs to the sphere of present percepts. Thus, the key to interpret the grand picture of universal time is either given in *present experience* or is not. What remains to be clarified is if the temporal succession that is primarily evident to us can or cannot be posited as subsistent independently of consciousness.

In order for temporal succession to be independent of consciousness, we should be able to *explain temporal succession through facts*. But ordinary spatiotemporal facts would obviously not do, since they are already taking place *in* time. What we could think is that the past is actually reducible to an actual state of affairs: for instance, to physiological traces in a brain. Indeed, an actual (presently real) state of affairs is the archetype model of what owes nothing to consciousness in order to exist. But the question is: can in principle a cerebral state account for temporal succession? This can be hardly argued, because the cerebral state is in the same condition as the mentioned sample of sedimentary rock: it needs 'somebody' to unfold and order what is actually just a state of affairs without any intrinsic order of succession. If we think of our memory like a trace on a Compact Disk, the trace can reproduce an order only if it is 'read' by a device that discerns the parts of the trace. But this is not enough: what is reproduced must be *retained as a past sequence in sight of a sequence to come*. Facts just do not have the explanatory resources to grasp and explicate temporal ordering. Only consciousness (or 'something' with the same functions) can account for orderings between *absent* elements, since consciousness can constitutively *refer to the inactual*.

The nature of the time-constituting traits of consciousness must be correctly understood, however. When we talk about universal or objective time

---

33   MEILLASSOUX, *After Finitude*, p. 14.

we could roughly define it as '*change* ordered in the form of *succession*'. Of the two mentioned elements, consciousness is decisive for the second, the order of succession, not for the first. That is, things happen, sensuous transcendence affects consciousness all the time, and this is *recognized by consciousness as independent from consciousness*. But when it comes to *ordering* events, the role of consciousness cannot be bypassed.

More generally, without an ordering (living) principle, without a preference for some traits instead of others, without the inclination to apprehend some events as salient instead of others, there are *no determinate events at all*. For any event in the universe, there could be *infinite* descriptions where we could change not only the classes of relevant categories (physical, chemical, biological, historical, etc.), but also the internal units, the levels of analyticity, the 'systems of reference', and the range of antecedents and consequents to be considered 'interesting'. Indeed, it should be clear that no event X in the universe has either a unique structure or clear-cut boundaries, such that at a certain point objectively X is no longer the *same* event, but a *different* one. The ordering role of consciousness (interests, saliences, sensitivity, aims, bodily dispositions, etc.) simply cannot be circumvented. This, however, does not mean that consciousness rules over reality. As we have seen, from a phenomenological point of view the transcendent sphere is recognized as independent; then, the most sensible way to accord the ordering role of consciousness with the independence of transcendent reality is by conceiving of consciousness as a *principle of selection*, which acknowledges an order among the indefinitely multiple orders that could be attributed to each instance of transcendent reality. Consciousness *selects* in transcendent reality what is pertinent to consciousness, it does *not* force together an haphazard, chaotic world.

To sum up, from a phenomenological perspective the irreducibility of reality and the legitimacy of talk about realities that are not manifest to consciousness can be granted. But any qualified talk about reality must involve its relation to consciousness and its acts, which provide the ground from which all meanings and truthful judgments (ancestral statements included) can be explained.

4. What is Right in Meillassoux's Claims?

Let us come to the last major objection that M. raises against the correlationist/phenomenologist. Without entering the discussion of the last pages, most orthodox Husserlian phenomenologists would have dismissed all of M.'s objections simply by noticing that he steadily mixes up the transcendental with the empirical level. When M. objects that the phenomenologist cannot account for a time when consciousness was not, he considers the transcendental position of consciousness and the related horizon of temporality as an empirical fact in time. If one recognizes that the two levels are not congruent, any further objection immediately fades away. Yet, we have chosen not to take here that traditional stance, because we believe that there is something *right* in M.'s objection. We have gone the way of illustrating the specific character of *transcendent reality* in a phenomenological framework, because the claim that empirical existence and transcendental subsistence are just *separate* dimensions is not wholly satisfactory.

The core of M.'s objection is the following:

> Objective bodies may not be a sufficient condition for the taking place of the transcendental, but they are certainly a necessary condition for it. We thereby discover that the time of science temporalizes and spatializes the emergence of living bodies; that is to say, *the emergence of the conditions for the taking place of the transcendental.*[34]

This objection is no refutation of transcendental views, because the conditions for the transcendental to *take place* are not conditions *of* the transcendental as such. But, on the other hand, and this is what we want to emphasize, even if transcendental meanings (conditions of possibility of actual experience) cannot be explained away by referring to factual experiences, this does not mean that factual experience is irrelevant for the *meaningfulness of the transcendental.*

What we want to say is that, granted that reality is no explanatory key of meaning, nevertheless the *experience* (and *meaning*) *of reality* is *motivationally* crucial for the activity of consciousness. Let us clarify this point.

Reality is something that consciousness recognizes and that therefore cannot be used to *explain* consciousness. *Causality* is the form that reality assumes in explanations. The notion of causality usually handled by realist accounts is *efficient causality*, that is, causality where all the powers of the successor are inherited from the powers of the antecedent, and so for each event in space-time. Causality is a constituted concept, not a self-evident fact of nature, and must be examined as any other concept, without taking for granted that its explanatory power has priority over all alternatives. Indeed, by far most philosophical analyses in the history of thought have doubted that causal explanations have much to say with regard to logical, axiological or transcendental relations, which should at least warn

---

34   *Ibid.*, p. 25.

against easy claims of self-sufficiency for ordinary, causal accounts. On the contrary, it cannot be denied that logical, axiological and transcendental (temporal) relations are already at work in the constitution of the *notion of causality*. That said, the fact that the features of efficient causality are the outcome of a specific conceptual reading of reality does not imply that the *instantiations* of causal relations are mere concepts: causality is an interpretation of a primal phenomenon, which we may call *efficaciousness*. By 'efficaciousness' we mean transcendent reality seen as *power*, as capability to have consequences (any kind of consequences), regardless of any more specific trait; all Aristotelian forms of causality or Schopenhauerian forms of sufficient reason are equally legitimate descriptions of 'efficaciousness'.

The experiential dimension that prompts the constitution of the notion of reality, that is, primarily, the experience of sensuous transcendence and efficaciousness, occupies in our lives a crucial position: it represents the primal existential challenge and therefore it is essentially a matter of *practical concern*.

Transcendent reality affects us and prompts reactions. Before being any spring of knowledge, it is a *source of motivation*. It induces us to assume certain stances, to appropriately react. In a specific sense, therefore, transcendent reality is a condition that *elicits* (not 'causes') *conscious acts*. Transcendent is both, what nourishes our perceptions while settling down in orders of succession, and anything that physiologically affects our conscious acts (the effects of a psychotropic drug, a painful disease, etc.). In *this* sense transcendent reality can be sensibly conceived as a *condition of possibility for the implementation of consciousness*. But it would be a naïve mistake to think that this essential role played by transcendent reality towards consciousness should be acknowledged in the form of an explanatory priority. Precisely because consciousness exists only in *relational* terms, transcendent reality is crucial for consciousness. But it is crucial at a *motivational* level, i.e. at the level of the meaningfulness of acts, not as a categorical contribution to explain acts.

This is indeed the point where the reasons of realism, and to some extent even of scientific realism, find vindication. M.'s attempt to oblige the phenomenologist to acknowledge her irreconcilable opposition to the claims of scientific realism is misplaced. The phenomenologist does not accept in general the explanatory superiority of scientific accounts, not because of dullness or envy, but for the very reasons that make scientific accounts *operatively* superior. The *criteria* of simplicity, manipulability, repeatability, measurability and aperspectival validity that define scientific practice have very dubious metaphysical grounds, but they have excellent *operational* motives: they represent methodological features that may turn the contingency of transcendent reality into the ground of effective action. This is how we can hope to limit and circumscribe our subordination to the self-givenness of being.

The question of scientific realism must be inscribed in the most general quest for *practical orientation*, which is the defining issue of *practical reason*. What we call scientific rationality provides the best knowledge available about *how* to correctly link acts and expectations. Transcendent reality as such is what specifically challenges the sense of action, and science, while silent about the nature of ends, is the preeminent authority about how to connect means and ends. It would be silly to denigrate science in neo-idealistic fashion by saying that it is mere 'utilitarian knowledge'. In fact science is after an ontology of causal relations, which cannot be a complete ontology for the very reasons that contribute to its peculiar value: because it always already pre-selects an ontological dimension (spatiotemporal extension) and a reading of efficaciousness (efficient causality) as the only legitimate sphere of reality. And an ontology of causal relations, while being a failure as full-fledged ontology, is certainly an important part of it: something that should not be ignored, but neither accepted at face value.

The dimension of *action* as value realization, historical change and personal commitment represents the threshold where traditionally the phenomenological analyses under *Epoché* (as much as Kantian 'pure reason' or Wittgensteinian 'language games') show their peculiar limits. All transcendental (conceptual) analysis can just reach the threshold of 'practical reason' without trespassing it. Transcendental (conceptual) analysis is concerned with meaning and with the relations of dependence between meanings. In this area it can attain certainties and apprehend essential boundaries. But this dimension of certainty and essentiality is obtained at the price of *not settling, of not moving from provisional probabilities to univocal commitments*. The field of what we can know only in provisional, probabilistic, partial or merely postulative ways is immense, and at the same time we are not in a condition to existentially abstain from taking a stance toward it.

When Kant realized the extent of what his critical analysis of metaphysical reasoning had expelled from the sphere of ascertainable knowledge, he made room for a different metaphysical dimension, which was treated in the form of practical reason, where the ideas of pure reason re-emerged in a different fashion. In fact, this question has been raised very early in the framework of phenomenological thought as well. While accepting the explanatory priority of phenomenological descriptions, most of Husserl's pupils at some point turned to reconsidering reality (Being) in forms, which raised claims that exceeded the outcomes of the analysis under *Epoché*. This is of course the case of Heidegger's reflection on the sense of *Being*, Scheler's project of a philosophical anthropology, Sartre's idea of historical commitment, etc.

5. Outline Of A Counter-Proposal To Meillassoux's Challenge

The fact that this turn (which can be labeled 'ontological', 'realist', 'metaphysical' or 'practical') has been often taken does not mean that its peculiar nature has been clearly perceived. Indeed, and this is the point where M.'s criticisms are appropriate, dealing with the urges and claims of transcendent reality has been definitely experienced as a challenge and a difficulty for the 'correlationist' approaches (actually more problematic for twentieth century thinkers than it was for Kant). I believe that this question will remain intractable until the irreducible nature of consciousness (i.e., of transcendental meanings) will not receive an interpretation in 'realistic' terms. Such interpretation, to be clear, should not try to *explain away* or *reduce* consciousness to fact, but just to show how consciousness can be properly positioned towards what consciousness recognizes as transcendent reality.

Phenomenological thought can account for transcendent reality and for the categories of scientific realism by saying that the reach of these notions can be made explicit only by examining their meaning, that is, their implications in terms of attitudes, operations, connections with other concepts, etc. But by this move phenomenological thought does not *invalidate* the accounts of scientific realism: it merely says that they are partial, while granting that they do play an important role. This has a crucial implication: *the peculiar position of consciousness that phenomenology claims should find room in an account informed by scientific realism.* Needless to say, to 'find room' does not mean to be conceptually reduced to the categories of scientific realism. It just means that we must find a way to *conceptualize* the *real* position of consciousness, and that this conceptualization must be *compatible* with realism, even scientific realism.

Although consciousness is not merely a fact, its activity is intrinsically correlated with the spatiotemporal world of facts. This means that actual implementations of consciousness *as such* must be describable in the spatiotemporal world of facts. When M. straightforwardly asks *when* consciousness has appeared on earth, he makes two different claims, one of which is legitimate: insofar as he is trying to *reduce* consciousness to the conceptuality of scientific realism (naturalism; physicalism), his claim is nonsensical; if, on the contrary, he is asking how could we make room in the reality of physical nature for the appearance of consciousness, he is raising a legitimate question.

A full-fledged answer to this question is far beyond the reach of what can be provided here, however, the general features of the main ingredients of such answer can be suggested. I would propose two main ways to tackle this question.

We should ask:

(I) How could we understand the position of consciousness in the time of nature or in 'natural history' (which is no 'arbitrary invention' of consciousness, but is transcendent change ordered by consciousness, in order to provide a causal history)?

(II) How could the activity of consciousness, in the midst of the causal operations of matter (inclusive of cerebral matter), be properly conceptualized?

Each phenomenologist (or correlationist) has informal opinions about them, although she often believes them to be rationally unjustifiable and therefore belonging to the sphere of private prejudice. But this need not be the case.

Question (I) could be tackled as follows. What we know of scientific accounts about the origins of life and consciousness would represent a difficulty only if it would force us (as M. believes it does) to choose between the reality of the material beginning of the implementations of consciousness and the validity of transcendental accounts. The two accounts would conflict only if transcendental accounts would not account for and reject objective time and existence, or insofar as naturalistic accounts wanted to explain away transcendental meanings. Neither should be granted. The alternative account that I would propose rests on conceiving of ontological properties as *emergent properties*. By 'ontological properties' I understand all properties that we recognize as endowed with efficaciousness; therefore each phenomenon bears witness to the subsistence of real properties of a kind: there is no such a thing as sheer epiphenomena.

Talk of emergent properties need not refer to any dualistic ontology: we can perfectly grant that there is just one 'substance' (monism) and we may even accept to call it, as scientific accounts would do, 'matter' (or 'matter-energy'). Such monism, however, cannot be just physicalist. We have to grant that the same state of affairs can be legitimately described through a plurality of rational descriptions (not just in the language of physical science). And we have to accept that the description of a whole is not reducible to the descriptions of its parts. As from the properties of Chlorine (*Cl*, a toxic gas) and Sodium (*Na*, a soft metal, exothermically reactive in water) we cannot logically *deduce* the properties of table salt (*NaCl*), similarly the properties of those specific ensembles that we call living matter and thinking matter cannot be deduced from the physical and chemical properties of its parts. This is not just an epistemic issue: after learning what the properties of the whole are, we can re-instantiate the same emergent properties by resorting to the same components; but the properties of the whole are *effective only* in the specific synthesis, which is what establishes its peculiar powers. Emergent properties of a whole X have 'downward causality', that is, they produce effects which cannot be produced either by the parts of X, or by any merely additive composition of such parts: only the specific formal synthesis of those parts produces its characteristic effects. Here is no place to diffusely dwell on the idea of emergent property,[35] but in the present context only two aspects have to be stressed on:

1) The idea of emergent property is perfectly compatible with all ordinary accounts of the temporal origins of the implementations of consciousness (and in fact with all accounts of natural history). Actually, in the absence of emergence all descriptions of qualitative *change* in nature are hardly intelligible.

2) Emergence makes manifest the heterogeneity between causal-ontological order and explanatory order. 'Materialism' is no antithesis to 'spirituality', to the extent that we do not take for granted a reductive understanding of what the properties of matter are. Since life and consciousness are not epiphenomena, life and consciousness must inhere in matter (in specifically *formed* matter). If we accept that 'matter' is not just what physical descriptions grants, but involves *all properties* (effects) *that we can experience*, then materialism loses all reductionist features and becomes perfectly compatible with accounts where consciousness is a constitutive correlate of the world.

From this point of view we can also tackle question (II). How can we try to account for the specific 'powers' of consciousness and its irreducible traits in a 'materialistic' context, where mind is constitutively affected by transcendent reality? The question can be transposed by asking: how should we conceive of the contents of thought and experience and of their irreducibility, if they can be influenced by transcendent reality and can influence it in turn? Here transcendent reality can be read as what Husserl calls *Ur-Hylé* or straightforwardly as 'matter', with the proviso that its *real* properties are all properties that we actually perceive in the world. Granted that the mind is materially implemented ('supervenes' on biological matter) and that is steadily affected by matter, how should we conceive of 'mental causation', if there is such a thing? Let us resort once more to Husserl's analyses. In *Ideas* II Husserl wrote that the spirit (*Geist*) is efficacious on nature, although it is

---

35   Cf. A. Zhok, *Emergentismo. Le proprietà emergenti della materia e lo spazio ontologico della coscienza nella riflessione contemporanea*, (Pisa: ETS, 2011).

not efficacious in the sense of efficient causality.[36] Yet, the efficaciousness of the spirit (mind, consciousness) is no more enigmatic than how ordinary causality is.[37] It is wrong to believe that we know *how* efficient causality works, while wondering just about the efficaciousness of the mind. In fact efficient causality is expressed in terms of succession, regularity, contiguity and the like, but is silent with regard to *how* something should produce something else or *what* should produce *what else*. As to the 'way' in which causes should produce the relevant effects, causality has no intrinsic features beyond the features that we perceive in the 'causing' event and the 'caused' one.

From this point of view, we can see that in the framework provided by the Husserlian analysis, the primal way in which 'meanings' (or 'essences') can be considered efficacious has little to do with efficient causality. As we said, the ordering role of consciousness is expressed in terms of interests, sa-liences, sensitivities, aims, bodily structure, etc., which bring to light events insofar as they are relevant to consciousness. In this sense consciousness can be said to operate as a *principle of selection*, which extracts from the infinite possibilities of transcendent reality the ones that are *pertinent to the life of consciousness*. This selection is not just a matter of 'mental activity', but belongs to embodied consciousness, to the living and sentient body as such. This *selection* can be roughly seen two ways: both as 'choice' of salient tran-scendent items by the living, and as 'selection' of realizable instantiations of living consciousness by the world (which would not be inappropriate to interpret in the general framework of 'natural selection'). The meaningful el-ements that consciousness can deal with are conditions of possibility for the World to *be for consciousness*. They are conditions that do not belong either to consciousness or to 'transcendent matter' taken separately, but to their irre-ducible and original mergence. The point in the efficaciousness of conscious-ness and its meanings is not that somewhere spirit turns into matter-energy and efficient causality (or the other way round). The point is that events and states of affairs in the world emerge by *taking shape* and their *form* (their *es-sence*) establishes how they can affect and be affected, how they can belong to the sphere of efficaciousness (ontology). Here there is room for a qualified recovery of the old notion of '*formal causality*', which should be understood as irreducible to, and more comprehensive than, efficient causality.[38]

---

36   HUSSERL, *Hua* IV, p. 283.
37   HUSSERL, *Hua* IV, pp. 259-260.
38   This is just the primitive sketch of a theoretical proposal, which merely suggests the direction of an answer, without exhaustively arguing for it. Some of the rele-vant arguments have been partially developed elsewhere (Zhok 2011a, 2011b, 2012) and should be soon elaborated in a book-length monograph.

X

PHENOMENOLOGY AND NEW REALISM: IN DEFENCE OF NAIVE REALISM

Luca Taddio

The following observations aim to defend the theoretical position of the 'naive realist', for a theory of knowledge of the external world. Through a 'direct' model of perception, the phenomenological analysis of the appearance of a thing is articulated by clarifying the concept of 'immediate experience.' The independence of the 'percept' from conceptual activity can make the phenomenology of perception compatible with realist theses, since phenomenal invariants are not strictly dependent on the subject, but are the conditions of the emergence of a phenomenon as such. Phenomena are complex, autopoietic properties emerging from matter.

The phenomenology outlined here has been referred to as 'heretical', because it not 'orthodox' with respect to that of Husserl. The realist phenomenology proposed here refers to another tradition: that of E. Mach and W. James and then, in an even more explicit way, the Gestalt tradition, up until the experimental phenomenology outlined by the latest generation of gestaltist thinkers, such as G. Kanizsa and P. Bozzi (I have also taken into account the work of J. J. Gibson, even if it's not directly quoted). The position of some supporters of new realism and speculative realism believe, for different reasons, that the appearance of things is incompatible with the realist position, since it implies a 'relationship' and, therefore, a form of 'correlationism.' However, as we intend to show, the relationships between relatively stable physical systems are not in contradiction with realism.

1. Immediate Experience

Let's analyse the concept of 'immediate experience' through the scheme that Paolo Bozzi called 'psycho-physical schema SD': it is a classic layout used in university classrooms, depicted on the blackboard so as to explain perception. The scene is the following: we see a man on the right perceiving a red cube placed to our left. The situation is represented on the blackboard by placing the source of the stimuli on the left: the physical object or distal stimulus, a solid coloured cube. On the right, instead, there are electromagnetic waves of a certain frequency. The structure determines the proximal stimulus that, reaching the retina, causes stimulation through the light beam that starts from the cube, whose surfaces are capable of reflecting light thanks to their physical-chemical nature. Continuing in the same direction of reading, we find the observer's eye. The images of the eye and the brain may, depending on the type of critical discussion, be more or less detailed. To the right we find the optic chiasm of the retina, the lateral geniculate nuclei, the area 17.

In this representation of perception, where do we place our immediate experience of the cube?

Conventionally, at the far right over the design of the brain, we symbolize the phenomenal perception of the thing, designating it as 'phi.' Phi represents the phenomenal perception of the cube directly experienced. The diagram on the chalkboard is the representation of any possible causal explanation of perception. It does not coincide with the direct experience one has in the first person; it represents, however, the situation in which someone looks at another person looking at something. Proceeding from the cube in the direction of the observer's head, along the various stages that make up the scheme, we never meet the direct experience of the perceiver as such: there is only the indirect representation, internal or external, of perception. Every single segment of the schema can be the subject of further, more or less extensive, scientific investigations, be they physical, chemical, physiological and so on.

The causal description of the perception of the thing is the result of an epistemic picture of reality. It aims to explain perception by analysing the situation – typically a laboratory situation – described earlier, where the investigator analyses and verifies what the subject observes in the first person. This situation should be distinguished from the phenomenological description where, on the contrary, the observation is in place as it is experienced firsthand. The descriptions of what is perceived here and now lie on a different level, that of the real, with respect to the causal relations that are a representation of it. A causal explanation of perception, being a theory, can be improved, falsified, implemented and therefore changes over time, while immediate experience as such is not falsifiable and does not vary historically: what varies may be the description of the event under observation or its interpretation, but not the experience itself.

In the fourth book of *De rerum natura,* Lucretius describes a horse that stops in the middle of the river; the rider looks at the horse's legs and, after a while, sees the water still, while feeling like himself and the horse are 'running away'. This phenomenon is called 'illusion of movement.' Anyone on horseback, after looking at the water for a while, has the impression of being on a sailing ship: the water acts as a reference system, and you feel like you're moving. The same thing happens at the railway station: when the train on the other platform departs, one has the feeling of moving in the opposite direction. Lucretius, incidentally, proves to be an extraordinary observer. It is true because it exists. This is the world encountered and unamendable. And that is as true today as it was in the first century BC. Today, as then, we discover the same facts. Experimental phenomenology is constituted as a science of the observable in act.

2. The Stimulus Error

To confuse what we know of the thing perceived – understood as a physical and scientific object (proper of a causal explanation) – with what is directly perceived means to make the stimulus error, as Wolfgang Köhler first put it. If, reporting the direct observation of the cube, we were to say that it is an aggregate of atoms, we would be committing the stimulus error, having indirectly applied 'physical' knowledge of the thing to direct experience. Correct phenomenal descriptions do not include propositions referring to knowledge that is not directly verifiable and inter-observable. For example, you cannot say that the red of the cube corresponds to a given frequency of the electromagnetic spectrum, since the dual nature of red (wave and particle) is not directly perceptible.

All of our phenomenic descriptions are guided by the cube that is there, with its directly detectable properties. The scientific investigation has the objective of explaining perception: deep as it may be, such an explanation shall say, in the end, why we perceive things as we do ('as such', Köhler would say). According to Köhler, the explanatory power of causal explanations depends on the size and depth of the phenomenological analysis and on new findings that experimental phenomenology is able to produce. The progress made by the discoveries of experimental phenomenology, as the science of observables in progress, constantly expands the *explanandum* that phenomenological theories of the processes underlying perception deal with. In phenomenology, each new discovery reduces the logical space of all logically possible theories and simultaneously falsifies existing ones.

If the discovery of a new fact can bring down the theories that explain perception through a causal model, the opposite case does not occur; since no new scientific discovery, internal to the psycho-physical schema SD, can falsify direct experience. This means that every new fact discovered by experimental phenomenology will lead to the disappearance of a number of theories aimed at explaining perception, while the correctness of a scientific theory does not modify nor alter the level of direct experience. Science, and the 'truth' it pursues, are created to determine what cannot be grasped directly through observation: observed data, strictly speaking, is neither true nor false. The 'truth,' according to a well-established philosophical tradition, belongs to the sphere of judgment and thought, not to the phenomenally explicit fact. In *The Analysis of Sensations*, Ernst Mach reminds us that the expression 'deception of the senses' implicitly demonstrates that we have not yet reached full consciousness of the fact that the senses do not give either wrong or right indications: the only right thing that can be said of the sense organs is that they, in different circumstances, evoke different feelings and perceptions.

4. The Müller-Lyer Illusion

Let us analyse a typical case of optical illusion, so as to discuss in what sense we believe that the senses deceive us. The illusion appears in its richness of expression as objectively 'illusory', first of all, by virtue of the stability of the observed phenomenon: i.e. for the intrinsic characteristics of the phenomenon itself. By changing the configuration of the appendages and the length of the segments, we vary the effect of expression accordingly. Instead, by changing our intention or subjective disposition, the phenomenon does not change in appearance and remains stable. What we observe is thus dependent on the characteristics of the 'thing' and not on our 'subjective disposition.'

In order to measure the phenomenon we must operate a 'spoliation' of the thing. The measurement involves a degree of abstraction with respect to the thing, as it is qualitatively experienced: it is independent from the appendices that determine the presence of the illusion as such. The ruler resting respectively on the two segments does not measure the complex phenomenon known as 'Müller-Lyer illusion', but only the length of the segments. So, in order to measure the phenomenon of the Müller-Lyer illusion, we have to isolate certain aspects of it, operating a spoliation and simplification so as to establish a certain purpose. We measure the segments without considering the presence of appendages and say that they have the same length; but the two segments without appendages not only have the same length, but also appear to be of the same length.

The reference system within which we operate changes: we move from aesthetic purposes to operational purposes. We decide to take into consideration *some* aspects of the phenomenon, rather than other ones, as a function of certain purposes. If the quantification of phenomena is what is most useful for their manipulation, then this establishes its reality: in the world of painting, appearance in a picture is the true reality, even at the expense of the ruler. The same thing happens with some statues whose head is made to appear larger, so as to seem proportionate in perspective; or with cubes drawn with distorted faces, in order for it to appear proportionate and regular.

To say that we measure the Müller-Lyer illusion in order to define the length of the figure is a simplification of what actually appears. We call it 'illusion' to classify a certain range of things that possess certain characteristics. The ruler does not measure the illusion. The phenomenon, in all its complexity, does not admit such a reductionism. To measure the illusion means, rather, to ask ourselves if we continue to see a segment longer than the other by trying to change the position of the appendages of the figure. This measurement, however, is not given by the ruler but by the eye; or rather, by our immediate experience of the event observed in its systematic variation, until we find the breaking point of its phenomenal stability (i.e., the permanence of the 'illusory' phenomenon).

The analysis of the phenomenon allows us to highlight the relevant epistemological aspects: 1) the event is repeatable; 2) the event is intersubjectively shared; 3) even after taking the measurement and *knowing* that the two segments are the same, we continue to see them as before: a longer one and a shorter one (this indicates a relative independence of the percept from the concept). These observations represent the first defence of our epistemological stance in defence of naive realism: perception is a fact, it is not part of the truth-value established by judgment, which implies the assumption of a reference system. We say that the phenomenon of 'Müller-Lyer illusion' is real because 'the event is repeatable' and 'intersubjectively shared': two signs of reality from which any scientific investigation can hardly prescind. Both requirements determine the attribution of scientific objectivity.

It could be argued that this case of optical-geometrical illusion is abstract and misleading because we cannot encounter it in nature. An example artfully contrived to deceive us. Then, let's analyze another classic case: the broken stick in the water, judged illusory because the stick is seen as a whole when out of the water. The comparison between situation A ('stick in the water)' and situation B ('stick out of the water') determines the judgment of situation A as an illusion, although in fact both have their own statute of objectivity, as intersubjectively shared and repeatable. In fact, every time the stick is dipped into water we see it broken: the stick in the water appears according to the modes of its own being in the water.

To see the 'same thing' differently, we have to necessarily change the conditions of observability of the phenomenon. We can say that the stick is the same without contradicting ourselves, precisely because it is not the same in respect to what we are talking about: two different situations are compared. Several reference systems – ecologically distinct – determine opposite responses, but not contradictory ones: 'broken' and 'whole' refer to two different respects of the thing. The stick in the water appears always broken: it would be a stimulus error to say that it is whole because we know it is whole. We can say that it remains whole in water only by changing the reference system, and comparing the *perceptual* reference system (our experience) with a *conceptual* reference system (what we know). In this case, the stick becomes an object or a representation of reality that is different from the reality we encounter. With so many good reasons, we can say that the stick in the water is broken.

Let us consider another case (the example is Bozzi's): water boils at different temperatures depending on whether you are at the beach or in the mountains. The same pot of water boils at 100°C at sea level but would boil at 75°C at three thousand metres in the mountains. What the thermometer indicates, say 75°C, is something different from the effect observable. We hypothesize that this is an illusion, and we affirm that the boiling of water is an appearance. The procedure to establish the existence of the illusion is opposite to that applied to the Müller-Lyer illusion: in that case, the measuring instrument indicates that segments are the same, while our experience shows they are different. In the case of boiling temperature, however, we see that the two cases are similar, while the measurement indicates they are different. Thanks to physics we know that, in the phenomenon of boiling, temperature is not the only factor involved but there is another variable, i.e. pressure, which the thermometer is unable to reveal.

Measuring instruments therefore provide a numerical scale that does not fit with the global reality of the phenomenon, but rather a single parameter that intervenes in the given phenomenon. If we say that the Müller-Lyer illusion is an optical illusion, we must also say that seeing water boil in the mountains is an illusion, thus creating a vicious circle with no way out. Asymmetries emerge that occur following the use of measuring instruments: in physics, they are found when an instrument reveals that two phenomena are different, while the 'physical status' observable decrees their equality; in psychology, they occur when the equality between two phenomena is provided by the operational criterion, while their inequality emerges from direct observation. The use of things in daily practice leads to the belief that measurements are true while observation is false, but what the instrument indicates is not reality but a cognitive integration: an attribute that is not detectable by observation. Cognitive integrations are not directly attributable to things, nor are they to be superimposed to them. The phenomenal appearance of the thing does not imply a dualism of the 'phenomenon vs. thing in itself': the phenomenon is the appearance of an aspect of the 'thing itself' caught in its immediacy.

5. Immediate Experience

To better understand the significance of the phenomenology of perception as a description of immediate experience that is 'complete and unprejudiced,' to use the words of Koffka, we can borrow an image provided by Leibniz in his *Monadology* (§17):

> It must be confessed, however, that perception, and that which depends upon it, are inexplicable by mechanical causes, that is to say, by figures and motions. Supposing that there were a machine whose structure produced thought, sensation, and perception, we could conceive of it as increased in size with the same proportions until one was able to enter into its interior, as he would into a mill. Now, on going into it he would find only pieces working upon one another, but never would he find anything to explain perception.

According to Leibniz's picture, visual perception corresponds to what we observe directly, and does not include the mechanisms underlying the direct perception of things that do not explain the sense of perception. As Wittgenstein puts it in his *Tractatus*, 'from nothing in the field of sight can it be concluded that it is seen from an eye' (5.633). In fact, perception is not perceived nor, normally, are we conscious of consciousness: we directly perceive things of the external world. We can observe that they present themselves in their objectivity; or, as sometimes happens, we can grasp them equally objectively for their character of 'subjectivity' (as in the case of consecutive images and the like) without departing from the observation in place, and without thereby referring to the neurophysiological processes underlying them.

The case described by Leibniz shows that direct perception is a different thing from the underlying transphenomenal mechanisms: the physiology of the brain corresponds to the mechanisms of the mill that do not give reason of the immediate experience of things, which is subject of investigation for experimental phenomenology. In a passage of Wittgenstein's *Remarks on the Philosophy of Psychology,* we find an idea symmetrical to that of Leibniz, namely the non-reducibility of immediate experience to the processes underlying perception:

> Let us assume that someone makes the following discovery. He investigates the processes in the retina of human beings who are seeing the figure now as a glass cube, now as a wire frame etc., and he finds out that these processes are like the ones that he observes when the subject sees now a glass cube, now a wire frame etc.... One would be inclined to regard such a discovery as a proof that we actually see the figure differently each time. But with what right? How can the experiment make any pronouncement upon the nature of the immediate experience?--It puts it in a particular class of phenomena.

Wittgenstein intends to emphasize the fact that it is the properties of 'immediate' perceptual experience that allow us to 'interpret' the optical apparatus, and not vice versa.

6. *Kanizsa's Triangle: Physical Description Vs. Phenomenal Description*

In the outside world we can find things that do not have a corresponding distal stimulation. Take the case of Kanizsa's triangle. What you see is a white equilateral triangle at the centre of the figure, slightly lighter than the remaining surface: in fact, for the triangle to be perceived, it is necessary that its colour differs from that of the surface. The distal stimulus of the triangle does not exist: there are only three round areas and three angles on paper. Kanizsa's triangle is a case of anomalous surface that is realized in the phenomenal field without any difference in luminance or reflectance between different regions of the stimulus.

In this figure we can distinguish between a phenomenal description (the encountered datum) and a physical-causal transphenomenal description. The latter aims to explain perception through the investigation of different fields, such as physics, chemistry, neurology and physiology. A physical-causal description of this figure would lead to the conclusion that the triangle does not exist in the reality of the outside world: ontologically, we could only claim the existence of black signs on the sheet of paper. In this case, the triangle as phenomenally evident is considered to be subjective.

The phenomenally evident triangle is 'corrected' by a kind of knowledge that consists of a physical description of the datum (the distal stimulus) under observation. Such 'correction' should be made with respect to an alleged 'objective datum' coincident with the physical (this observation is taken from W. Metzger). It is in this way that the ontological contrast arises together with possible contradictions between different levels of reality (the description of the phenomenon and the description of the underlying reality). For the same event, therefore, two types of descriptions that are not comparable (being defined on two different sets of properties) end up overlapping.

Kanizsa's triangle exemplifies the inadequacy of concepts that lead us to reduce reality to physical reality or to non-reality on the basis of a correspondence with the physical object: the distal stimulus. The phenomenal presence of the triangle does not depend on the subject but on the respect of the proportions and the way in which the figure is drawn: this phenomenon can be found or not, but it is an emergent property that depends on the organization of matter. In this sense, Kanizsa's triangle is just as real as our conscience. We speak of illusions after identifying a parameter of comparison. A rainbow, for example, is not considered an illusion but a natural phenomenon, while the perception of a broken pencil in water is considered to be an illusion, based on the fact that it can be seen as a whole in an empty glass.

The mechanisms that regulate perception are the basis of our understanding of the ecological environment. In the immediate experience of the world sometimes we see what is not there, as in Kanizsa's triangle, and we do not see what is there, as in cases of 'masking'. In our behavioural phenomenal environment, we can also see that which cannot exist: take the case of an 'impossible object' like the Penrose triangle. Such a thing would be impossible to build in our three-dimensional Euclidean space: it follows that the existence of physical objects is not a necessary condition for their phenomenal existence. In this sense, the physical world is a subset of the phenomenal world.

In addition to this, there is the false idea that we see things because we have learned to see them: we cannot have seen an object like the Penrose triangle, nor will we ever see it in the physical world. Therefore, in theory, we could not be able to observe it now, but this is against factual evidence that we do (see Vicario 2001). These examples teach us to take on the appearance of the thing according to the modes of the phenomenon encountered, following a principle of phenomenal location that makes visual perception of the outside world ostensible by definition. The appearance of the thing, be it an illusion or not, is always a phenomenon that appears to us in its immediacy, complexity and inter-subjectivity.

7. Chromatic Induction

Let us analyse another case: chromatic induction. Let's take a 2 cm^2 grey square located at the centre of a 15 cm^2 blue square. We observe the blue induce yellow on the grey square: 'Yellow is a function of the surrounding blue.' Now let's complicate the phenomenon: let's take a half-black and half-white disc and let's spin it at melting speed. The disc will appear grey: if *esse est percipi*, the disc is grey. Let's now make a 2 cm hole in the centre of the blue square. If we apply the square on the grey disc, a streak of yellow will appear in the hole: if *esse est percipi*, the hole is yellow. The term 'appears' refers to what you see. The 'appearance' should not be placed in opposition to the 'reality': the reality is the appearance of the thing determined by the yellow hole and the grey disc as the result of 'a phenomenal property acting over another phenomenal property.'

This example shows how misleading it is to ask the question 'what is reality?' in contrast to the appearance of phenomena. Rather, we should ask ourselves where, and not what, reality is with respect to appearance. Whenever we locate reality, we encounter the phenomenon and never reality itself. The white and black disc is not the reality with respect to the grey disc in motion, since the black and white disc is actually grey when in motion. Similarly, the movies we moving at the cinema are real, that is, we do not consider them as the sum of the movement of frames or pixels.

As we have pointed out, the grey square inscribed in a blue frame turns yellow; if you decrease the size of the blue frame, the yellow induced by the blue becomes clearer: it is said, then, that the intensity of the yellow is a function of the blue. There is a point where the blue frame decreases and the yellow disappears, becoming a grey square. This is explained by a linguistic formulation such as 'the apparent colour is too weak to appear', while it should be recognized that, in the real world, blue and yellow become independent. Such considerations allow for a first phenomenological distancing from the statements asserting the necessity that 'everything is related to everything.' Once again, we have to specify the reference system to which this statement belongs.

At the phenomenological level, it is not true that everything is in relation to something else: in a given state of things, there are relations that, if altered, change the thing observed, while others leave it indifferent. Let's take once again the example of the small grey square within a larger blue square. The blue induces the vein of yellow as in the case just described. By progressively increasing the size of the grey square and, consequently, decreasing the surface area of the blue square, at a certain point the yellow disappears. While the blue area is not equal to zero, we say that the yellow ceases to exist. Believing that the yellow exists but is not seen, because (being a function given by the inducing area to the induced) it is below the threshold of perceptibility, means to be committing the stimulus error.

The idea that sensations below the threshold of perception diminish by following the curve of the function perceived above the threshold is incongruous at the level of phenomenal reality: it should be possible to produce an apparent but invisible yellow, which is a contradiction in terms. In fact, a perception that is not perceived is a contradictory concept in itself. Imagine a scale where, below a certain threshold, an aspect of the thing is no longer perceived but continues to exist according to a certain function, as within the visible spectrum. This is a hypothesis, a representation of reality, but it is not the reality of the world appearing in immediate experience. On the basis of what do we affirm the existence of the inducing action, if it is defined and exists only when we observe that something acts on something else?

The confirmation of the presence of yellow is in fact synonymous with inducing action, but if we no longer observe the yellow, talking about inducing action becomes senseless. By modifying the areas of the squares, there continues to be a visible relationship between two states of affairs, while the actual or presumed inducing influence becomes an image, an operationally manageable object, provided by physics or related disciplines. 'The experience system in place is characterized by absolute independence: whenever an observable is not sensibly affected by changes while others change their state, it is absolutely independent of them.'

For the experiment of chromatic induction we can provide two explanations: 1) the intensity of the yellow becomes too weak to be perceived, as it depends on the relation between the inducing area and the induced area; 2) this induction does no longer exist even if the inducing area is different from zero. In the first case, we postulate that sensations continue to decrease even under the perceptual threshold, according to a function similar to that which determines their decrease above the threshold: the relationship between the two areas – inducing and induced – would continue to produce the 'yellow', only it would be an invisible yellow. However, in this regard, one cannot speak of inducing relationship: an inducing action exists when you see the effect of one thing on another. In our case, the end of the effect also determines the end of the action or influence, and therefore there is no reason to still speak of induction. The mistake is to conclude that there is a cause and effect relationship between the variation of the relation between the inducing and induced areas, and the visibility of the colour.

Yet the supposed cause does not cease when its effect ceases to exist:

there is the paradox of perfectly knowing a cause producing a fact that does not exist. The two facts, then, are perfectly independent of each other, and their very independence allows experimental phenomenology to discover the mechanics of their functional dependencies. We cannot only consider the colour as the perceptual effect of the action on the retina of electromagnetic waves. We know that to produce a colour it is enough to stimulate the eye mechanically, chemically, or electrically. In order to see a colour, according to the physiology of the eye, it is sufficient to cause a modification of the electrical impulses in the optic nerve. From a theoretical point of view, we can imagine a prosthesis capable of inducing electric shocks perfectly calibrated to make the eye 'see' the colour.

8. Gelb's Experiment: Antidualism

Now I shall dwell for a while on the effect discovered by Gelb. Imagine we hang a black disk on the threshold between two dimly lit places and light it up with a projector, so that the shadow of the disk falls in a position invisible to the observer. As a result, the black disk is seen as white and weakly lit: 'the phenomenal split between enlightened and enlightening does not intervene to ensure the constancy of the colour of the object, but it seems to depend only on the intensity of the light reflected by the object itself.' Let's introduce a piece of white paper near the black disk in the same light cone: 'the disc is perceived as black or nearly so, therefore you have first scission and then constancy.' One might suppose that the cause of the original effect is ignorance on the part of the observer as regards to the lighting conditions of the disk. However, this hypothesis is proven false because, if you turn away, the white piece of paper that allows one to understand the real illumination, the observer returns to perceiving the disk as white.

Next to the effect discovered by Gelb, there is that of Kardos, from which just as many theoretical implications emerge. Let's take an illuminated room in which we place the observer. In the doorway, we hang a white disk lit by a projector. Between the projector and the disk we place a screen that casts its shadow on the disk without allowing the observer to see the shadow. If we ask the observer, she will answer that she sees a black disk illuminated. Moving the shadow we will reveal the previous colour of the disk; however, even knowing that it is a shadow, as soon as we restore the conditions of the experiment, the observer will go back to perceiving a black disk. This demonstrates the independence of the phenomenon from the experience and knowledge of the subject. The theoretical core that characterizes the experiment is the questioning of the dichotomy between appearance and reality.

To strengthen our argument, we can also resort to the following experiment. The situation is this: at the bottom of a wall we suspend a black cardboard disk projecting on it a powerful circular beam of light, so that the edges of the light beam coincide with the edges of the cardboard. Looking at the board, the observer will say that she sees it 'bright silver.' Subsequently, the person who controls the beam of light makes it slightly spill over, so to speak: the observer will then see the black cardboard. One would think that in the experiment, in reality, the stimulus is black, a material capable of absorbing all the light rays and reflect very few of them, but apparently visual perception gives us the illusion of brilliance. This typical description of the experiment inevitably creates a dualism between the reality of the physical stimuli and the phenomenal appearance – between stimuli and perceptions. A jargon like this impoverishes the reality of the situation by introducing a non-existent duplicity. In fact, if we stop considering the observer as a guinea pig in the hands of the investigator, forced to an immobility that is alien to everyday experience, we will see that, in the presence of the disk of silvery colour, the observer will naturally get closer to it.

In this way we will see a different set of perceptions, and an itinerary that will take the observer as its starting point and the experimenter as the point of arrival, since we can move the beam of the projector at will. By varying the conditions of observation the observed object changes, and this does not imply any form of dualism. If we consider the route from the observer to the observed object we will find that, in taking this route, the observing conditions vary continuously. There will be no wonder if, at the end of the path, we will see an object that we are forced to describe differently. In all these experiments, therefore, there is no shadow of dualism. To say that the disk is 'really' black, but 'apparently' brilliant, we have to assume a dualistic metaphysics. Yet, the disk is brilliant until there are certain conditions of observation; when these are changed the disk is no longer so. We can say the same for the broken stick in the water; the stick appears visually broken and looks like this whenever observed in water: these are the properties of those two things, stick and water, placed in that given relationship.

But as per the attempt to locate reality with respect to appearance in the experiments by Gelb-Kardos, what does it mean? Consider the circumstance in which the black disk is the result of Maxwell's rotating disk, composed of white and black portions fused together by virtue of the rotation of the disk. According to what principle can we favour a reality over another, and which one should we go for? We could say that the still disk is real with respect to the black rotating disc that if illuminated appears white; or we may say that the white illuminated disk is real; or the black disk in rotation that appears white if illuminated, and that with the addition of a piece of white paper looks black, but in reality is black and white. At this rate, how many levels of reality should we find?

Whenever we locate a reality, we affirm a new appearance, but to do so we lose the reality of the phenomenon, which is no longer directly visible. If instead we observe the appearance and affirm that there is an underlying reality, what we assume as such is subordinated to the observable, to what appears 'so and so' at that time and in that particular way (as in Gelb's effect). If we change the conditions of observation do we discover an underlying reality, or do we just see something different? What appears different is also identified in a different way, according to its appearance at the given time. So, to affirm the reality of the black disk against its white appearance, for example, we have to insert a piece of white paper, or change the cone of light: all these changes mean there is no dualism, but rather testify to phenomenal monism – the reality of the world encountered.

The antidualist observations of Gelb's experiment are equally valid for many other experiments in psychology. In fact, the conditions of observability of the object are organized by the investigator in such a way that they can then describe a reality that the investigator knows, and an appearance that the subject undergoes. The observer is in a position to take the place of the experimenter. The problem is not to put a reality against an appearance, but rather to consider an event observed in different conditions in a given reference system. Objects do not have any 'noumenal structure' placed beyond appearance: they are as we encounter them in direct observation, but can be described in different ways in relation to the measuring instruments we apply to them. This means that, strictly speaking, the term 'illusion', as opposed to 'reality,' has no ontological or epistemological significance.

Every time we give a description of the object based not on immediate experience, but rather on the application of measuring instruments, we give a reductive description of it: one that excludes certain parameters in favour of a more accurate analysis of those examined. A reductive description is useful for scientific purposes, but should be considered with caution when it comes to perception. What's the risk? The loss of the reality of the world around us. Subject and world are inscribed in reality, in that same reality that scientific knowledge intends to bring to light.

9. The Tunnel Effect: Independent and Dependent Invariants

In order to understand if and how the situation considered depends on a distinct aspect of it, take for example the 'tunnel effect'. Before doing this in the laboratory, this experiment can be implemented in everyday life. Let's observe a vehicle that passes behind a building. We feel no surprise at seeing the same vehicle disappear and then reappear on the opposite side: we are absolutely convinced that objects continue to exist, even when they are not directly part of our visual field. We say that the car has 'passed behind' the building – the phenomenon of 'passing behind' is precisely what we want to explain here. Now let's move to a laboratory of experimental phenomenology to examine the variables involved in determining this phenomenon, as well as those which leave it unchanged. An experimental approach shows us that it is situated on the level of phenomenal organization and not on that of judgment or past experience: we do not see the vehicle 'pass behind' on the basis of habit, as Hume would want it, or more generally because we know that cars in general pass behind buildings. As a result, we would see it 'so and so' because it corresponds to a situation that *de facto* was proven in the past a number of times.

If we abstract the shapes of the vehicle and the building, we will get a figure that is equally seen pass behind another, bigger shape. Therefore, we can note that the phenomenon of 'passing behind' is independent of the particular characterizations of the two figures: getting rid of the identifying characteristics of the vehicle and the building has no influence on the perception of the phenomenon. We can also come to the point of using two patches of light, and our perception of the 'passing behind' phenomenon will not change. Differently, by expanding the time of entry and exit, or by increasing or altering the size of the building and the vehicle, we operate changes that can affect our perception of the phenomenon under consideration. We can therefore conclude that the kinetic and temporal relations are conditions that allow us to observe the 'passing behind', while other elements (such as knowing what a car or a building is) leave it unchanged. So it is not our judgment that determines the phenomenon, but vice versa: it is the phenomenal property of events that produces our cognitive integrations. In summary: if the time interval between the disappearance of A and the appearance of B is respected, we can 'see' the movement of an object that passes from side to side. We may think that this interval corresponds to the physical time that it would take a real object to pass behind the screen. In fact, the most effective interval is less than the time taken by a real object (about 15% less).

Incidentally, this observation raises the question of why a perceptually continuous motion requires less time than the physical continuity. The experiments taken from experimental phenomenology show how we are able to isolate the condition of appearance of a given phenomenon, according to the laws intrinsic to the material taken into consideration: in fact, the dependent and independent variables on which we act belong to the same level of reality, being there in the world. The observer represents a constant that does not determine the conditions for the appearance of the phenomenon under consideration. In this sense, we can say that the stability of an emerging phenomenon of the matter is determined by certain properties of the material itself and not by the representative function of the subject: this applies to the phenomena of 'transparency', 'chromatic induction', 'unification' and to all other cases when the visible sphere is examined by experimental phenomenology.

10. Conclusions. Sufficient Conditions, but not Necessary Ones

Let's take the psycho-physical scheme SD on the one hand and the hypothesis of the evil genius on the other. Now, where, or in what part, could we put the latter within the former? In *any* segment, because the whole scheme is a causal explanation of the appearance of the thing. It could replace the physical object (distal stimulus) and electromagnetic waves, it may lie in a part of the brain or replace it entirely, it could take the place of the proximal stimulus, that of the retinal image and so forth. Every piece is a 'cause' of perception, just like the genius can be the cause of the alleged evidence of the outside world. It could replace every part, except the immediate phenomenal experience of the thing with which it must necessarily coincide.

Our phenomenal experience is independent of the metaphysics underlying the phenomenon, or, if you prefer, we can regard it as a metaphysical level zero: neutral with respect to all metaphysics. No transphenomenal causal explanation captures perceptual experience as such: that is, it cannot be located within the psychic-physical schema. As Köhler would put it, no explanation can change a phenomenon or its location. Immediate experience lies not in the stimuli, nor in the retina, nor in the physiology of the brain. The problem is not to define correctly the 'concept' of perception, but rather to describe experience in an appropriate manner. 'Experimental phenomenology' identifies the conditions of appearance of a given phenomenon without departing from the observables in place: the dependent and independent variables are conditions that lie in the world, and never in the subject that determines the implicit reference system through his or her body.

The conditions highlighted for the appearance of phenomena are valid in all possible worlds, so the phenomenon *juxta propria principia* is no longer something contingent, but necessary. We may doubt the cause of appearances, but not appearing as such. As I said, the cause of appearance must, in the end, explain why the world 'appears as it does'. Immediate phenomenal experience, with respect to the underlying reality, only has rights and no duties except that of being what it is – an observable fact. This fact, taken within an ecological reference system, constitutes the beginning of knowledge, the beginning of the appearance of truth. The thing cannot but be offered from a certain phenomenological perspective to complement-implement itself phenomenologically. Without such a 'limit' we cannot talk about *Lebensform*: the limit structures our behaviour, our *in-der-Welt-sein*, as Heidegger would say. The structure of the visible-invisible event depends on the reference system determined by our body, as a system of reference in relation to the surrounding environment.

Our being a physical body in reference to other bodies determines spaces and perspective limits on things – hence the visible-invisible relation. These 'limits' (the fact that we only see a part of the thing, for example, a cube) do not represent limits to knowledge, but the presupposition of knowledge itself. It is not possible to know a cube – the most classic example from the phenomenological tradition – as an object that has six equal sides: knowledge is always in perspective. It depends on our point of view and on our being situated in the world. If we were not simply located, we would not be. For this reason there can be no absolute knowledge, but only relative knowledge. This does not imply that there is no truth because 'everything is relative,' as we often hear. On the contrary, relativism is the prerequisite to be able to say 'truth.'

We can further investigate the expression 'such that' by resuming the example of the cube: suppose you have a red cube on the left and an observer to the right. We could ask someone why the observer sees the red cube. The interlocutor may respond, for example, 'because the cube, or at least its surfaces exposed to observation, are made of a certain chemical substance that absorbs all wavelengths except the one narrow strip that, in the visible spectrum, is indicated with good approximation (being really a fuzzy set) as red.' We could argue that it is not 'that particular chemical', since any chemical that presented the same characteristics of absorption and reflection in relation to the spectrum should work just as well. Different materials, with different chemical characteristics, possess the same properties. The other party will agree with us, and admit that the material, whatever it is, must be 'such that' some frequencies of the electromagnetic waves are absorbed and others are reflected. That material, in the contingent case, 'is thus a sufficient condition to perceive the red, but not a necessary one: in fact many other chemically different materials would propagate in the environment frequencies of that magnitude, instrumentally detectable and visible.'

The problem seems to affect the properties of radiation, not those of the materials: in this way we move the problem further to the right in the scheme SD. It is not only the action of electromagnetic waves on the retina that leads to the perception of a colour; we get the same effect by mechanical, chemical and electrical stimulation of the eye. So to see a colour, at the optical level, it is necessary to intervene on the electrical impulses in the optic nerve. The photochemical process of receptors is one of the elements that produce these electrical pulses, but it is not the only one. It can be assumed to apply to the optic nerve electrical stimuli that are perfectly adequate to induce the vision of a colour. 'It is theoretically possible to imagine a prosthetic so refined, and in logical analysis the theoretically possible is decisive.'

In summary, Bozzi's thesis is that, if we could apply ideal prostheses to each individual part of the SD scheme, these prostheses would have perfectly defined material properties capable of rendering the same qualities of the thing under observation or, more generally, of the outside world. As much as we investigate the physiological processes occurring in the central nervous system, 'we will never find the last, irreplaceable process, which is identified with mental life. Or again: the usefulness of studying and describing the physiological processes concurrent with mental life – aiming at the explanation of the latter – is dubious, because they are sufficient conditions but not necessary ones.'

The expression 'such that' can be useful with respect to the starting point – the possibility of doubting the immediate experience of the thing – because that concept can be made to coincide with Descartes' evil genius or Berkeley's God. We see the outside world 'as if' behind there were Descartes' genius, or 'as if' there were a certain metaphysics, or theory of information, or more. Instead, as is clear from our reflections, immediate experience may be accepted irrespective of the underlying metaphysical circumstances: phenomenological analysis is thus intertwined with the ontological level. The meeting point is, in my opinion, indicated by the term 'realism' – the phenomenal level of immanence independent of the subject.

Our body determines the reference system within our perception thresholds. Through Descartes' hyperbolic doubt, the sceptic doubts not what appears, nor the appearance of the thing, but its cause – the metaphysics underlying ir. Experimental phenomenology as the science of observables can prescind from the metaphysical level to capture the phenomenon as such (regardless of whether it is the result of the will of an evil genius or not), because the immanent level of phenomenal reality is, as such, safe from doubt. This independence of the phenomenal level within which experimental phenomenology operates – identifying the dependent and independent variables of the phenomenon (conditions of phenomenal appearance for all possible worlds) – is the central point for a new realism of a phenomenological matrix.

INTERVIEWS
By Sarah De Sanctis

INTERVIEW WITH LEE BRAVER[1]

Lee Braver is Associate Professor of Philosophy at the University of South Florida. His main interests lie in continental philosophy (especially Heidegger and Foucault), Wittgenstein, realism, and the dialogue between continental and analytic philosophy. He is the author of *A Thing of This World: A History of Continental Anti-Realism* (Northwestern, 2007), *Heidegger's Later Writings: A Reader's Guide* (Bloomsbury, 2009), *Groundless Grounds: A Study of Wittgenstein and Heidegger* (MIT, 2012), *Heidegger: Thinking of Being* (Polity, 2014), and editor of *Division III of Being and Time: Heidegger's Unanswered Question of Being* (MIT, 2015), as well as a number of articles and book chapters.

1) The words "realism" and "anti-realism" are ancient words, almost as old as the history of Western philosophy itself. Yet these are empty concepts if they are not contextualized: one has to specify the classes of objects to which these words refer. So, can you explain on what basis you use different approaches depending on the class of objects under consideration?

Yes, they are somewhat tricky terms which have meant different things at different times. In my first book, *A Thing of This World: A History of Continental Anti-Realism* (Northwestern University Press, 2007), I constructed a matrix of six ideas, derived largely from analytic philosophers, to capture the various aspects of realism. These were: mind-independence, correspondence theory of truth, commitment to a single description of reality, truth bivalence, the subject's passive copying of reality in knowing it, and the unchanging structure of the subject's mind. Anti-realism consists in the denial of some subset of these. I then plotted a number of continental figures onto this matrix to see which ideas each took up and how they

---

1   The present interview, as well as those with Tristan Garcia and Graham Harman, have already appeared in *Philosophical Readings* VI.2 (2014).

adapted them. This provided a fine-grained analysis of each thinker's position that plotted how they related to each other with some precision.

I think this approach is important because, while the independence of reality from the mind is perhaps the central idea of realism, many other notions naturally accrue to it. Anti-realism is similarly complex, for one may reject some of these theses but accept others, or alter them significantly.

Another way to specify the movement is, as you note, by denoting particular subject matters one is realist or anti-realist about. One might, for example, be a realist about the past but an anti-realist about math, if one thinks that the past exists independently of us, whereas math is just a set of practices we have created that doesn't track a separate realm of entities. Traditionally, most continental philosophers have been global anti-realists, in my opinion, meaning that they have not made this kind of limited application; analytic philosophers are more prone to do so.

2) Relativism has often been treated as an extreme and necessary outcome of antirealism. Is that so? And, if not, what is the difference between relativism and antirealism?

Realism generally prevents relativism. If the good is determined by a set of objects or properties that don't change, then values cannot differ. Of course this solution leads to problems of its own. For instance, what does it mean to say that there is a *thing* that is goodness? How can an object be a value? Doesn't this conflate ought and is? Wouldn't such objects be what Mackie calls "metaphysically queer?" Also, there's no guarantee that these external anchors of value cannot change and if they do, then a realist ethics would be relativist as good and bad would change with them.

Furthermore, there is the problem of connecting such abstract, transcendent objects to daily life. Human actions are good by participating in or corresponding to the Good on this theory, but this participation or instantiation muddies and compromises the purity of the Good in itself. If it must be integrated, necessarily partially and imperfectly, into behaviour, then interpretation enters: one must figure out how the transcendent Good applies to one's present situation and, since this cannot be done perfectly, it opens the backdoor to relativism. There are many ways to approximate the Good, none of which may be the clear winner.

Ironically, it is the very separation from us, which is supposed to ensure its objectivity, that lets in relativism. It's like with stereos. They strive for fidelity, but to what? The only way to hear music is in specific situations through particular equipment, each of which affects the sound. There is no music-in-itself, at least none that we can access; we can only hear music as played through particular equipment in specific places. Hence, music can sound better and worse, but not right or wrong. These qualities cannot get purchase on the various instantiations of music.

3) Relativism is particularly hard to refute in ethics. What can be the consequences of adopting a realist perspective, from this point of view?

Plato would be an excellent example of an ethical realist: good things and actions are good by virtue of the Forms, which exist entirely independently of us. This move confers objectivity onto ethical judgments and prevents relativism since the Good never changes.

To be an anti-realist about ethics, on the other hand, is to claim that there is no set of objects or properties external to us and independent of our judgments and practices that determines right and wrong answers about what is right and wrong. Goodness, on this view, depends upon us.

Now, relativism follows from anti-realism if we can legitimately vary in our evaluative practices. For instance, I think that Nietzsche is a value anti-realist — "Whatever has *value* in our world now does not have value in itself, according to its nature — nature is always value-less, but has been *given* value at some time, as a present — and it was *we* who gave and bestowed it" (*Gay Science* §301) — and he is also an ethical relativist, at least most of the time, because we who value are constantly changing — "we ourselves keep growing, keep changing, we shed our old bark, we shed our skins every spring" (ibid. §371). Since values come from us and we change, values change, hence what is good will differ depending on various factors, in particular the psychological makeup of the valuer. Kant, on the other hand, is able to preserve a universal ethics by keeping all reason the same, hence the importance of the 6th thesis of my matrix: the unchanging subject. (Just to confuse matters, there is a reading of Nietzsche according to which he bases values on life which has some unchanging characteristics, making ethics non-relativistic. Deleuze and Heidegger give versions of this reading).

Therefore, relativism is not a necessary outcome of anti-realism; it depends on other facets of one's commitments. This is why we must recognize the nuances of the topic.

4) Why is it that new realism is essentially continental? Is it true that, as Quentin Meillassoux put it, "in analytic philosophy there is so much realism that they can't be amazed by the capacity of realism"? And, if it is true, what distinguishes analytic realism from continental realism?

It's not true, as is sometimes stated, that analytic philosophy simply is realist whereas continental philosophy is anti-realist (this is not what Meillassoux is saying here). There have been many quite prominent anti-realists in analytic philosophy: Putnam in his middle period, Goodman, Dummett, later Wittgenstein on some readings (including mine), Davidson on some readings. However, realism is far more prevalent in analytic philosophy, to the point of being the default position, I think. Continental philosophy, in my opinion, has been largely anti-realist, which does indeed make realism more exotic for continental thinkers rather than the humdrum self-evident position it holds for many analytics.

Analytic philosophy inherited, primarily from Russell and Moore, a strong sense of common sense. They are the ones holding onto plain, simple truths unlike those wacky continentals who cultivate the absurd. In Russell's day that position was held primarily by Hegel and the British Idealists, but others have held it since then—Heidegger and Derrida perhaps most prominently. Continental philosophers have, I think, drawn more surprising and counterintuitive implications from realism, whereas analytic thinkers often use it as a bulwark to defend more common sense ideas. This has led some, such as Searle, to portray the division as one between those committed to truth, justice and civilization, versus those who want to tear down everything good and righteous in this world.

5) What is, in your opinion, the (possible or yet-to-come) relationship between speculative realism and aesthetics, understood both as a theory of perception – *à la* Baumgarten – and as a philosophy of art?

Well, speculative realism is committed to the existence of a reality wholly independent of us. This does not commit one to its unintelligibility *à la* Kant, but it does commit one to the *possibility* that it operates according to rules we cannot fathom, which simply don't fit into human-shaped heads. This is called "non-epistemic truth" in analytic philosophy — the idea is that truth has nothing to do with our epistemic practices, i.e. what we find intelligible; it is denied by people like Rorty and Dummett. Now if this is a genuine possibility then we have to ask how we can approach or describe this unknowable, insensible world. I believe, and am currently exploring the idea in what I am calling "transgressive realism," that art may be better at intimating the unintelligible than science or philosophy. Heidegger, for example, in his later work, was very interested in what surpasses our ability to grasp, and he frequently says that assertions are worse at indicating it than poetry.

INTERVIEW WITH MAURIZIO FERRARIS

Maurizio Ferraris is full Professor of Philosophy at the University of Turin. A pupil of Gianni Vattimo, and influenced by Jacques Derrida, Ferraris has worked in the field of aesthetics, hermeneutics and social ontology, attaching his name to the theory of Documentality and Italian New Realism. New Realism, sharing significant similarities with Speculative Realism and Object Oriented Ontology, has been the subject of several debates and international conferences, having a significant impact even in non-philosophical areas. He wrote almost fifty books that have been translated into several languages.

1) The words 'realism' and 'anti-realism' are ancient words, almost as old as the history of Western philosophy itself. Yet these are empty concepts if they are not contextualized: one has to specify the classes of objects to which these words refer. So, can you explain on what basis you use different approaches depending on the class of objects under consideration?

I distinguish three classes of objects: *social objects*, which exist in space and time depending on the subjects; *natural objects*, which exist in space and time depending on the subjects; and *ideal objects*, which exist outside of space and time independently of the subjects. It is clear that a social object is more dependent on the context than a natural object or an ideal object. I can decide to stipulate a contract, and this contract will depend on me. In this context, correlationism is inevitable: if there were no subjects, there would be no contracts (just as there would be no artworks, taxes, or philosophy departments).

Should we conclude – as suggested by John Searle, whom I believe to be much more antirealist than he is willing to admit – that social objects completely depend on our will and even our imagination? I don't think so. As for Searle, I have the impression that collective intentionality, on which he makes social reality depend, is simply a repeat of Rousseau's "volonté générale" and has the same flaws as the social contract. In this view, society was born from a deliberate act, as a result of an agreement between people who already knew what a contract, a language or a society are. Clearly this was not the case.

Under the genetic profile, i.e. from the point of view of the origin of society, I think we are rather dealing with a process of emergence. There was a time when humanity decided to believe in Jupiter and Juno, or to prohibit incest, or to submit to the authority of the sovereign. There has been a long process starting from our animal past that progressively solidified into institutions and reached a reflexive clarity (this latter step in fact is rarely reached: in most cases social behaviour consists in following the rules blindly, without thinking of their meaning).

From this point of view, I think it is inevitable to adopt a philosophy of history *à la* Vico: *homo non intelligendo fit omnia.* And this seems to me a profoundly realist thought, because it posits the emergence of society from the world, which is exactly the opposite of social constructionism. There is something else that should not be overlooked: that is, the fact that this social emergence has not been completed yet, and it never will. There was a time when slavery was considered unacceptable, then another in which women's subalternity appeared unacceptable, and finally – it is the current era – a time in which the critique of speciesism began. None of this is the result of an individual decision, no more than Zeus, Juno or monotheism are the result of an individual decision.

Obviously, when, in a given society, I perform a social act (for example, when I stipulate a contract) I construct an object. But – this is the second realistic thesis that distinguishes my perspective from that of the theorists of collective intentionality – this does not mean that the object I constructed is totally dependent on my will (in that case, constructing social objects would not make sense). The object I constructed has become part of the external world. In fact, the external world is not "the world external to the mind" (this is a vague and contestable concept). It is the world external to our conceptual schemes, as in the case of natural and ideal objects, which would have the same properties even if we knew nothing of them. It is the world external to our will.

This world is the world of social objects, on which we can intervene, which are dependent on us, but which have properties independently of our will and our knowledge. There may be a recession even if nobody in the world is aware that there is a recession.

2) Relativism has often been treated as an extreme and necessary outcome of antirealism. Is that so? And, if not, what is the difference between relativism and antirealism?

I would suggest there are three types of relativism. The old one, *à la* Protagoras, posits that man is the measure of all things and is a form of anthropocentrism. The modern one posits that the world is not at the centre of the universe, and (simplifying) I would call it a form of heliocentrism. Finally, postmodern relativism posits that part of reality is socially constructed. The only relativism that seems radically problematic is the old one, precisely because it manifests an anthropocentrism that we are no longer willing to accept (also, I'm not sure that Protagoras would include slaves among men). The other two are fine. There is no doubt that we inhabit a marginal planet and there is no doubt that part of reality is socially constructed.

The real limitation we should set is this: the part of reality being socially constructed is much smaller than what is thought by not only radical constructivists, but also common sense. Not only natural objects and ideal objects are not socially constructed but, as we have seen, social objects are, in most cases, socially dependent, but not socially constructed.

In short, relativism (which I generally consider a good thing) is not the necessary outcome of antirealism, if not in the minds of antirealists. Antirealists have often defended their position by suggesting that in order to have a free society, one that is tolerant and far from fundamentalism, it is necessary – if not to deny the existence of the external world – at least to argue that there are no facts, only interpretations. Which is obviously absurd.

3) Relativism is particularly hard to refute in ethics. What can be the consequences of adopting a realist perspective, from this point of view?

In my opinion there is no direct link between epistemological realism and ethical realism. The fundamental thesis of realism in ethics, in my view, is that there is a difference between saying that values are socially constructed and saying that they are socially dependent. I think it's perfectly reasonable to argue that values are socially dependent: without a society, it would be very difficult to talk about "values", as they are not things that are found in nature.

But, even in this case, it is important to note that values are not constructed as a contract. A law decreeing that theft is legal would merely legalize a negative value: it would not transvalue a value. In short, in order to transform good into evil the will is not enough, just as it is not enough to turn beauty into ugliness or vice versa. These ambitions can be left to the witches in *Macbeth* when they sing "Fair is foul, and foul is fair."

In this regard I would like to point out that Derrida himself (who is commonly regarded as a champion of antirealism) felt the need to say that "justice is undeconstructable" – there are thresholds that cannot be crossed. Supporting, say, the legitimacy of genocide as the outcome of a fine deconstructive exercise is unacceptable. What Derrida does not say (and is the reason for my own call for realism) is that the proposition "justice is undeconstructable" ontologically depends on an even more fundamental proposition: that is, "reality is unamendable". That is to say, reality is given and independent from our conceptual schemes and perceptual apparatuses – it cannot be amended at will.

Therefore, what I think is radically problematic is epistemological relativism, which calls into question the argument that reality is unamendable. A doctor who claimed that any treatment goes would be denying the obvious, namely the fact that people now live much longer than they used to and infant mortality has decreased, precisely through the use of specific treatments to defeat specific diseases. This is what proves that modern medicine has done better than witchery. In the same way, a hermeneutist claiming that any interpretation goes would be denying another obvious fact: namely, that there are interpretations better than others. Above all, both him and the doctor would be denying their *raison d'être*: why be a doctor, if a witch could do the same job? Why engage in hermeneutics, if any interpretation goes? I'd also like to note that if the nihilist doctor is a fictional character, being a pure intellectual hypothesis, the nihilist hermeneutist is well represented in the cultural landscape. Which I personally find inexplicable.

4) Why is it that new realism is essentially continental? Is it true that, as Quentin Meillassoux put it, "in analytic philosophy there is so much realism that they can't be amazed by the capacity of realism"? And, if it is true, what distinguishes analytic realism from continental realism?

Continental philosophy has always been much more prone to counter common sense than analytic philosophy. It was already the case with the rationalism of the seventeenth and eighteenth centuries. In the nineteenth and twentieth centuries, the continental taste for paradox was tinged with political nuances: philosophy must not only interpret the world, it must change it. And – for reasons that one may understand historically, but not justify theoretically – it was concluded, against all evidence and reason, that denying reality is a revolutionary attitude, while recognizing it would be reactionary. However, it is clearly not so: acknowledging reality is the prerequisite of every transformation and is not at all tantamount to accepting the existing state of things. Moreover, much more than in the analytic tradition, continental philosophy is aimed at a wide audience, therefore, also in this case, the paradox works better than common sense: the news is not that a dog bites a man, but that a man bites a dog.

This explains continental anti-realism sociologically. But behind it all there is something even more radical, on which it is worth spending a few words. The various families of anti-realism have a common root, i.e. what I call "transcendental fallacy", the confusion between ontology (what there is) and epistemology (what we know, or think we know). It is a very natural confusion, something very similar to the "stimulus error": in it someone, after closing their eyes and being asked what they see, says "nothing" (while the truth is that they are seeing phosphenes, consecutive images and so on). The subject is not giving a description, s/he is proposing a naive theory of vision: the eye is like a camera, so when the lens is closed there is nothing or perfect darkness. But even if the confusion is natural, it is not natural, nor sensible, to theorize it. And yet, this is the standard move of what I would call the average continental philosophy (of course there are also analytical thinkers doing this, but usually they are more cautious with radical and blatant statements).

The fundamental thesis of this attitude – claiming to be beyond realism and anti-realism, but being instead the expression of a radical confusion between ontology and epistemology – is what I would call, based on Meillassoux, the *correlationist thesis*:

"There are not a subject and an object, there is only the relation between subject and object"

From which follows that:

"There are not ontology and epistemology, there is only the relation between ontology and epistemology"

This statement describes the cognitive process by which a person knows an object (epistemology) as what is known (ontology), which, in hindsight, collapses the distinction between knowledge of the outside world and introspection. It does not take into account that between being and knowing there is an essential asymmetry, which is constitutive of being as much as of knowledge. In fact, without knowledge there would still be whole regions of being (all natural objects and all social objects), while without being there would be no form of knowledge, which is always *knowledge of* something.

Those supporting the thesis that "There are not a subject and an object, there is only the relation between subject and object"should be asked to show clearly where the subject ends and the object begins. If they answered with a punctual statement (for instance, that the subject ends at the level of the looking eye, while the object is what is being looked at by the eye) this would prove that the previous statement is false. It is not true that "There are not a subject and an object, there is only the relation between subject and object" because the answer (be it right or wrong) shows that it is in principle possible to distinguish the subject from the object. If instead – as is much more likely – they replied with something indistinct, restating the indistinguishability of object and subject, then they should explain why they keep talking about objects and subjects. In fact, it follows from this thesis that they can only know a subject, their own, in a radical form of solipsism.

Of course, this happens when you consider the thesis in the ontological form, that is, precisely in the formulation "There are not a subject and an object, there is only the relation between subject and object". On the contrary, if one simply claimed that knowledge is the relationship between a knowing subject and a known object, in which the main interest is directed to the latter, one would affirm something totally obvious and understandable. What appeared to be a bold ontological theory proves to be an epistemological platitude, a principle of common sense that nobody would ever deny, but that, because of this, is not very interesting.

My modest proposal and answer to the correlationist thesis is therefore:

> "Knowledge is *knowledge of* something different and independent of knowledge, otherwise it is not knowledge".

I would define this as a *differentialist thesis*: the observer observes in the observed something different and independent of the observer, otherwise what s/he is doing is not observation, but introspection.

It is banal to observe that:

> *Knowledge of reality* is the result of a constructive process.

Instead, it is trivially false to say that:

> *Reality* is the result of a constructive process.

It's better to be trivial than to make trivially false statements.

5) What is, in your opinion, the (possible or yet-to-come) relationship between speculative realism and aesthetics, understood both as a theory of perception – *à la* Baumgarten – and as a philosophy of art?

Postmodern anti-realism claimed that between art and reality there is no difference, as in both cases we are dealing with simulacra and simulations. I think that, on the contrary, art itself cannot exist without reality, and in particular without the part of reality we call sensible perception. For example, the fact that the assent we give to artworks is not a purely intellectual assent (I speak of those works from which we expect aesthetic pleasure, not conceptual ones) says a lot about the importance of perception. It shows how limited correlationism is in its postulating not a dependency of the object on the subject, but a dependency, in the subject, of perception on thought.

For me, the first step to overcome the transcendental fallacy and resolve the confusion between ontology and epistemology has lied in understanding that perception is autonomous from thought and that it is false that (as posited by Descartes and then many so-called post-Cartesians) what sees is not the eye but the spirit. As put by Gaetano Kanizsa, the great Gestalt theorist: even if we posited that the eye thinks, it would still think in its own way. This seems to me a definitive answer to the Kantian thesis that "intuitions without concepts are blind". In conclusion, as exotic as it may be, the Berkeleyan thesis according to which we know nothing but ideas collapses before Reid's crucial objection: if we only know ideas, how come does a needle sting while the idea of a needle doesn't?

INTERVIEW WITH TRISTAN GARCIA

Tristan Garcia was born in 1981 in Toulouse and attended the École Normale Supérieure in Paris, where he specialized in philosophy. He is the author of the influential *Form and Object* (Edinburgh University Press, 2014). He is also a fiction writer and author of *Hate: A Romance* (Faber & Faber, 2012).

1) The words 'realism' and 'anti-realism' are ancient words, almost as old as the history of Western philosophy itself. Yet these are empty concepts if they are not contextualized : one has to specify the classes of objects to which these words refer. So, can you explain on what basis you use different approaches depending on the class of objects under consideration?

Realism is not primarily defined by a content, but rather by an attitude. Realism is not the recognition of reality: it is the idea that any object determines its understanding and not the other way round (i.e. that the understanding determines the object). If by "understanding" we simply mean the fact of relating to something, we can say that a realist spirit is one that believes that everything he thinks of depends on what he thinks (i.e. the object of his thought is what the thought of the object depends on): a realist and Cantorian mathematician believes that her demonstration follows the object of her demonstration, while the anti-realist mathematician thinks that the object of the demonstration is constructed by the demonstration itself (and there are a thousand ways not to be a realist in philosophy of mathematics). Regarding perception, the realist believes that what he sees (the object of his seeing) determines what he sees; the anti-realist believes that his seeing determines what he sees. They both refer to the same relation, but in opposite directions.

Therefore, realism – in theory of knowledge, but also in ethics or politics – does not essentially proceed from the real; realism is rather the attitude of the spirit which finds its own strength in the recognition of a superior strength. The realist recognizes in what he sees a greater strength than his own seeing; she recognizes in what she judges a greater strength than her own judgement. The realist admits that everything he can understand proceeds from what he understands (the object of his understanding): he celebrates the superior power of the perceived over the perceiver.

Thus, there may be as many realisms as the possible objects of perception or thought: everything that we relate to can give rise to a realism, provided that what one relates to outweighs those who relate to it. There is thus, I believe, a realism of matter (Engels' Anti-Dühring), a realism of Evolution (evolutionary psychology), a realism of society (Durkheim's "social realism", according to which society is independent of the individuals who compose it and conceive of it), a realism of culture, a realism of History, a realism of the everyday and the ordinary; there is even a realism of the possible.

This could also be a definition of Speculative Realism: that is, a realist attitude applied not to the real, but to the possible. Realistically relating to the possible means believing that the possible object has greater strength than understanding and than the conception of the possible object. It therefore means judging that the possible is not an extension of our human cognitive apparatus or of what actually exists, but that the possible accessed by thought exists independently of thought's ability to conceive of it. There are certainly as many realisms as the possible determinations of everything that is: perhaps the realism of the possible is the widest in scope.

2) Relativism has often been treated as an extreme and necessary outcome of antirealism. Is that so? And, if not, what is the difference between relativism and antirealism?

If realism is the idea that the object determines its understanding, and if anti-realism is the idea that the understanding of the object determines the object, it could be argued that both are in some way relativisms: realism makes the understander of an object relative to the object; anti-realism makes the object relative to whoever understands it as an object. Of course, we usually mean by relativism an anti-realist position, which makes the object depend on its understanding, and not vice versa.

The anti-realist relativism consists in specifying the conditions under which an object is always understood, namely, what it should be related to in order to be determined. Outside of those conditions, a relativist does not assert that the object does not exist, but that it is not what it is. A work of art out of context, a rule or moral law out of the culture that has enacted it, a historic-specific behaviour out of its time: they all exist, but they are no longer what they are. Understood in another context, in another culture, in another era, they are a different object. The relativist antirealist is one who states that the singular being of any object depends on certain conditions of its understanding; if these conditions are changed, the object is changed at the same time. When Nelson Goodman says that an object is a work of art under the terms of its presentation and its exposition, he makes a good example of aesthetic relativism. If the being of an object depends on the conditions of its understanding, the challenge for thought becomes to discover the conditions that, when changed, change the understanding of an object to the point of altering its identity. What are the conditions that make something what it is and that, upon changing, will make the object into something else?

Following the answer I have given, it seems to me that there are different degrees of determination of relativism. When expressing the dependence of any proposition, any truth, any value vis-à-vis a cultural, historical or social position, relativism affirms the triumph of the particular over the singular and the universal: there is nothing universal, nothing is singular because everything that is thought, said or perceived is particularized by the conditions of its perception, its conception, its enunciation. This first relativism is particularist. It says that everything that makes an object particular determines it to the point that, if the conditions of its particularity change, its uniqueness will also change: it will no longer be what it is.

Obviously, the very statement of this relativism is either universal or particular. In the first case, the particularity itself is particular. We could then say that this relativism is not completely false, but that it is only true for those who give it a form of truth: it embodies this strange and fascinating thought that will only begin to be true when one wants to take it for true. In the second case, the particularity is universal: even those who believe they escaped it are stuck in it. What I think depends on my social status, my education, my gender, my historical situation, my language, the grammar of my language, the configuration of my body, the part of the light spectrum I see, the part of the sound spectrum I hear, my belonging to the human race ... If I were poorer or richer, if I had not done the same studies, I were a woman and not a man, if I were not standing on two legs, if I saw what a cat sees, if I heard what a dolphin hears, all the objects in the world which I relate to would be different, and everything I take to be true might become false. Obviously, particularism then appears to be a necessary exception to its own rule: even if I were radically different, it would still be true that everything I know and perceive depends on my particularities.

Nothing is universal, except for the negation of the universal itself.

Once we accept this formula, it becomes necessary to consider a second kind of relativism, one with more important consequences, that no longer has to do with the particularity of the conditions of access to an object, but the universal conditions of the relation of any subject with any object. This universal rather than particularistic relativism becomes a statement on knowledge which postulates that there is no object without a subject of this object (that is, without a conscience, without a cognitive apparatus that identifies it, recognizes it, names it and attributes qualities to it). Any object is under the condition of that which it is the object of. Since this relativism is universal, it is necessary that the subject of the relation can relate to itself as to an object among others: the object does not come first, since it is determined by the subject who understands it, but the latter may become at any time a relative object him or herself (a relativist sociologist transforms his sociology into an object of study, the moralist who says 'Truth on this side of the Pyrenees, error on the other side' passes to the other side of the mountains...).

What is left ? What is left is the relation. And universal relativism always ends up turning into relational universality.

The dependence of the object on the subject is nothing but a special case of dependence of the object on another object. In this latter form of relativism, any entity in general is what it is only insofar as it is connected to another entity. In relation to a given object or class of objects, I am like this; but in relation to another object or to any other class of objects, I am like that. All changes, even my maxims on the variation of all things. The subject of universal relativism is ready to submit her relativism to relativity. What remains is the relation: in relation to itself, relativism is true; in relation to its refutation, it is wrong. Relational relativism does not say that everything is relative, but that everything is related. It argues that there is no support for these relations outside of these relations themselves, and that what is related is an effect of the relations themselves.

When it is perfectly consequent, then, I think that any relativism, step by step, leads not to the idea that everything is relative (this is simply a possible content of relativism), but that there is nothing in reality but relations, and relations of relations.

3) Relativism is particularly hard to refute in ethics. What can be the consequences of adopting a realist perspective, from this point of view?

There is an ethical promise in any relativism, without which it would not be attractive: the promise to treat equally everything I can get in relation with, and to respect the uniqueness of every object I perceive or think of. Relativism, especially moral and political, promises to adapt its understanding of a phenomenon to what the phenomenon is, rather than adapting the phenomenon to the understanding we want to have of it. This is a very worthy ideal: to treat equally the other and the same, to find an equal footing to account for everything that occurs.

I think the Achilles' heel of relativism, when it is expressed in ethics, is always the confusion it ends up making between equality and equivalence. Initially, a relativist position is appealing to the democratic spirit because it promises equal dignity to every position, every belief, every thought, every perception of an object: everything that is something is something equally. The great ontological strength of relativism is to suggest that everything which we can get in relation with (by perceiving, imagining, thinking it) is something. And no thing is more or less than another. Relativism, being a kind of realism of the relations, regards everything that enters into a relation as equally real: what is not in relation to anything is nothing.

But if we reverse the proposition, a relation is never a relation with nothing. And as it is a relation, it cannot be a relation with everything because in that way there would not be the everything that comes into relation with it. The relation thus ensures that everything that appears is neither nothing nor everything. It is something. It is something more or something less, but it is never more or less anything, it is equally something.

But by relating equal possibilities, relational relativism makes them equivalent, and therefore replaceable by one another. The relativist therefore thinks that what is equal is replaceable by anything, because anything else is worth it. What is unique thus becomes common. Equality is supposed to ensure the uniqueness of each entity. But equivalence transforms this singularity into a non-singular character: nothing is more common than being singular... In the eyes of the relativist, everything is equally singular, so nothing is. Wanting to establish the uniqueness of every possibility, the relational relativist ultimately makes any possibility replaceable by another: instead of an irreducible singularity, she produces a common and exchangeable singularity, she founds universal equivalence, which allows her to say that anything goes, in a certain sense.

Thus the relational relativist is unable to fulfil her ethical promise: it is precisely in the name of singularity that she destroys it. And this is, I think, the weakness of relativism, its counter-productive character: pretending to respect the singularity of everyone, it assimilates everyone to anyone. It absolutizes the relation and makes the terms of the relation replaceable. The relativist remains the same, regardless of the position she faces; and she loses what she claims to make us gain: the recognition of the uniqueness of each thing.

I believe that the most effective way to challenge relativism is to separate equality and equivalence, to think that what is equal is not equivalent, so that equality is never achieved by relation. One has to think that the singularity of a thing, that which makes it what it is, is certainly not its relation with other things; on the contrary, one thing is something quite apart from its relation with other things. When this is something, nothing else is. There is always only one thing at a time. As the thing is what can be neither more nor less, equality is achieved in solitude: things are never equal, they are equal because each is only the exclusion of others. When things are equal, they are not together: they are absolutely not equivalent, since we cannot compare them and, *a fortiori*, we cannot substitute one for the other.

Equality is distributive and exclusive; equivalence is collective and common. Relativism, which is a realism of relations, treats its entities as if they were equal and therefore equivalent. Instead, I argue in *Form and Object* that everything is equal in the precise sense that anything is something, and there is no order or relation of things, so that nothing is comparable. Each entity has its own luck. Everything is equal, nothing is equivalent: this is the only magic formula that enables one to avoid a relativism that threatens both anti-realism and realism.

INTERVIEW WITH GRAHAM HARMAN

Graham Harman is Distinguished University Professor at the American University in Cairo, where he has worked since 2000. He is a founding member of the well-known Speculative Realism movement, and the chief exponent (since the late 1990's) of object-oriented philosophy. In 2014 he was ranked by *ArtReview*, along with his Speculative Realist colleagues, as #68 of the most powerful influences in the contemporary art world.

1) The words 'realism' and 'anti-realism' are ancient words, almost as old as the history of Western philosophy itself. Yet these are empty concepts if they are not contextualized: one has to specify the classes of objects to which these words refer. So, can you explain on what basis you use different approaches depending on the class of objects under consideration?

"Realism" obviously has different senses in philosophy, politics, mathematics, the art of the novel, and in other areas. But we all more or less know what it means in philosophy— the commitment to a world existing independently from the mind.

That's only a rough approximation, of course. One of the chief merits of Lee Braver's candidly anti-realist masterpiece *A Thing of This World: A History of Continental Realism* is that Braver carefully distinguishes between six possible meanings of realism and their six possible anti-realist counterparts (R1-R6 and A1-A6, respectively). This gives Braver a neat technical shorthand that allows him to say things like "Philosopher X combines R1 realism of the external world with A3 and A5 antirealist positions on related issues," and so forth.

However, Braver neglects a key *seventh* realist thesis that in my review of the book I called R7, with a counterpart antirealist A7. Thesis R7 would run as follows: "the human-world relation is no different in kind from any other relation." And this to me is the key. A good example of an R7 philosopher would be Alfred North Whitehead, who does not treat the human-world relation as different in ontological kind from that of raindrops and a wooden roof. There is at best a difference in degree between these kinds of relations. With Kant, however, it is quite different. Even if we might read Kant as an R1 realist who believes very strongly in the independence of the thing-in-itself from the mind (which is how I read him), he still definitely counts as an A7 philosopher for whom the human-world relation is special, since it mediates all our talk of all other relations. Whitehead lets us talk straightaway about raindrops striking wood, whereas Kant would say even this talk is mediated by the twelve categories of the understanding as well as space and time, none of them necessarily applicable beyond the realm of appearance.

The fact that the human-world relation is not special also has consequences for the scope of our knowledge. I see all relation as a matter of translation. There is no possible direct access to reality that gives us that reality in the flesh, without relation or mediation. This holds for human knowledge, animal awareness, plant life, and even inanimate collision. The human mind has no especial entanglement in error and no special capacity for direct contact with the real. This is the point where I seem to disagree with my colleagues Maurizio Ferraris and Markus Gabriel, not to mention Quentin Meillassoux, all of whom seem to hold that realism also marks an end to the relativity of perspectives. For me, by contrast, realism entails the very opposite: the *impossibility* of ever gaining direct knowledge of the world. In analytic philosophy, I believe Nancy Cartwright has said something similar: that she's an ontological realist but a theory anti-realist, or something along those lines. That's more or less my position as well.

2) Relativism has often been treated as an extreme and necessary outcome of antirealism. Is that so? And, if not, what is the difference between relativism and antirealism?

Allow me to approach this question from the opposite end instead: anti-relativism has often been treated as a necessary consequence of realism! Many people are moved to pursue a realist ontology precisely because what they worry about most is relativism. Personally, I'm a lot more worried by idealism than by relativism. A certain plurality of perspectives is inevitable. Indeed, realism requires this, if we allow that the real can never be equalled or exhausted by any particular perspective.

One of my most observant readers, Joseph Goodson of Michigan, has noted the following difference between my position and postmodern relativism. The relativists are all hung up on the incommensurability of perspectives *with each other*, while for me this is uninteresting, and the real problem is the incommensurability of any perspective *with the real*. It's less a matter of the conflict between perspectives than the internal conflict *within* a perspective to measure up to a real that eludes it.

3) Relativism is particularly hard to refute in ethics. What can be the consequences of adopting a realist perspective, from this point of view?

One frequent assumption about realist ethics is that it would require the same objective rules to be followed by everyone, rules somehow grounded in the nature of reality itself — an "ought" grounded in an "is." This follows the same assumption found elsewhere in philosophy: namely, that realism does not just mean the existence of a world outside the mind, but also the ability of the mind to *know* it.

But this is a counter-philosophical attitude from the start. Philosophy is *philosophia*, or love of wisdom rather than wisdom itself. Note that Socrates is never able to give us a definition of friendship, justice, virtue, or love, however much he searches for one. Socrates is not a knower, and we do not escape sophistry through knowledge claims.

So in a sense, I conclude the opposite of what your question might have suspected. For me, a realist ethics entails the *failure* of objective rules of behaviour. Any ethical rule can be no more than a rough approximation of the reality it attempts to address. Such approximation is necessary for social existence — we can't necessarily affirm a wildcat planet of ethical freelancers who invent their own standards at every moment. Nonetheless, each of us has broken basic ethical rules at various times (not too brazenly, one hopes) precisely because ethics often requires this. It is easy to imagine moments when stating a cold, hard truth would amount to needless cruelty, for instance. For any ethical rule, we can probably dream up an exceptional situation that would strongly encourage its violation.

In fact, this to me is the key fact of ethics: everyone seems to be allowed certain ethical exceptions on a fairly constant basis. There is my colleague who regularly speaks of dirty jokes in class streams, and this in culturally conservative Egypt. If you or I were to do it, we would quickly be terminated, since there would no doubt be a certain ugly edge to it. But my colleague is able to pull off the "crazy uncle" persona that allows him to get away with this pretty regularly despite a number of close calls. Women generally get away with certain sorts of things that men generally do not, and certainly vice versa. It is by no means the case that we treat everyone the same. And while this may sometimes be the result of "hypocrisy" or a "double standard," the most interesting cases are those in which it may be a double standard but not mere hypocrisy. Though the surface value of two actions may be equivalent, their underlying character may be completely different in the two cases, based on who carries them out.

4) Why is it that new realism is essentially continental? Is it true that, as Quentin Meillassoux put it, "in analytic philosophy there is so much realism that they can't be amazed by the capacity of realism"? And, if it is true, what distinguishes analytic realism from continental realism?

In the first place, Meillassoux's statement is basically correct. Realism has always been a live option for analytic philosophy, whereas in the continental tradition one has always risked becoming a laughingstock even by *posing the question* of realism vs. antirealism. Thanks to the phenomenological tradition (which I love for other reasons, unlike Meillassoux) we have been trained to treat the problem of realism as a pseudo-problem. After all, thought is "always already outside itself in intending an object." However, we can also intend hallucinatory or otherwise delusional objects, which does not make them "real" in any defensible sense of the term.

Husserl is a full-blown idealist, though also an object-oriented realist— the first to merit that description in the history of philosophy. There were other philosophers such as Kasimir Twardowski (Husserl's true predecessor in the Brentano School) who insisted on a doubling, with an object outside the mind and a content inside the mind. We are quick to see that Husserl got rid of the "outside the mind" part but rarely notice that he *preserved* Twarodwski's dualism, while ingeniously imploding both terms into the phenomenal realm. The British Empiricist tradition disdained objects and analysed them away as "bundles of qualities," but for Husserl the object remains somewhat constant, robust enough to withstand numerous changes in qualities. The object comes first, and its adumbrations swirl atop its surface. Rather than objects being bundles of qualities, it is qualities that become the slaves of objects— consider Merleau-Ponty's remarks about how the black of a pen's ink and the black of an executioner's hood are utterly different even if they are exactly the same in objective hue. The object bends its qualities to do its bidding.

But we need more than Husserl, who remains an idealist. This is why I cannot remain a phenomenologist. I've tried to read Heidegger as a realist through the tool-analysis, though there are problems with considering Heidegger a realist in the *bona fide* sense. First, it's all about the Dasein-Sein correlate for him. Like Kant, in whose cold shadow he works, Heidegger places the human-world relation in a position of superiority to all others; any discussion of object-object relations would make sense, for Heidegger as for Kant, only if we consider how it is mediated by the categories or horizon of human reality. And this is not yet realism. Second, there is the problem that Heidegger's "real" (much like Lacan's, or that of Parmenides or the early Levinas) is generally treated as a lump-real not articulated into parts until we encounter it. We see this in the early Heidegger with his frequent misunderstanding of the being/beings duality not just as absence/ presence (which is justified) but also as one/many (which is not).

As for realism in analytic philosophy, it tends to involve too much science-worship for my tasts. Consider Kripke's brilliant *Naming and Necessity*, a book I adore until it turns out that what is rigidly designated by the word "gold" is its number of protons! Moreover, "Nixon" turns out to be a man produced by two specific parents, which I don't believe is even true in terms of genetics (though extremely unlikely, the same Nixon DNA might have been generated by two totally different parents than the ones he had). There's the lingering notion in most analytic realism that some privileged layer explains the reality that can't quite be found in mid- or large-sized entities, accompanied by the parallel notion that the natural sciences are doing such a good job with that privileged ultimate layer that we simply ought to limp along like servants and explain why Master Science is so successful. Continental philosophy has the opposite problem of excessive *contempt* for the natural sciences (we are only now beginning to pull out of this prejudice). But given the remarkable prestige of the sciences these days and the widespread contempt for the humanities, there is little intellectual thrust to be gained by ratifying the present-day worship of natural science. (I'm speaking here of intellectual circles, of course, since I'm well aware of the ongoing stream of news stories about how science knowledge in the general public is at an all-time low, etc. etc.)

5) What is, in your opinion, the (possible or yet-to-come) relationship between speculative realism and aesthetics, understood both as a theory of perception – *à la* Baumgarten – and as a philosophy of art?

The original four Speculative Realists as a whole were just ranked in October 2014 as the #68 most powerful force in the contemporary art (see http://artreview.com/power_100/).

For my own part, I've written one article entitled "Aesthetics as First Philosophy," and another called "The Third Table" that proposes the arts as a model for the next four centuries of philosophies, much as the natural sciences or deductive geometry were taken as models during the past four centuries.

For me, philosophy is all about the tensions between two types of objects (the real and the sensual) and their two types of qualities (also the real and the sensual). This leads to four basic tensions in the cosmos that I have identified in *The Quadruple Object* and elsewhere as time, space, essence, and eidos. I've also tried to show that aesthetics results from just such a tension, again placing aesthetics at the centre of philosophy.

Even Meillassoux, who rates mathematics rather than aesthetics as the highest discipline, has written a brilliant book on Mallarmé. I do think Meillassoux will have problems extending the marvellous use of his mathematical method (707 as Mallarmé's secret number) into other authors, painters, and musicians.

The one type of Speculative Realism that is bound to have difficulty with aesthetics is the nihilistic, science-worshipping kind of Speculative Realism. In a sense, aesthetics is the very opposite of an angry scream against the futility of existence, and thus any philosophy that asserts such futility is to display a deft touch in the unlikely event that it ever turns to Wordsworth, Cézanne, or Schönberg.

GENERAL BIBLIOGRAPHY

ALLISON, H. E., *Kant's Transcendental Idealism: An Interpretation and Defense*, Revised and enlarged edition (New Haven: Yale University Press, 2004).

ASH, M. G., *Gestalt Psychology in German Culture 1890-1967* (Cambridge, Cambridge University Press, 2004).

BARBARAS, R., *Dynamique de la manifestation* (Paris: Librairie Philosophique J. Vrin, 2013).

BASHOUR, B. and MULLER, H. (Ed.), *Contemporary Philosophical Naturalism and Its implications*, (London and New York: Routledge, 2014).

BECK, L. White, *Essays on Kant and Hume* (New Haven: Yale University Press, 1978).

BENJAMIN, W., *Selected Writings, Volume 1, 1913-1926*, edited by Marcus Bullock and Michael W. Jennings (Cambridge, Massachusetts: The Belknap Press of Harvard University Press).

BENNET, J., *Vibrant Matter: A Political Ecology of Things* (Durham and London: Duke University Press, 2010).

BERTHOZ, A., *The Brain's Sense of Movement* (Cambridge: Harvard University Press, 2000).

BOGHOSSIAN, P., *Fear of Knowledge* (New York: Oxford University Press, 2007)

BOZZI, P., *Fenomenologia sperimentale* (Bologna: Il Mulino, 1989).

BOZZI, P., *Un mondo sotto osservazione*, (Milano-Udine: Mimesis, 2007).

BRASSIER, R., *Nihil Unbound. Enlightenment and extinction* (London: Palgrave Macmillan, 2007).

BRASSIER, R., "The View from Nowhere", in *Identities: Journal for Politics, Gender, and Culture* 8:2 (2011).

BRASSIER, R., "Behold the Non-Rabbit: Kant, Quine, and Laruelle", in *Pli: The Warwick Journal of Philosophy*, N° 12 (2001), pp. 50-82.

BRAVER, L., *A Thing of This World: An History of Continental Anti-Realism* (Evanston: Northwestern University Press, 2007).

BRYANT, L., *The Democracy of Objects* (Ann Arbor: OPEN HUMANITIES PRESS, 2011).

BROUWER, J., MULDER, A. and SPUYBROEK, L. (Ed.), *The Politics of the Impure* (Rotterdam: NAI Publishers 2010).

BRYANT, HARMAN and SRNICEK (Ed.), *The Speculative Turn: Continental Materialism and Realism*, (Melbourne: re-press, 2010).

BURN, S., *Conversations with David Foster Wallace*, (Jackson: University Press of Mississipi, 2012.

CARNAP, R., *Logical Syntax of Language* (London: Routledge, 2000).

CARNAP, R., "Empiricism, Semantics, and Ontology", in *Analytic Philosophy: An Anthology,* edited by Martinich (Malden: Blackwell Publishing, 2001).

CARUSS, A. W., *Carnap and Twentieth-Century Thought: Explication as Enlightenment* (Cambridge: CUP, 2007).

CHURCHLAND, P. M., *Plato's Camera: How the Physical Brain Captures a Landscape of Abstract Universals* (Massachusett: MIT Press, 2012).

COFFA, A., *The Semantic Tradition from Kant to Carnap: to the Vienna Station* (Cambridge: CUP, 1991).

COLLINGWOOD, R. G., *An Essay on Metaphysics* (Oxford: Clarendon Press, 1940).

DELANDA, M., *War in the age of intelligent machines* (Cambridge, MA: Zone Books, 1991).

DELANDA, M., *Intensive Science and Virtual Philosophy* (London: Continuum, 2002).

DELANDA, M., *Philosophy and simulation: the emergence of synthetic reason* (London : Continuum 2011).

DELEUZE, G., *Logic of sense* (London: Continuum 2004).

DELEUZE, G., *Difference and Repetition,* trans. by Paul Patton (New York: Columbia University Press, 1994).

DELEUZE, G., 'Immanence: A Life', in *Pure Immanence, Essays on A Life* (New York: Urzone Inc., 2001).

DELEUZE, G., and GUATTARI, F., *What is Philosophy?,* (New York: Columbia University Press, 1994).

DENNETT, D., *Consciousness Explained* (New York: Back Bay Books, 1991).

DERRIDA, J., *The Work of Mourning,* edited by Brault, Pascale-Anne and Naas, Michael (Chicago: University of Chicago Press, 2001).

ENNIS, P. J., CONTINENTAL REALISM (WINCHESTER: ZERO BOOKS, 2011).

ENNIS, P. J., "The Transcendental Core of Correlationism", in *Cosmos and History: The Journal of Natural and Social Philosophy,* 7:1 (2011), pp. 37-48

FERRARIS, M., *Goodbye Kant! What Still Stands of the Critique of Pure Reason* (Albany: SUNY, 2013).

FERRARIS, M., *Manifesto of new Realism* (New York: Sany Press, 2014).

FERRARIS, M., *Il mondo esterno* (Milano: Bompiani, 2001).

FOUCAULT, M., *The Hermeneutics of the Subject, Lectures at the Collège de France, 1981-82,* (New York: Palgrave Macmillan, 2005).

FRIEDMAN, M., *Dynamics of Reason* (Stanford: CSLI Publications, 1999).

FRIEDMAN, M., *Kant's Construction of Nature: A Reading of the Metaphysical Foundations of Natural Science* (Cambridge: CUP, 2013).

FRIEDMAN, M., "Reconsidering the Dynamics of Reason: Response to Ferrari, Mormann, Nordmann, and Uebel", in *Studies in History and Philosophy of Science Part A,* 43: 1 (2012), pp. 47–53.

FRIEDMAN, M., "Kantian Themes in Contemporary Philosophy", in *Aristotelian Society Supplementary Volume,* 72: 1 (1998), pp. 111–30.

GABRIEL, M., *Il senso dell'esistenza* (Roma: Carocci, 2012).

GARCIA, T., *Forme et objet* (Paris: PUF, 2011).

GIBSON, J., *The Perception of Visual World* (Boston: Houghton Mifflin, 1950)

GIBSON, J., *The Ecological Approach to Visual Perception* (Boston, Houghton Mifflin, 1979).

GRANT, I., "Movements of the World", in *Analecta Hermeneutica*, n° 3 (2011), pp. 1-17.

GRATTON, P., *Speculative Realism: Problems and Prospects* (London: Continuum, 2014).

GREEN, G. W., *The Aporia of Inner Sense: The Self-Knowledge of Reason and the Critique of Metaphysics in Kant* (Leiden: Koninklijke Brill, 2010).

GRIER, M., *Kant's Doctrine of Transcendental Illusion* (Cambridge: Cambridge University Press, 2001).

Guyer, P., *Kant and the Claims of Knowledge* (Cambridge: Cambridge University Press, 1987).

GUYER, P. (edited by), *The Cambridge Companion to Kant and Modern Philosophy* (Cambridge: CUP, 2006).

HARMAN, G., *Quentin Meillassoux: Philosophy in the Making* (Edinburgh, Edinburgh University Press, 2011).

HARMAN, G., *The Quadruple Object* (London: Zero Books, 2011).

HARMAN, G., "The Current State of Speculative Realism", in *Speculations*, N° IV (2013), pp. 22-28.

HEGEL, G. W. F., *Phenomenology of Spirit* (Oxford: Oxford University Press, 1977).

HEIDEGGER, M., *Being and Time* (Oxford: Basil Blackwell, 1962).

HERZOGENRATH, B. (Ed.), *Deleuze/Guattari & Ecology* (London: Palgrave Macmillan, 2009).

HUSSERL, E., *The Crisis of European Sciences and Transcendental Phenomenology* (Evanston: Northwestern University Press, 1970).

HUSSERL, E., *Cartesianische Meditationen und Pariser Vorträge*, edited by Strasser (Den Haag: Martinus Nijhoff, 1973).

HUSSERL, E., *Die Idee der Phanomenologie. Funf Vorlesungen*, edited by Biemel (The Hague: MartinusNijhoff, 1973).

HUSSERL, E. (1952), *Ideen zu einer reinen Phänomenologie und phänomenologischen Philosophie. Zweites Buch. Phänomenologische Untersuchungen zur Konstitution*, Husserliana IV, edited by M. Biemel (Den Haag: Martinus Nijhoff, 1952).

HUSSERL, E., *Die Krisis der Europäischen Wissenschaften und die transzendentale Phänomenologie*, edited by Biemel (Den Haag: Martinus Nijhoff, 1954).

HUSSERL, E., *Vorlesungen zur Phänomenologie des inneren Zeitbewusstseins (1893-1917)*, edited by Böhm (Den Haag: Martinus Nijhoff, 1966).

HUSSERL, E., *Späte Texte über Zeitkonstitution (1929-1934). Die C-Manuskripte*, edited by Lohmar (Dordrecht: Springer, 2006).

HUSSERL, E., *Zur phänomenologischen Reduktion. Texte aus dem Nachlass (1926-1935)*, edited by Luft, Husserliana XXXIV (Dordrecht: Kluwer Academic Publishers, 2002).

IEVEN, B., SCHUILENBURG, M., VAN TUINEN, S. and VAN ROODEN, A. (Ed.), *De Nieuwe Franse Filosofie* (Amsterdam: Boom 2011).

JAMES, W., *Essays in Radical Empiricism* (Mineola, New York: Dover Publications, Inc., 2003).

JÄRVILEHTO, L., "Concepts and the Real in C. I. Lewis' Epistemology", in *Realism, Science and Pragmatism*, edited by Kenneth Westphal (London and New York: Routledge, 2014).

KANISZA, G., *Organization in Vision: Essays on Gestalt Perception* (Westport: Praeger Publishers, 1979).

KANT, I., *Correspondence*, edited by Zweig, Arnulf (Cambridge: Cambridge University Press, 2007).

KANT, I., *Critique of Pure Reason*, edited by Guyer and Wood (Cambridge: Cambridge University Press, 1988).

KANT, I., *Notes and Fragments*, edited by Bowman and Rauscher (Cambridge: Cambridge University Press, 2010).

KANT, I., *Theoretical Philosophy, 1755-1770*, edited by Walford and Meerbote, Ralf (Cambridge : Cambridge University Press, 1992).

KANT, I., *Theoretical Philosophy After 1781*, ed. by Allison, Henry and Heath (Cambridge: Cambridge University Press, 2002).

KARDOS, L., *Ding und Schatten* (Leipzig: Barth, 1934).

KEUPNIK, A. and SHIEH, S. (Ed.), *The Limits of Logical Empiricism*, (Dordrecht: Springer, 2006).

KÖHLET, W., *Gestalt Psychology* (New York: Liveright, 1929).

KOHNKE, K. C., *The Rise of Neo-Kantianism: German Academic Philosophy Between Idealism and Positivism* (Cambridge: CUP, 1991).

KOFFKA, K., *Principles of Gestalt Psychology* (London: Routledge, 1935).

KUEHN, M., "Kant's Conception of "Hume's Problem"", in *Journal of the History of Philosophy*, 21:2 (1983), pp. 175-193.

KUHN, T., "Dubbing and Redubbing: The Vulnerability of Rigid Designation", in *Minnesota Studies in the Philosophy of Science*, edited by Savage, Conant, and Haugeland (Minneapolis: University of Minnesota Press, 1990).

KUHN, T., *The Road since Structure: Philosophical Essays, 1970-1993, with an Autobiographical Interview*, edited by Conant and Haugeland (Chicago: The University of Chicago Press, 2000).

LACOSTE, Jean-Yves, *Expérience et Absolu* (Paris: Presses Universitaires de France, 1994).

LACAN, J., *On Feminine Sexuality. The Limits of Love and Knowledge*, ed. by Jacques-Allain Miller, (New York: W.W. Norton & Company, 1999).

LADEN, S., *Reasoning: A Social Picture* (Oxford: OUP, 2012).

LAKATOS, I., *The Methodology of Scientific Research Programmes: Philosophical Papers* (Cambridge: CUP, 1978).

LAND, N., *Fanged Noumena: Collected Writings 1987-2007*, edited by Brassier and Mackay (Falmouth: Urbanomic, 2011).

LATOUR, B., *We have never been Modern* (Cambridge: Harvard University Press, 1993)

LATOUR, B., "Irreductions", in *The Pasteurization of France* (Cambridge: Harvard University Press, 1993).

LATOUR, B., *On the Modern Cult of the Factish Gods* (Durham and London, Duke University Press, 2010).

LATOUR, B., *Rejoicing or the Torments of Religious Speech* (Cambridge: Polity Press, 2013).

LATOUR, B., HARMAN, G., and ERDÉLYI, P. (Ed.), *The Prince and the Wolf: Latour and Harman at the LSE* (Winchester: Zero Books 2011).

LATOUR, B. and WEIBEL, P. (Ed.), *Making Things Public: Atmosphere of Democracy* (Cambridge, MA: MIT Press, 2005).

LEIBNIZ, G. W., *New Essays on the Human Understanding* (Cambridge: Cambridge University Press, 1982).

LEIBNIZ, G. W., *Monadology* (New York: Courier Dover Publications, 2012).

LEWIS, C. I., *An Analysis of Knowledge and Valuation* (La Salle, IL: Open Court, 1946).

LEWIS, C. I., *Mind and the World-Order: Outline of a Theory of Knowledge* (New York: Dover, 1956).

LIGOTTI, T., *The conspiracy against the human race*, (New York: Hippocampus Press, 2010).

LONGUENESSE, B., "Kant's Deconstruction of the Principle of Sufficient Reason", in *The Harvard Review of Philosophy* N° IX, 2001.

LYOTARD, Jean-François, *The Inhuman: Reflections on Time,* (Stanford: Stanford University Press, 1991).

LYOTARD, Jean-François, 'A Postmodern Fable', *Yale Journal of Criticism*, 6:1 (1993), p. 237.

MACBETH, D., *Realizing Reason: A Narrative of Truth and Knowing* (Oxford: OUP, 2014).

MACKAY, R. (ed.), *Collapse: Philosophical Research and Development,* vol. II (Falmouth: Urbanomic, 2007).

MACKAY, R. (ed.), *Collapse: Philosophical Research and Development,* vol. III (Falmouth: Urbanomic, 2007).

MACKAY, R. (ed.), *Collapse: Concept Horror,* vol. IV (Falmouth: Urbanomic, 2008).

MADDY, P., *Second Philosophy: A Naturalistic Method* (Oxford: OUP, 2007).

MACH, E., *The Analysis of Sensations* (Chicago: Open Court, 1897).

MALLARMÉ, S., *Collected Poems and Other Verses* (Oxford: Oxford University Press, 2006).

MALLARMÉ, S., *Divagations* (Cambridge, MA: Belknap Press of Harvard University Press).

MALLARMÉ, S., *Igitur, Divagations, Un coup de dès*, edited by Bertrand Marchal (Paris: Editions Gallimard, 2003).

MASSIRONI, M., *Fenomenologia della percezione visiva*, Bologna: il Mulino, 1998)

METZGER, W., *Psychologie* (Darmstadt: Steinkopff, 1954).

MCMULLIN, E., *Newton on Matter and Activity* (Notre Dame: University of Notre Dame Press, 1978).

MEILLASSOUX, Q., *After Finitude: essay on the necessity of contingency,* (London: Continuum, 2007).

MEILLASSOUX, Q., *Métaphisique et fiction des mondes hors science* (Paris: Aux forges du volcan, 2013).

MEILLASSOUX, Q., "Time Without Becoming", talk presented at Middlesex University, 8 May 2008.

MEILLASSOUX, Q., "Iteration, Reiteration, Repetition: A Speculative Analysis of the Meaningless Sign", in *Spekulative Poetik* (Freie Universität, Berlin, 20 April 2012).

MERLEAU-PONTY, M., *The Visible and the Invisible* (Evanston: Northwestern University Press, 1968).

MERLEAU-PONTY, M., *The Primacy of Perception* (Evanston, IL: Northwestern University Press, 1964).

MERLEAU-PONTY, M., *L'institution. La passivité. Notes de cours au Collège de France (1954-1955)*, (Paris : Editions Belin, 2003).

METZINGER, T., *Being No One: The Self-Model Theory of Subjectivity* (Massachusetts: MIT Press 2003).

MILLER, A. S., *Speculative Grace: Bruno Latour and Object-Oriented Theology* (New York: Fordham University Press, 2013).

MORMANN, T., "Carnap's Boundless Ocean of Unlimited Possibilities: Between Enlightenment and Romanticism", in *Carnap's Ideal of Explication and Naturalism*, edited by Wagner (Basingstoke: Palgrave Macmillan, 2012).

NIETZCHE, F., *Philosophy and Truth: Selections from Nietzsche's Notebooks of the Early 1870s*, edited by Daniel Breazeale (Atlantic Highlands, New Jersey: Humanities Press, 1979).

O'SHEA, J., *Wilfrid Sellars: Naturalism with a Normative Turn* (Malden: Polity, 2007).

PAP, A., *The A Priori in Physical Theory* (New York: King's Crown Press, 1946).

PEIRCE, C. S., *Reasoning and the Logic of Things*, edited by Laine Ketner (Cambridge (MA): Harvard University Press, 1992).

PIPPIN, R., *Kant's Theory of Form: An Essay on the Critique of Pure Reason* (New Haven: Yale University Press, 1982).

PUTNAM, H., *Realism and Reason: Philosophical Papers* (Cambridge: CUP, 1983).

REICHENBACH, H., *The Theory of Relativity and A Priori Knowledge* (Berkeley and Los Angeles: University of California Press, 1965).

REICHENBACH, H., *Selected Writings, 1909-1953,* edited by Reichenbach and Cohen (Dordrecht: Reidel, 1978).

RICHARDSON, A., *Carnap's construction of the World: The Aufbau and the Emergence of Logical Empiricism* (Cambridge: CUP, 1998).

ROBINSON, H., "The Priority of Inner Sense", in *Kant Studien* N° 79 (1988), pp. 165-182.

ROBINSON, H., "A New Fragment of Immanuel Kant: On Inner Sense", in *International Philosophical Quarterly*, 29:3 (1989).

ROBINSON, H., "Inner Sense and the Leningrad Reflexion", in *International Philosophical Quarterly* 29:3 (1989).

ROSENBERG, J., *Wilfrid Sellars: Fusing the Images* (Oxford: OUP, 2007).

SACHS, C. B., *Intentionality and the Myths of the Given* (London: Pickering and Chatto, 2014).

SACILOTTO, D., "Realism and Representation: On the Ontological Turn, in *Speculations* N° IV (2013), pp. 53-64.

SARTRE, Jean-Paul, *The transcendence of the ego. An existentialist theory of consciousness*, (New York: Hill and Wang, 1960).

SELLARS, W., *Science, Perception, and Reality* (Atascadero: Ridgeview, 1963).

SELLARS, W., *Science and Metaphysics: Variations on Kantian Themes* (London: Routledge and Kegan Paul, 1968).

SELLARS, W., *Essays on Philosophy and its History* (Dordrecht: Riedel, 1974).

SELLARS, W., *Pure Pragmatics and Possible Worlds* (Atascadero: Ridgeview, 1980).

SCHELLING, F. W. J., *System of Transcendental Idealism* (Charlottesville: University of Virgina Press, 1978).

SCHELLING, F. W. J., *Philosophical Inquiries into the Essence of Human Freedom* (Peru: Open Court, 1986).

SCHELLING, F. W. J., *The Philosophy of Art* (Minneapolis: University of Minnesota Press, 1989).

SPIEGELBERG, H., *The Phenomenological Movement: A Historical Introduction* (The Hague: Nijhoff Stewart, 1960).

STENGERS, I., *The invention of modern science* (Minneapolis: University of Minnesota Press, 2000).

STRAWSON, P., *Bounds of Sense: An Essay on Kant's Critique of Pure Reason* (London: Methuen & Co Ltd, 1966).

STRAWSON, P., Individuals: An Essay in Descriptive Metaphysics (London: Routledge, 1996).

SLOTERDIJK, P., *La compétition des Bonnes Nouvelles: Nietzsche évangéliste* (Paris, Mille et une nuits, 2002).

TADDIO, L., *Fenomenologia eretica* (Milano-Udine : Mimesis, 2011).

TAHKO, T. E., "Boring Infinite Descent," in *Metaphilosophy,* 45: 2 (2014).

TSOU, J. Y., "Putnam's Account of Apriority and Scientific Change: Its Historical and Contemporary Interest", *Synthese* 176: 3 (2009), pp. 429-45.

VALERY, P., *Variation sur une* Pensée, in *Variété I et II* (Paris: Editions Gallimard, 1924-1930).

WHITEHEAD, A. N., *Process and Reality* (New York: The Free Press, 1979).

WILSON, M., *Wandering Significance: An Essay in Conceptual Behavior* (Oxford: Clarendon, 2006).

WIMSATT, W., *Re-Engineering Philosophy for Limited Beings: Piecewise Approximations to Reality* (Cambridge (MA): Harvard University Press, 2007).

WITTGENSTEIN, L., *Tractatus Logico-Philosophicus* (New York: Cosimo Inc., 2010).

WITTGENSTEIN, L., *Remarks on the Philosophy of Psychology* (Oxford: Blackwell, 1980).

ZOELLER, G., "Making Sense out of Inner Sense", in *International Philosophical Quarterly,* 29:3 (1989).

AUTHORS

Erik Bordeleau is researcher at the SenseLab (Concordia University). He is the author of *Foucault anonymat* (Le Quartanier, 2012, Spirale Eva-Legrand 2013 award) and of *Comment sauver le commun du communisme?* (Le Quartanier, 2014). He is interested in the speculative turn in continental contemporary thought and is working on the mode of presence of spirits, gods and other surexistential forces in East-Asian Cinema. He is a member of Épopée, an action group in cinema which directed *Rupture* (2015) and *Insurgence* (2013), two movies about the 2012 student strike in Quebec.

Gabriel Catren (PhD in Physics, University of Buenos Aires; PhD in Philosophy, University of Paris) works as a researcher in the institute *SPHERE - Sciences, Philosophie, Histoire* (UMR 7219), University Paris Diderot – French National Centre for Scientific Research (CNRS).

Sarah De Sanctis is a member of the Research Centre LabOnt at the University of Turin, where she also works as an academic translator specializing in philosophy. She has translated several books, including Maurizio Ferraris' *Where Are You? An Ontology of the Cell Phone* (Fordham University Press, with a foreword by Umberto Eco) and *Introduction to New Realism* (Bloomsbury University Press, with an introduction by Iain Hamilton Grant), to which she also co-wrote the Afterword. She lives in London and collaborates with several literary agencies.

Paul J. Ennis is a Research Fellow in the School of Business, Trinity College Dublin. He is the author of *Continental Realism* (Zero Books, 2011), co-editor with Edia Connole and Nicola Masciandaro of *True Detection* (Schism Press, 2014), co-editor with Peter Gratton of *The Meillassoux Dictionary* (Edinburgh University Press, 2014) and co-editor with Tziovanis Georgakis of *Twenty-First Century Heidegger* (Springer, forthcoming).

Fabio Gironi is an IRC Postdoctoral Research Fellow in the School of Philosophy, University College Dublin. He previously studied at the University of Rome "La Sapienza," the University of London, and Cardiff University, where he obtained his Ph.D. His work focuses on the philosophy of science and the history of scientific conceptual frameworks, drawing from both analytic and continental sources. He's the editor of the journal *Speculations*.

Matthijs Kouw (PBL Netherlands Environmental Assessment Agency and IVM Institute for Environmental Studies, VU University Amsterdam) works on smart cities, climate change, and various issues on the science-policy interface, such as data visualization and framing. In 2012, he completed his PhD at Maastricht University. In his doctoral thesis, Matthijs discusses how simulations and models make knowledge of risks more or less visible, and to what extent their use makes technological cultures susceptible to risks. Matthijs has an MA in Philosophy and an MSc in Science and Technology Studies (cum laude) from the University of Amsterdam.

Anna Longo (PhD in Aesthetics at Université Paris 1 – Panthéon Sorbonne) works on the relations between artistic creation and complex systems of scientific research. For MimesisiInternational, she has already published the book *Time without becoming*, with Quentin Meillassoux. She lives in Paris.

Liam Sprod is a philosopher and writer. He is currently a Doctoral Research Student at the London Graduate School, working on the debate between realism and idealism through the asymmetry of space and time in the work of Immanuel Kant and his philosophical legacy. His most recent book is *Nuclear Futurism: The work of art in the age of remainderless destruction* (Zero Books, 2012). He has also collaborated on a series of ongoing projects concerned with futurity, fragments, ruins and technology with artist Linda Persson.

Sjoerd van Tuinen is Assistant Professor in Philosophy at Erasmus University Rotterdam and Coordinator of the Centre for Art and Philosophy (www.caponline.org). He holds a PhD in Philosophy from Ghent University. He is editor of several books, including *Deleuze and The Fold. A Critical Reader* (Basingstoke: Palgrave Macmillan, 2010), *De nieuwe Franse filosofie* (Amsterdam: Boom, 2011), *Giving and Taking. Antidotes to a Culture of Greed* (Rotterdam: V2/Nai) and has authored *Sloterdijk.*

Binnenstebuiten denken (Kampen: Klement, 2004). Van Tuinen is currently preparing a book in which he proposes a speculative concept of Mannerism, entitled *Matter, Manner, Idea: Deleuze and Mannerism*. See also: www.svtuinen.nl.

Ben Woodard is a PhD student in Theory and Criticism at Western University. His dissertation is on the relation of space, motion, and naturalism in the work of FWJ von Schelling. He has published numerous articles on the philosophy of nature, ecology, feminism, materialism, pessimism, as well as horror and weird fiction. He has published two monographs: *Slime Dynamics: Generation, Mutation, and the Creep of Life* (Zero, 2012) and *On an Ungrounded Earth: Towards a New Geophilosophy* (Punctum, 2013).

Luca Taddio has been Adjunct Professor of Aesthetics at the University of Udine, Trieste and Ferrara, where he now teaches. He has curated and personally supervised several series including "Volti", "Estetica e Architettura" and "Sx/Quaderni Fortuna". He has edited several books, including P. Bozzi, *Un mondo sotto osservazione*; W. James, *Empirismo radicale*; E. Severino, *La guerra e il mortale* and the volume of aesthetics of architecture *Costruire Abitare e Pensare*. He published *Spazi immaginali* (2004), *Fenomenologia eretica* (2011), *L'affermazione dell'architettura* (with Damiano Cantone, 2011), *Global Revolution* (2012), *I due misteri* (2012), *Verso un nuovo realismo* (2013).

Andrea Zhok has studied at the universities of Trieste, Milan, Vienna and Essex. He has taught Philosophy of History and is now teaching Philosophical Anthropology at the Philosophy Department of the University of Milan. Among his monographs, there are *Fenomenologia e genealogia della verità* (*Phenomenology and Genealogy of Truth*,1998), *L'etica del metodo. Saggio su Ludwig Wittgenstein* (*Ethics of Method. An Essay on Ludwig Wittgenstein*, 2001), *Il concetto di valore: dall'etica all'economia* (*On the Notion of Value: From Ethics to Economics*, 2002), *Lo spirito del denaro e la liquidazione del mondo* (*The Meaning of Money and the World Destructuration*, 2006), *La realtà e i suoi sensi* (*Reality and Its Senses*, 2012).

MIMESIS GROUP
www.mimesis-group.com

MIMESIS INTERNATIONAL
www.mimesisinternational.com
info@mimesisinternational.com

MIMESIS EDIZIONI
www.mimesisedizioni.it
mimesis@mimesisedizioni.it

ÉDITIONS MIMÉSIS
www.editionsmimesis.fr
info@editionsmimesis.fr

MIMESIS AFRICA
www.mimesisafrica.com
info@mimesisafrica.com

MIMESIS COMMUNICATION
www.mim-c.net

MIMESIS EU
www.mim-eu.com

.

Printed by Digital Team

Fano (PU) in March 2015